Getting StartED with Windows 7

Joseph Moran

Kevin Otnes

friendsof ED

an Apress® company

GETTING STARTED WITH WINDOWS 7

Copyright © 2009 by Joseph Moran and Kevin Otnes

ISBN-13 (pbk): 978-1-4302-2503-4

ISBN-13 (electronic): 978-1-4302-2504-1

Printed and bound in the United States of America 9 8 7 6 5 4 3 2 1

Trademarked names may appear in this book. Rather than use a trademark symbol with every occurrence of a trademarked name, we use the names only in an editorial fashion and to the benefit of the trademark owner, with no intention of infringement of the trademark.

Distributed to the book trade worldwide by Springer-Verlag New York, Inc., 233 Spring Street, 6th Floor, New York, NY 10013. Phone 1-800-SPRINGER, fax 201-348-4505, e-mail orders-ny@springer-sbm.com, or visit www.springeronline.com.

For information on translations, please e-mail info@apress.com, or visit www.apress.com.

Apress and friends of ED books may be purchased in bulk for academic, corporate, or promotional use. eBook versions and licenses are also available for most titles. For more information, reference our Special Bulk Sales–eBook Licensing web page at http://www.apress.com/info/bulksales.

The information in this book is distributed on an "as is" basis, without warranty. Although every precaution has been taken in the preparation of this work, neither the author(s) nor Apress shall have any liability to any person or entity with respect to any loss or damage caused or alleged to be caused directly or indirectly by the information contained in this work.

The source code for this book is freely available to readers at www.friendsofed.com in the Downloads section.

Credits

Lead Editor: Matthew Moodie	**Coordinating Editor**: Kelly Moritz
Technical Reviewer: Peter Membrey	**Copy Editor**: Kim Wimpsett and Sharon Wilkey
Editorial Board: Clay Andres, Steve Anglin, Mark Beckner, Ewan Buckingham, Tony Campbell, Gary Cornell, Jonathan Gennick, Michelle Lowman, Matthew Moodie, Jeffrey Pepper, Frank Pohlmann, Ben Renow-Clarke, Dominic Shakeshaft, Matt Wade, Tom Welsh	**Indexers**: BIM Indexing and e-Services
	Compositors MacPS, LLC
	Cover Image Designer: Margaret Artley
	Interior and Cover Designer: Anna Ishchenko

To my Mom, who set the ball rolling by buying me my first computer many years ago, and to my wife, for all her love and support.

—Joseph Moran

To my father, who gave me writing genes, and my mother who made me blue jeans. To my wife, for sharing our dreams.

—Kevin Otnes

Contents at a Glance

Contents

About the Authors

Joseph Moran has been using Windows since the operating system was sold on a half-dozen floppy disks. He's a long time technology writer who has penned articles for numerous web sites, magazines, and newspapers, and has worked in technology public relations and as a corporate IT manager.

When he's not in front of a computer, he tries to work on his tennis game where he recently upgraded his skills from comical to competent.

Kevin Otnes is a technical writer in the Seattle, Washington area, where he has worked for Boeing, Microsoft, and EMC. At Microsoft, he wrote online help for numerous Windows releases, from Windows 95 to Windows XP. He served on the front lines of the Internet Explorer/Netscape Navigator browser wars as an award-winning writer for Internet Explorer help. During his tenure on the Windows documentation teams, he also worked on many other Windows and MSN features, including Outlook Express, MSN Mail, NetMeeting, instant messaging, chat, Windows XP Embedded, and Windows Mobile Embedded. Today, he writes documentation peacefully outside of Microsoft for a market leader in enterprise-level backup and recovery software and hardware products.

About the Technical Reviewer

Peter Membrey lives in Hong Kong and is actively promoting open source in all its various forms and guises, especially in education. He has had the honor of working for Red Hat and received his first RHCE at the tender age of 17. He is now a Chartered IT Professional and one of the world's first professionally registered ICT Technicians. Currently studying for a master's degree in IT, he hopes to study locally and earn a Ph.D in the not-too-distant future. He lives with his wife Sarah and is desperately trying (and sadly failing) to come to grips with Cantonese.

Acknowledgments

Thanks to Karen Offermann, who recommended me for this project and who years ago gave me my first shot in the tech industry following a spirited discussion about modem standards.

I also want to thank all the folks at Apress for their guidance and support throughout the project. Last but not least, thank you to my wonderful wife Andrea, for all her encouragement and for sharing my interest in technology.

—Joseph Moran

I feel almost guilty saying that I wrote half of this book by myself. I could never have done this without the experiences I gained working over the years with several different Windows writing teams at Microsoft. Several managers and leads stand out, who made the work fun, challenging, and rewarding: Kat Cordell, Bob Lee, Sarah Norton, among others. I also want to thank Bret Muzzey and Dan Simpson, for planting the idea of putting what I know into a computer book. Once this idea was planted, several friends provided key encouragement to pursue this dream and opportunity. Nancy Raiken, Debbie Frederickson, Karen Weber, Katharine Enos, Diane Stielstra, and Colleen Dunham—your support has been priceless.

All those experiences and knowledge would all be for naught if I hadn't hooked up with the wonderful team at Apress, who turned this into a book. I really appreciate the professionalism and patience of all of the editing staff we worked with on this book: Steve Anglin, Matthew Moodie, Kelly Moritz, Sharon Wilkey, and Kim Wimpsett. They make us look so good. Thanks too to Pete Membrey, for his thorough and essential technical reviews.

I want to thank my coauthor, Joe Moran, for bringing me into this book, and for enabling me to write about some really fun stuff.

Last, but most of all, thank you to my best friend, my wife Lori, for your unfaltering support every day, every year, in every way.

—Kevin Otnes

Introduction

Each time a new version of Windows comes out, it improves upon the one it replaces in some way, but we can say without hyperbole that Windows 7 is very likely Microsoft's best operating system ever, and we believe it will have as large an impact on how people use computers as Windows 95 did well over a decade ago. Windows 7 is the second new version of Windows in less than three years (Windows Vista launched in early 2007). While Windows Vista quickly developed a reputation, fairly or not, as being inferior to its predecessor in many ways, Windows 7, the first Windows version to be made available to the general public while still in beta (test) form, has made a positive impression on nearly everyone that's used it.

For the visual experience, Windows 7 brings a more efficient Taskbar that better manages program windows on your desktop, provides useful thumbnail previews of open windows, and a myriad customization options. For your peace of mind, Windows 7 continues Microsoft's ongoing improvement in security to make your PC experience safer and more secure. You'll also get improved notification from Windows when there are problems with software, devices, or security. The User Account Control now provides additional settings so that you can keep a high-level of security on your computer while making it less obtrusive to you when you are trying to do other things on your computer. Only a few years ago, homes with more than one computer were an exception. Now multiple-computer homes and home networks are becoming the norm. Windows 7 adds HomeGroups for simplified networking between computers running Windows 7 and many other networking improvements that make it easier to connect to older computers running Windows Vista or Windows XP. These network improvements are also handy for sharing your pictures, music, and videos between computers on your network. Behind the scenes, under the hood, in the background—however you want to say it—Windows 7 contains a lot of improvements in performance. It not only looks better, it runs better, faster, and safer.

Getting StartED with Windows 7 is your guide to hitting the ground running without becoming a computer geek or becoming enslaved to it. Windows 7 is fun. It's something to get excited about. You can have fun and enjoy your computer and still get your job or work done better.

It was a real joy for us to explore Windows 7 and write this book. We hope you'll have just as much fun reading this book and exploring Windows 7.

Who this book is for

As the title implies, *Getting StartED with Windows 7* isn't geared toward computer enthusiasts or "techies". Rather, it's intended for those who have little to no experience with Windows and want to understand the basics of getting things done with Windows 7, or even for those who may be familiar with a prior version of Windows and want to know more about the new and improved features that Windows 7 brings.

You won't find lots of buzzwords or technical jargon in this book. What you will find is lots of practical information about Windows 7's interface and its most important features, along with step-by-step instructions on how to get the most of the operating system by making it do the things you want it to.

How this book is structured

Whether you are new to computers, Windows, or new to Windows 7, *Getting StartED with Windows 7* will help you get up and running with Windows 7 quickly. You can start this book from the beginning and read it end-to-end, or you may want to dive into an area that is most important to you at the moment. If you've been using Windows Vista, Windows 7 will be very familiar to you. If you've been using Windows XP, or an even older version of Windows, you'll find some things have been moved, rearranged, or renamed. Many people will want to start with Chapter 1 to find their way around Windows and the desktop. If you're new Windows 7 computer is replacing another computer, you may want to start with Chapter 10 to quickly move your files and settings from the old to the new computer. Here's a short summary of what you'll find:

Chapter 1 Navigating Windows 7 In this chapter, you'll get a tour of the Windows 7 user interface and see how to use it to accomplish your day-to-day computing chores. Some of the things you'll learn include how to find and run programs from the Start menu, how the Taskbar helps you manage running programs (and open new ones), and some ways to customize each. You'll also see how Jump Lists give you easy access to frequently used files and program functions, and learn how to easily manipulate and switch between program windows using keyboard and mouse commands.

Chapter 2 Managing User Accounts One of Windows 7's strengths is its ability to accommodate multiple users and allow each to customize the operating system to his or her own tastes. In this chapter you'll be introduced to the different Windows 7 user account types and understand why you should create separate accounts for different members of your household. You'll learn how to create accounts and protect them with passwords, as well as how to use parental controls to limit when and how a child can use the computer.

Chapter 3 Working with Files and Folders In this chapter, you'll see how Windows 7 sets up a series of special folders for each user (and for all users collectively) to store various forms of personal data such as documents, pictures, or music. Then you'll learn how Windows 7 uses libraries to help you organize similar types of files that are stored in different places. You will learn how to use the search feature to quickly find information like files, programs, or configuration settings.

Chapter 4 Personalizing Windows Windows 7 is more than just a new pretty face. It offers new ways to customize how Windows looks and behaves, from your desktop colors to the way your mouse works. By personalizing Windows, you can make it more fun, simpler, and convenient for you to use. In this chapter, you'll learn how to customize the appearance of Windows by changing the desktop background, Windows colors, and your screen saver. You'll also learn how to make the screen easier to use, and adjust other settings to make your computer more accessible for visual, audio, and mobility needs.

Chapter 5 Fixing Problems from A to Ctrl+Z Windows 7 is a wonderful operating system; it's easy, reliable, and safe to use. Occasionally things don't go the way you want them to. It could a problem with settings in Windows, new software you installed, or a new device you just hooked up. In this chapter, you'll learn how to use Windows features like troubleshooters, Safe Mode, System Restore, Advanced Recovery, and Help and Support Center to fix problems. You'll also learn practical tips for fixing everyday problems within programs, and practical steps for avoiding or preventing problems before they happen.

Chapter 6 Protecting Your Data It won't be long before your Windows 7 computer is filled with all kinds of important, if not irreplaceable, personal data, and this chapter will show you how to make sure that data isn't lost as the result of an unexpected computer trouble. You'll learn how to configure Windows 7 to back up your personal files and/or make a copy of the entire computer contents (including your programs and Windows 7 itself) so that you're prepared and protected in case of a problem. You'll also learn how to restore the previous version of a file in case you accidentally overwrite it with unwanted changes.

Chapter 7 Creating a Home Network Whether you use a single computer connected directly to the Internet, or connect to other computers within your home, you are using a network. Windows 7 provides new features and improvements to make it easier to connect to the Internet and other computers, and share printers, files and storage. In this chapter, you will learn how to use the new HomeGroup feature, and the improved Network and Sharing Center. You'll also learn how to set up your network to protect your files and access.

Chapter 8 Using Windows 7 Programs Windows 7 includes lots of handy built-in programs to help you with your daily computer chores, and in this chapter we'll take a look at some of them. Some of the things you'll learn include how to browse the web with Internet Explorer, how to play music and video with Windows Media Player, and how to scan documents using Windows Fax and Scan. You'll also learn how to add and remove your own programs, and how to control what program is run when you open a certain type of file. In addition, we'll tell you how to configure Windows 7 to run a particular program or perform a particular task when you use items like Audio CDs, DVD movies, or external storage devices.

Chapter 9 Safeguarding Your Computer This probably isn't the first chapter you wanted to read. But maybe it should be. One bad computer virus can really ruin your day. Or week. Fortunately Windows 7 comes out of the box (or onto your computer) with new and improved security features to protect you and your computer. But computer hackers are working round the clock to find new ways to attack computers. So there are several things you need to set up to keep your computer protected today and tomorrow. In this chapter, we'll cover how to use Windows 7 to protect your computer with features like Automatic Update, Windows Firewall, User Accounts, antispyware, and third party virus protection programs. You'll also learn practical ways to use your computer safely in daily use, including surfing the Internet and exchanging e-mail.

Chapter 10 Moving Files and Settings to Your Windows 7 Computer Windows 7 provides some professional help to make your move to a new computer less stressful: Windows Easy Transfer. With Windows Easy Transfer, you can copy files and settings from your old computer, even another computer running Windows 7, to your new computer running Windows 7. In this chapter, you'll go through the common tasks associated with getting a new computer, such as moving files and settings with Windows Easy Transfer or alternate methods, installing programs on your new computer, upgrading a computer to Windows 7 from a previous version of Windows, and using or disposing of your old computer.

About the Boxes in the Series

There are three tip boxes sprinkled throughout the book that we will use to call out information that we think is important for you in some way. They are: NotED, ExplainED, and LinkED, and they look like this:

NotED

A NotED box will tell you something that you might find useful, but that you don't need to know in order to get the most from this book and the subject you're learning. They contain things that are worth noting that you can use in your own projects, or that you may want to come back to when it suits you.

ExplainED

An ExplainED box will give you more information on the subject under discussion. They add more detail to the main text and explain additional concepts that you may find useful as you read. We'll also use them for recapping relevant information that you may have forgotten from previous chapters.

LinkED

A LinkED box will provide you with a link to somewhere you can find more information on a subject. This may be a reference to a website, somewhere you can see the topic you're discussing come to life, or simply a link to another chapter in the book where a discussion is continued.

Any of the boxes can be skipped if you want to focus on the chapter and come back to them at a later time, or you can pause at each one and spend some time investigating the information they give before returning to the chapter. It's up to you.

Chapter 1

Navigating Windows 7

In this chapter, you'll explore the basics of the Windows 7 interface, which is often referred to as the **desktop** (Figure 1-1). You'll learn how to use the Start menu to run programs, how the taskbar helps you organize and keep track of multiple running programs (and launch new ones), how the notification area provides access to system information and settings, and how to manage open windows.

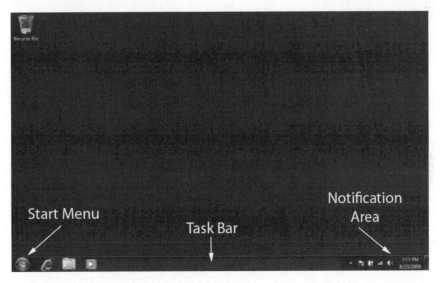

Figure 1-1. The Windows 7 desktop

The Start menu

The Start menu will often be the first place you visit when you begin using the computer and the last place you visit when you're done, because from here you can perform tasks such as run programs, search for and open files and folders, change system settings, shut down the system, and so on. Click the Start button, the round Windows logo in the lower-left corner of the screen, to display the Start menu (Figure 1-2).

Getting Started ▶

Windows Media Center

Calculator

Sticky Notes

Snipping Tool

Paint

Magnifier

Solitaire

▶ All Programs

Search programs and files 🔍

Andrea

Documents

Pictures

Music

Games

Computer

Control Panel

Devices and Printers

Default Programs

Help and Support

Shut down ▶

Figure 1-2. The Start menu is your jumping-off point for accessing programs, system settings, and more. (Note: The items displayed on the left side of your Start menu won't necessarily be the same as the ones shown here.)

AdvancED

Pressing the Windows key will also open the Start *menu.*

Running programs

You can find and run programs from the `Start` menu's left pane, where you'll see a group of default programs as well as some you've recently used. Just click a program to run it. If the program you want isn't in the list, click `All Programs` to browse through a menu listing all the programs installed on your system (Figure 1-3).

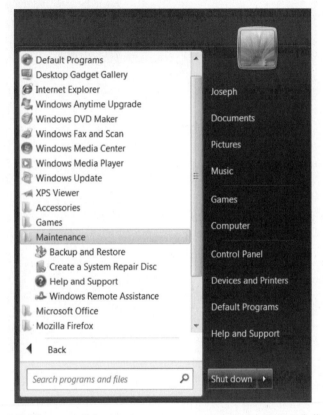

Figure 1-3. When you click `All Programs`, you can browse a menu of all the software installed on your system.

3

Start menu items with a folder icon represent a group of related items. When you click one, the list will expand to show each item in the group.

Finding programs

When you want to run a particular program but aren't sure where to find it, you don't need to wade through a series of menus looking for it because the *Start* menu's search box can help you locate it quickly. Just type in the name of the program—or even the first few letters of the name—to display a menu containing a list of full or partial matches (Figure 1-4).

You can start typing a search term as soon as you open the *Start* menu; you don't need to click the search box first. Also, the search results will update automatically as you type; click the X to clear what you've typed and start over.

We'll be using the *Start* menu's search box extensively throughout this book, because it can be a quick and efficient alternative to navigating through menus when you need to locate not just a program but settings, files, and folders as well. To follow along with the examples in the book, you'll want to use our suggested keywords, but we encourage you to experiment with your own as you get familiar with Windows 7.

4

Figure 1-4. Type all or part of a program (or setting or filename) into the `Start` menu's search box to get a list of matches.

In Figure 1-4, for example, you'll notice that typing `back` produces program matches for both `Backup and Restore` and `Internet Backgammon`, along with a variety of setting matches. If there were any files or folders with `back` in the name, they'd appear in the list of search results as well.

LinkED

For more on searching for files and folders, see Chapter 3.

Customizing the program list

One way to ensure your favorite programs are easily accessible is to make them immediately visible when the Start menu appears by **pinning** them to the Start menu. To pin a program to the Start menu, pick the program you want—it can be in the recently used list, it can be in the All Programs menu, or you can find it with the search box. Then right-click the program and choose Pin to Start Menu (Figure 1-5).

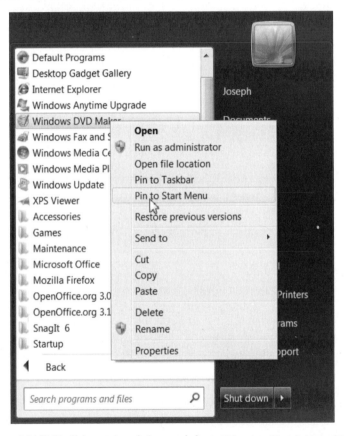

Figure 1-5. Right-click a program's icon and choose Pin to Start Menu to permanently add it to the top of the menu.

Programs that are pinned to the Start menu will appear at the top of the program list and be separated from other programs by a thin line, as shown in Figure 1-6.

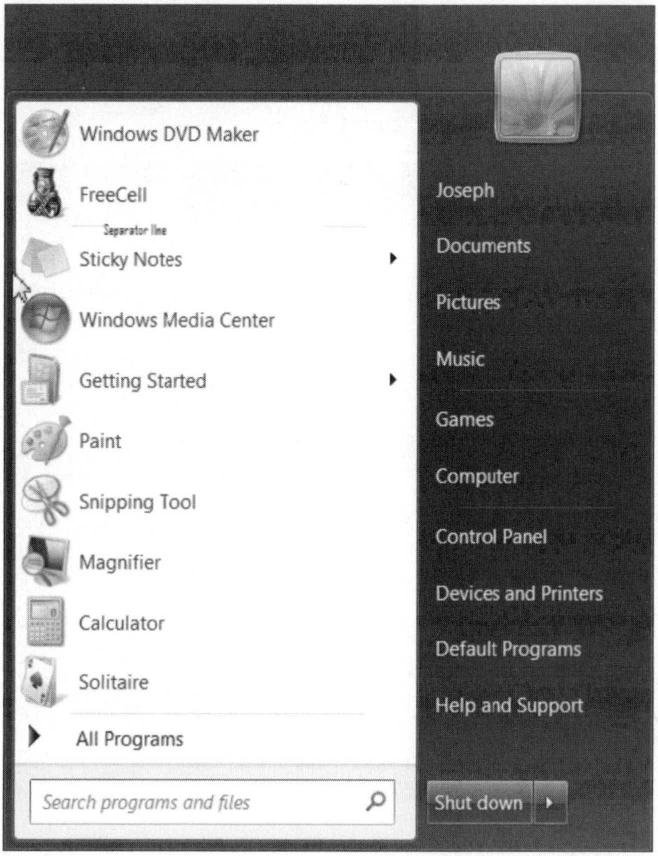

Figure 1-6. In this Start menu, both Windows DVD Maker and FreeCell are pinned.

You can also pin a default or recently used program to the Start menu by dragging its icon toward the top-left corner of the Start menu until the icon displays a Pin to Start menu label, as shown in Figure 1-7.

Figure 1-7. You can pin programs by dragging them toward the upper left of the
Start menu.

To remove a pinned, default, or recently used program from the Start
menu, right-click the item and choose Remove from this list.

LinkED

Another way to keep programs within easy reach is to pin them to the taskbar, which we'll outline later in this chapter.

Using Jump Lists to open files and run programs

Sometimes a program listed in your `Start` menu will include a small right arrow. This arrow means the program has a **Jump List**—a special menu that offers convenient access to recently used files (and, in some cases, common tasks that are related to the program).

To view a Jump List, just leave the mouse pointer over the program listing for a moment. The Jump List in Figure 1-8, for example, lists images recently opened with the Paint program.

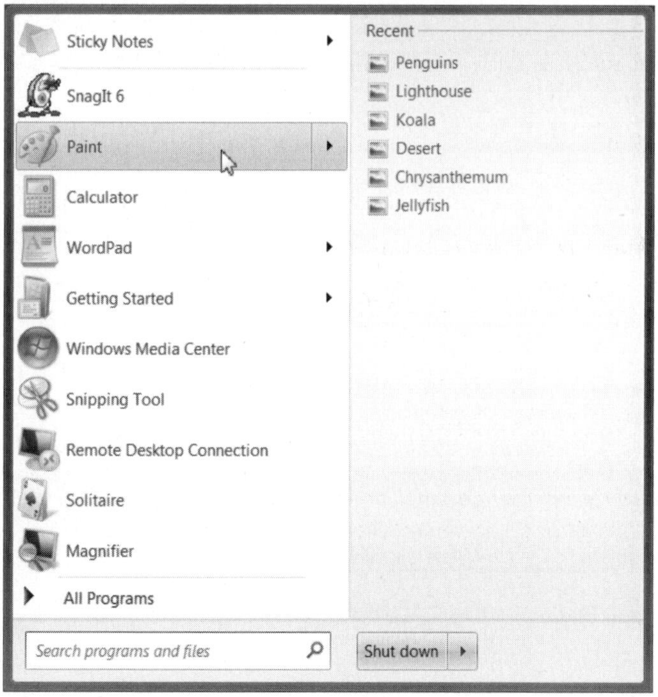

Figure 1-8. Jump Lists provide convenient access to a program's recently used files.

Jump Lists don't appear when you use the Start menu to search for programs.

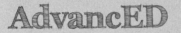

To have an item permanently appear on the Jump List, highlight it and click the pushpin icon that pops up.

Browsing folders and settings

The Start menu's right pane provides numerous shortcuts to commonly used areas of Windows 7. The top section (the portion above the first horizontal line) contains a shortcut to a user's personal account folders—click the account name in the upper right to view them (Figure 1-9). You can also click the three individual shortcuts for direct access to Documents, Pictures, or Music.

Figure 1-9. Click the name in the upper right of the Start menu to view the account's personal folders.

After you click the account name, a window will open displaying a group of account folders (Figure 1-10). Double-click a folder to view its contents.

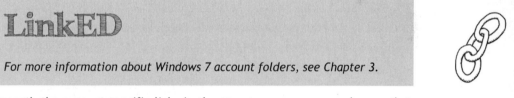

Figure 1-10. The personal folders for an account

LinkED

For more information about Windows 7 account folders, see Chapter 3.

Beneath the account-specific links in the `Start` menu are several more that you can use to perform tasks such as browse storage devices (`Computer`), find system settings (`Control Panel`), get help, and more. Figure 1-11 shows the `Control Panel` window that opens when you click the `Control Panel` link.

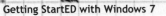

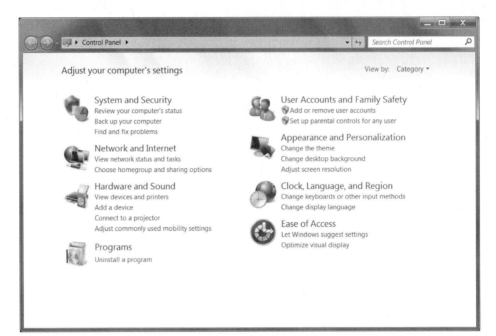

Figure 1-11. The `Start` menu's `Control Panel` link provides a menu of system settings.

AdvancED

We won't visit the Control Panel very often in this book since we'll be using Windows 7's search feature to find specific settings directly. However, the Control Panel is a good jumping-off point when you want to view or adjust Windows 7 settings.

Shutting down and logging off

Clicking the `Shut down` button (Figure 1-12) will begin the process of shutting down Windows 7 and turning off your computer. By clicking the arrow to the right of the `Shut down` button, you can choose to log off your account, lock the system, restart the computer, or put it into a power-saving mode.

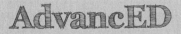

Figure 1-12. Click Shut down to immediately turn off the computer, or click the adjacent arrow to choose other related options.

LinkED

For more on the Log off *and* Lock *options, see Chapter 2.*

AdvancED

If you try to shut down the system while a program has an unsaved file open, the program will interrupt the shutdown and display a window asking if you want to save the file. You should avoid shutting down the system while someone else is already logged into it. If you try, Windows 7 will display a warning message telling you that shutting down might cause other users to lose data and asking you to confirm that you really want to shut down.

The taskbar

The **taskbar** is the narrow horizontal bar that runs across the bottom of the screen (Figure 1-13). The taskbar allows you to easily switch between open programs or windows and, like the Start menu, can provide convenient access to frequently used programs. Three programs are already included on the taskbar by default—they are Internet Explorer, Windows Explorer, and Windows Media Player.

Whenever you run a program or open a file or folder, a button representing that item's window will appear on the taskbar, and clicking an item's taskbar button will make its window active and bring it to the forefront.

Figure 1-13. The taskbar lets you easily launch programs and switch between those already running.

AdvancED

Another way to activate taskbar buttons is by holding down the Windows button and pressing the number key that corresponds to a button's position on the taskbar (going from left to right and not counting the Start button). For the taskbar shown in Figure 1-13, pressing Windows+2 will open Windows Explorer.

There are three different kinds of taskbar buttons (as shown in Figure 1-14).

A button representing an open window is framed to appear "pressed" (in Figure 1-14, the three buttons on the far right)

A button representing an active window (the one in front of all the others) appears highlighted (in Figure 1-14, the button containing the document with the large letter *A*).

AdvancED

If you click an empty part of the taskbar while there are windows open, the button for the active window will no longer be highlighted, though it will still be in front.

Buttons that are neither framed nor highlighted represent program shortcuts (in Figure 1-14, the three buttons directly to the right of the Start button). We'll discuss these a little later in this chapter.

Figure 1-14. Taskbar buttons that look "pressed" represent open windows, while a highlighted button (the one with the letter *A* in this shot) shows which window is active.

Previewing program windows

You don't necessarily need to click a program's taskbar button to see what the window contains. If you simply place the mouse pointer over a taskbar button, a preview window will pop up displaying the program's name (as well of that of an open file, if applicable) and a thumbnail image of the window (Figure 1-15).

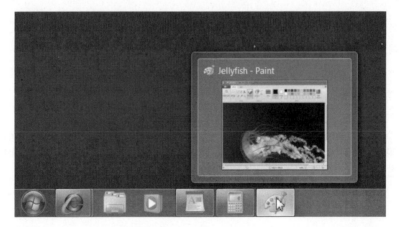

Figure 1-15. Place the mouse pointer over an open window's taskbar button to get a glimpse at the program it represents.

Sometimes a taskbar thumbnail image provides only limited information about the program. For example, most people would be hard-pressed to read the tiny letters in the thumbnail image of a text document. In this case, moving the mouse pointer over the thumbnail image will reveal the corresponding program window while reducing all other open windows to transparent outlines (Figure 1-16).

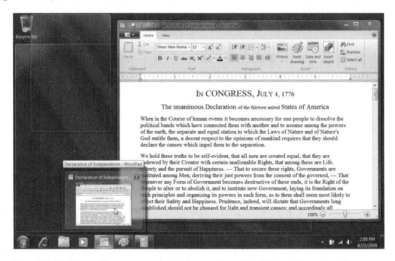

Figure 1-16. Place the mouse pointer over a thumbnail image to reveal its program window.

AdvancED

Windows 7 Starter Edition, which is common on netbooks, doesn't include the ability to preview windows via taskbar buttons.

LinkED

For more on netbooks, see Getting StartED with Netbooks *by Nancy Nicolaisen and Karen Offermann (friends of ED, 2009).*

When a program has more than one window open (for example, if you've opened two websites with Internet Explorer), all windows are grouped together under a single taskbar button. You can tell when a button has more than one window because it will look like several buttons stacked on top of each other, as shown in Figure 1-17.

Figure 1-17. The extra line to the right of the Internet Explorer button means the program has two windows open. In the case of the Windows Explorer button to its right, there are three open.

When you click or place the mouse pointer over a taskbar button with multiple windows attached, you'll see thumbnail previews of each window, as shown in Figure 1-18. Click a particular thumbnail to switch to that window. You can also place the mouse pointer over a thumbnail to bring that window to the forefront and temporarily hide all others, as shown in Figure 1-19.

Figure 1-18. Click a taskbar button with multiple windows to display thumbnail views of each.

Figure 1-19. Put the mouse pointer over a thumbnail to bring the window to the forefront and temporarily hide other windows.

AdvancED

The small x you see in the upper-right corner when you put the mouse pointer over a thumbnail will close that window when clicked.

Adding program buttons to the taskbar

The taskbar isn't only for switching between programs that are already running. Just as you can make favorite programs easier to access by pinning them to the Start menu, you can also create taskbar buttons for them by pinning them to the taskbar. As mentioned earlier, Windows 7 pins a few programs—Internet Explorer, Windows Explorer, and Windows Media Player—to the Start menu in advance.

To create a taskbar button for a program, find the program (in the Start menu, for example) and then right-click it and choose Pin to Taskbar (Figure 1-20). (Note: If you pin a Start menu item to the taskbar, it will be removed from the Start menu.)

AdvancED

You will also see the `Pin to Taskbar` *option when you drag a program icon to the taskbar.*

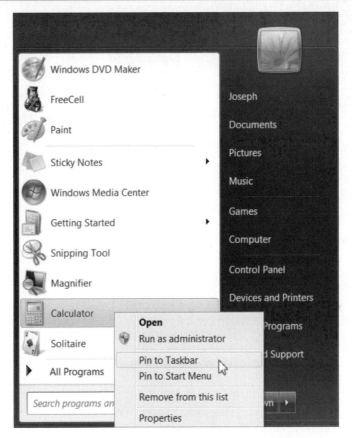

Figure 1-20. Pinning a program to the taskbar creates a button for it.

After you pin a program to the taskbar, you'll see a new button for it (Figure 1-21).

Figure 1-21. The taskbar, with a button for the Calculator program added

AdvancED

The order of taskbar buttons remains the same whether they represent open windows or pinned programs. You can click and drag buttons around the taskbar to rearrange them into whatever order you choose, and you'll always be able to tell which buttons represent open windows, because those buttons will be framed or highlighted as described earlier.

To unpin a program from the taskbar, right-click the button and choose `Unpin this program from taskbar`.

Using Jump Lists from the taskbar

Jump Lists aren't just limited to the `Start` menu—you can use them from the taskbar too.

ExplainED

You may recall from earlier in this chapter that Jump Lists are shortcuts to recently used files or commonly used tasks for a program.

Right-click a taskbar button—it doesn't matter whether it's for a program that's running or not—and a Jump List will appear giving you access to recently opened files and common tasks (and, in the case of Internet Explorer, recent websites, as shown in Figure 1-22).

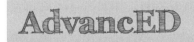

Figure 1-22. Jump Lists provide convenient access to recently used items and common tasks.

AdvancED

Some programs—especially ones released prior to Windows 7—may not offer Jump Lists in either the Start *menu or the taskbar.*

If you right-click the taskbar and select Properties, *you can change aspects of the taskbar's appearance, behavior, and location.*

Using the notification area

On the right side of the taskbar you'll find the **notification area**, which includes a time and date display along with a group of small icons that provide information about and access to various system or program settings (Figure 1-23).

Figure 1-23. The notification area provides system information and quick access to important settings.

On desktop systems, the notification area consists of three icons. The first two (viewed from right to left) let you view and change audio volume and network settings, respectively, while the third icon—the one that looks like a pennant—opens the Action Center, where you can view messages regarding potential system problems. On laptop systems, there's a extra icon for managing power settings, as you can see in Figure 1-23.

We cover the Action Center in more detail in Chapter 9.

Programs you install on your system will often include their own notification area icons, but Windows 7 automatically hides these to reduce clutter and minimize use of taskbar space. If you see an arrow to the left of the notification area, it means at least one icon is hidden from view. Click the arrow to see the hidden icons (Figure 1-24); to see a hidden icon at all times, click and drag it to the notification area.

Figure 1-24. Click the notification area arrow to expose any hidden icons.

To change the setting for several notification area icons at once, click `Customize` to display the `Notification Area Icons` window (Figure 1-25).

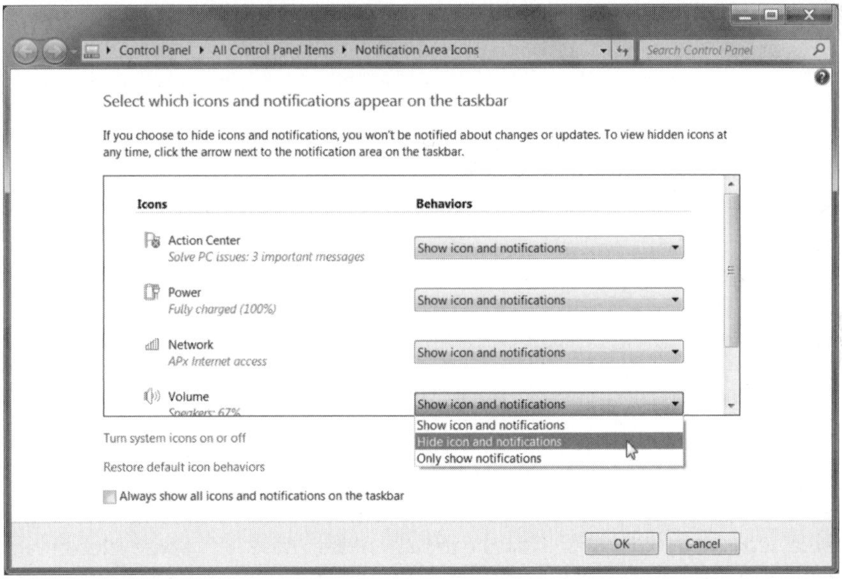

Figure 1-25. The `Notification Area Icons` window lets you decide which icons will appear there.

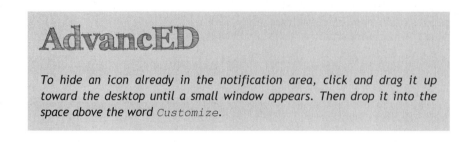

AdvancED

To hide an icon already in the notification area, click and drag it up toward the desktop until a small window appears. Then drop it into the space above the word Customize.

Manipulating windows with the mouse

Every window includes a trio of buttons in the upper-right corner that you can use to minimize, maximize, and close the window (Figure 1-26). When the window is maximized, you can resize it by placing the mouse pointer anywhere along a window's edge (or in the corners) until the pointer changes to a double-headed arrow and then clicking and dragging to make the window larger or smaller.

Figure 1-26. These buttons let you minimize, maximize, or close a window, respectively.

Windows 7 also offers several handy shortcuts you can use to change the size or position of windows.

Stretching a window vertically

Stretching a window vertically to make it as tall as possible can make viewing certain types of information easier, such as a long text document or a web page.

To maximize a window to the full height of the screen without making it any wider (as shown in Figure 1-27), position the mouse pointer at the upper or lower edge of the window until the pointer becomes a double vertical arrow; then double-click. Repeat the process or drag the window downward slightly to return it to its original size and orientation.

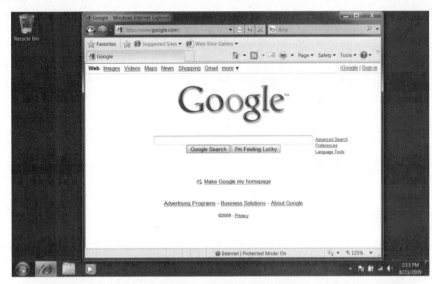

Figure 1-27. Click the top or bottom edge of a window to stretch it to full height while keeping its width the same.

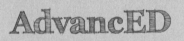

AdvancED

Double-click a window's top bar (or press Windows+up arrow) to maximize it to full-screen.

Arranging windows side-by-side

There may be times when you need to work with two large windows side-by-side (such as when copying or moving files between locations or viewing two programs simultaneously). Manually moving and sizing windows into this orientation can be cumbersome, but Windows 7 allows you to do it relatively easily with a feature called Snap.

To arrange two windows in an adjacent and nonoverlapping position, hold the left mouse button down while the mouse pointer is over a window's top bar, and then drag it over to the left or right edge of the screen. When you see the outline appear filling half the screen, let go of the window (Figure 1-28).

To minimize how far you need to move the mouse while dragging a window, grab it on the side in which you're going to move (that is, don't grab the left side of a window and drag to the right).

Figure 1-28. Drag a window to the edge of the screen, and it will resize to take up that half of the desktop.

Repeat the process on the opposite side of the screen with another window, and when you're finished, the two will be arranged exactly side-by-side, as shown in Figure 1-29.

Figure 1-29. Viewing two windows side-by-side

AdvancED

You can also snap windows to the edges of the screen with the keyboard. Click the window, hold the Windows key, and press either the left or right arrow to move it to that edge. Hold the Windows key and press the opposite arrow to undo it.

To return a window to normal size, double-click its top bar, or drag the window away from the edge of the screen.

LinkED

For more on the Snap feature, see http://windows.microsoft.com/en-us/windows7/products/features/snap.

Minimizing background windows

You can take advantage of Windows 7's Aero Shake feature to focus on a single window without being distracted by others in the background. Just click and hold the top bar of a window you want to focus on, and then quickly shake the mouse pointer back and forth (either left/right, up/down, or diagonal) to quickly minimize all but the window you've selected. Repeat the process, and the minimized windows will reappear.

AdvancED

Shaking a window is easy with a mouse but can be trickier with some other pointing devices, such as the touchpad found with most notebooks. To minimize all but the active window using the keyboard, use the keystroke Windows+Home.

LinkED

For more on Aero Shake, see http://windows.microsoft.com/en-us/windows7/products/features/aero-shake.

Minimizing all windows

When multiple overlapping windows are open, they often block your view of items on the Windows 7 desktop. To see what's beneath them, put the mouse pointer over the small vertical rectangle at the extreme right edge of the taskbar. All open windows will temporarily become transparent outlines, allowing you to view the items below (Figure 1-30). Click this rectangle to immediately minimize all open windows, and then click it again to restore them to their original positions.

Figure 1-30. Take a peek behind open windows by moving the mouse pointer to the rectangle in the lower-right corner of the screen.

AdvancED

Windows 7's Aero Peek feature lets you see behind open windows without using the mouse. Just hold down the Windows key and tap the spacebar— the windows will turn to outlines and reappear when you let go of the Windows key. To minimize all windows, hold down the Windows key and press D; then do it again to reopen them.

LinkED

The ability to see through open windows comes in handy when you use desktop gadgets, which we'll discuss in Chapter 8.

LinkED

For more on Aero Peek, see http://windows.microsoft.com/en-us/windows7/products/features/aero-peek.

Browsing open windows with the keyboard

Windows 7 gives you three ways to browse and select from among all the open windows on your desktop using the keyboard:

- Alt+Tab
- Windows+Tab
- Alt+Esc

Alt+Tab

Hold down the Alt key while pressing Tab, and a box will pop up displaying thumbnail images of every open window, beginning with the active one (Figure 1-31). Continue holding down Alt and press Tab repeatedly to cycle through the thumbnail images, and release the keys when you find the one you want. As you select each thumbnail, the window it represents will be brought to the forefront of the desktop, while the remaining open windows are replaced with outlines.

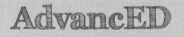

You can also press Shift+Alt+Tab to cycle backward.

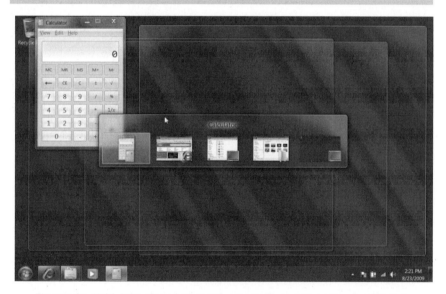

Figure 1-31. Hold down Alt and press Tab repeatedly to browse thumbnails of open windows.

Windows+Tab

The thumbnail images displayed by Alt+Tab aren't large enough to let you see window details, but by holding down the Windows key while pressing Tab repeatedly, you can cycle through a series of larger, three-dimensional thumbnails, which will provide a closer look at each window's content (Figure 1-32).

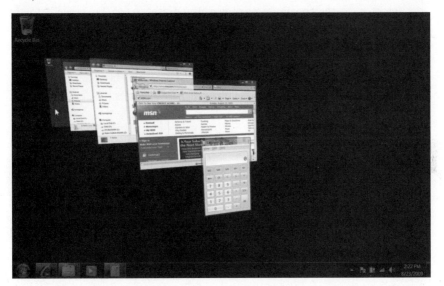

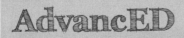

Figure1-32. Hold down the Windows key while pressing Tab to see larger, three-dimensional window thumbnails.

Alt+Esc

This option is a way to switch between open windows directly without displaying thumbnails first. Hold down Alt while pressing Esc repeatedly to make each open window active.

AdvancED

The Alt+Tab and Windows+Tab methods each provide a desktop thumbnail that will automatically minimize all open windows but not restore them all at once.

Summary

Here's a review of what you've learned in this chapter:

- How to use the `Start` menu to find and run programs, view account folders, access other Windows 7 features, and shut down your system
- How to use Jump Lists to open files and run programs
- How to use the taskbar to manage open windows and run programs
- How to pin programs to the `Start` menu and taskbar
- What the notification area does and how to customize it
- How to manipulate Windows with the mouse and how to browse open windows with the keyboard

Chapter 2

Managing User Accounts

User accounts in Windows 7 serve two main purposes. The first is to allow different people to customize the operating system to their own personal preferences, and the second is to make sure that people can't gain access to each other's files.

For example, imagine if you sat down at the computer and found that characteristics such as the background wallpaper, colors, and menu options were different from the last time you were there because someone else had come along and changed all the settings. Similarly, you probably wouldn't want other members of your household to be able to read, change, move, or delete your important personal files.

User accounts can make sure this kind of thing doesn't happen. Through user accounts, each person who uses the computer gets to customize the "look and feel" of Windows 7 the way they want, and everyone's personal files are kept separate and private.

The other purpose of user accounts is to control what somewhat can do in Windows 7 and what kinds of settings they can change. You might not want a child or a houseguest to be able to install their own software or change critical settings that could damage the system. Making sure each user has the right type of account can prevent this.

In a nutshell, user accounts make it easier and safer for multiple people to share access to the same computer.

Exploring Windows 7 account types

Windows 7 provides three types of user accounts: standard, administrator, and guest. Each offers a different level of access to the computer:

- **Standard**: The standard account provides you with a lot of control over how you use the computer, but not enough to affect other users. For example, a standard account lets you access personal files and customize many operating system settings, but it doesn't allow you to use other people's files, change security-related settings, or install new hardware or software.
- **Administrator**: The administrator account provides complete and unrestricted access to all Windows 7 settings (including those of other users) and all of a computer's files and folders. You can also use an administrator account to create, delete, or change accounts that belong to other users.
- **Guest**: The guest account is a special type of limited-access account that's primarily designed for infrequent or temporary users.

Windows 7 requires the computer to have at least one administrator account, but the standard account is appropriate for most users because it limits the amount of control they have over the operating system while still allowing them to get things done.

Even if you're the person in charge of controlling and maintaining the computer (that is, the administrator), you should still use a standard account for day-to-day computing because it can keep you from accidentally making potentially undesirable changes to Windows and can help prevent similarly harmful modifications from being made without your knowledge by malicious programs or websites.

If you use a standard account and try to make a change that requires an administrator account, such as creating a new account, as described next, you'll still be able to do it, but Windows 7 will pop up a window confirming the action and requiring you to type an administrator account password to proceed.

Creating a user account

To create a new user account, perform the following steps:

1. Click the `Start` button, and then type `add users` into the search box. Choose `Add or Remove user` accounts from the list of search results, and you'll open the `Manage Accounts` window (Figure 2-1).

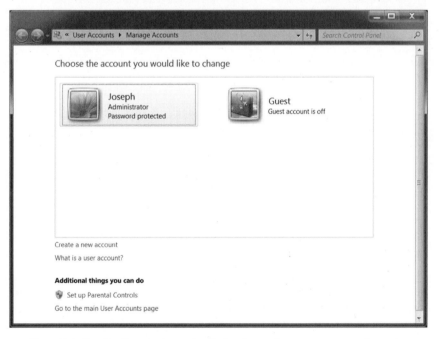

Figure 2-1. Use the Manage Accounts window to create new user accounts.

2. Click `Create a new account`, type a name in the `New account name` box (such as `Andrea` in this example), and choose whether you want the account to be a standard user or an administrator (Figure 2-2).

ExplainED

Remember, standard accounts are preferred because unlike administrator accounts, they don't let you change critical settings or those that affect other users.

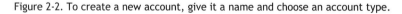

Figure 2-2. To create a new account, give it a name and choose an account type.

3. Click the `Create Account` button to set up the new account. You'll return to the `Manage Accounts` window, where you can see the account you just created (Figure 2-3). Use the `Create a new account` link again if you need to create additional accounts.

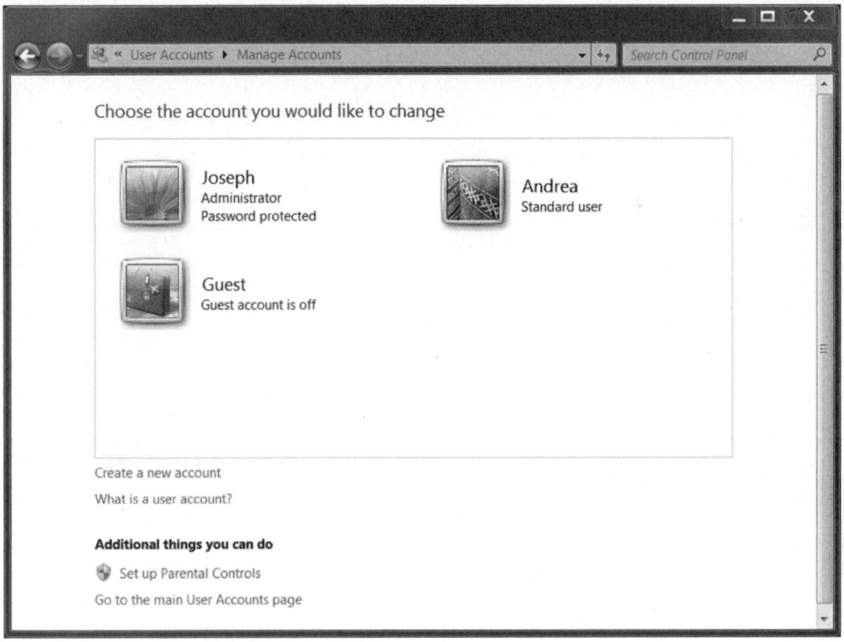

Figure 2-3. Presto! You've created a new account.

Using the guest account

Windows 7's guest account lets you give someone access to the computer without having to set up a personal account for them or let them use someone else's account. For example, if visiting friends or family want to use your computer to check e-mail or browse the Web, they can do so with the guest account. The guest account is extremely limited; it can't change most settings, install software or hardware, or even have a password assigned to it (more on passwords in a moment).

No matter how much you trust a visitor, friend, or relative, it is not a good idea to give them access to your user account. If you want them to have fuller access to the computer than what a guest account allows, add a standard account for them. When they no longer need access to the computer, you can delete the account.

Before you can use the guest account, you need to turn it on. To do so, start from the `Manage Accounts` window shown in Figure 2-3, and click the guest account's suitcase icon. Then click the `Turn On` button (Figure 2-4).

Figure 2-4. You need to turn on the guest account before you can use it.

Logging off an account

When you no longer need to use the computer, you can log off your account, which will close all your programs but not turn off the computer. To log off, click the `Start` button, click the arrow next to the `Shut down` button (not the button itself), and select `Log off` (Figure 2-5). If you have any programs with unsaved files open, you'll be prompted to save them before your account is logged off.

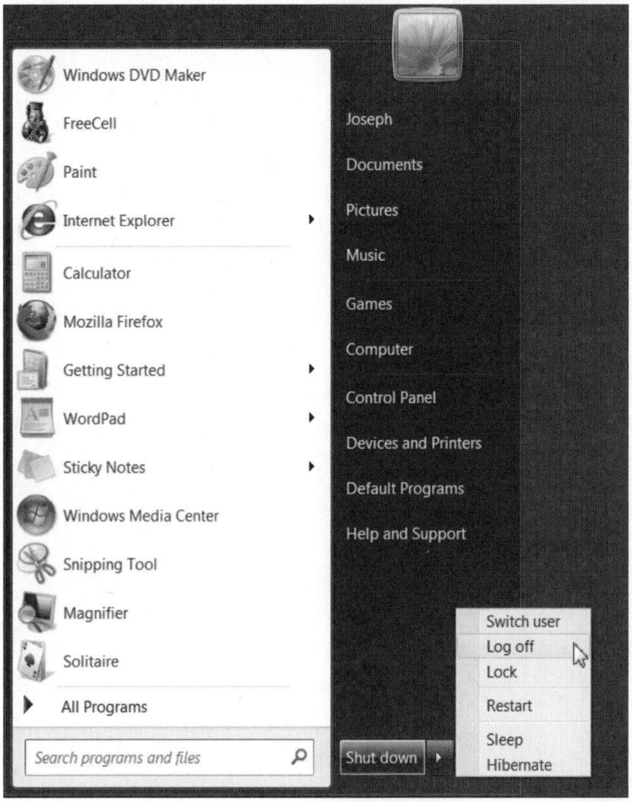

Figure 2-5. Use the `Log off` option when you're done using the computer.

You don't need to log off your account every time you walk away from the computer. Many users find it more convenient to stay logged in unless they expect to be away from the computer for an extended period of time. As you're about to see, keeping an account logged in doesn't prevent other people from using their own accounts.

Switching between accounts

Although only one person can sit in front of the computer to use their account at a time, Windows 7 does allow multiple accounts to be logged in simultaneously, which is handy because it lets others use the computer while you're away from it, even if you didn't log off your account. To make the computer available for someone else to use in your absence without logging off your account, go to the `Shut down` menu shown in Figure 2-5, and click `Switch user`.

This will keep your account running but will return the computer to the Windows 7 welcome screen so another user can log in (Figure 2-6).

LinkED

For information about shutting down the computer, including what happens if you try to shut down while someone else is logged in, see Chapter 3.

Figure 2-6. Even when someone else is already logged into Windows 7, you can also log in from the welcome screen by clicking your account icon.

Another option is to press the Windows+L, which will "lock" your account and allow someone else to log in from the welcome screen after clicking the `Switch User` button (Figure 2-7).

Figure 2-7. The Switch User button (Figure 2-7).

Figure 2-7. The Switch User button lets you log into a computer that's already in use.

Windows 7 will allow two, three, four, or even more accounts to remain logged in at the same time. However, depending how much memory is installed in your computer (and how many programs each of the logged-in accounts has running), having too many accounts logged in at the same time may noticeably slow down the computer's performance and cause it to take a long time to switch between accounts. In addition, some programs may not work properly when multiple accounts are using them simultaneously, so you may need to close certain programs in one account before you can use them in another. (Apple iTunes is a good example.)

Setting up account passwords

Windows 7 doesn't require you to set passwords on user accounts, but it's a good idea to have one to protect each user account. This is especially true for administrator accounts because of the unrestricted access they provide, but ideally you should make sure a password is assigned to each account to prevent the wrong person from using it—either intentionally or by accident.

ExplainED

Remember that the guest account can't have a password, so it's available to anyone.

Creating an account password

The first time you start Windows on a new computer or after Windows 7 has been installed, you're prompted to create a password for the first account you add. If you didn't specify a password or your account was added later after installation, you should set a password for it.

To create a password for your own account, make sure you're logged into the account, and then perform the following steps:

1. Type `account password` in the `Start` menu's search box, and then select `Create or remove your account password` to display the `User Accounts` window shown in Figure 2-8.

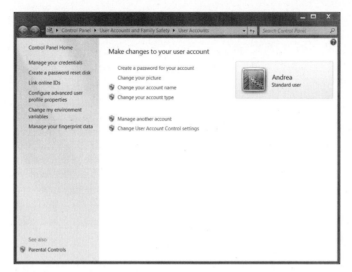

Figure 2-8. You should create a password for each new account.

2. **Click** `Create a password for your account;` in the `Create Your Password` window, type your chosen password in the `New password` box. Then type it again in the `Confirm new password` box. This ensures you typed it the same way twice—you'll see dots in place of the letters and numbers you type (Figure 2-9).

Figure 2-9. Type your password twice to confirm it.

AdvancED

Passwords should be at least eight characters long and not contain names or even real words. Click How to create a strong password *for additional tips.*

3. Type in a password hint that will be displayed in the event you ever forget your password (the hint will appear only after you've typed in an incorrect password). This step is optional but highly recommended.

ExplainED

As the warning states, the hint you create is visible to anyone who uses the computer, so it should be meaningful only to you. Otherwise, someone might be able to use it to guess your password and get access to your account.

4. Click the Create password button to return to the User Accounts window.

Changing an existing password

Once your user account has a password, you can change it in a couple of ways. One is to type change password in the Start menu's search box and choose Change your Windows password. This will display the same User Accounts window that's shown in Figure 2-8, except the Create a password option will be replaced with one labeled Change your password (Figure 2-10).

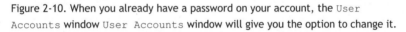

Figure 2-10. When you already have a password on your account, the User
Accounts window User Accounts window will give you the option to change it.

The second way to change a password is to press Ctrl+Alt+Delete while logged
into your account and then click Change a password (Figure 2-11).

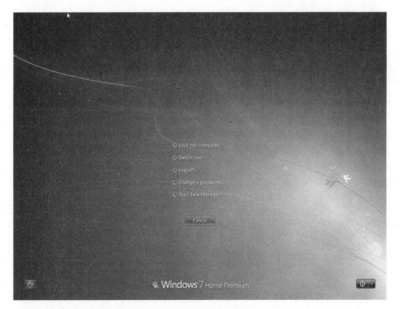

Figure 2-11. Pressing Ctrl+Alt+Delete will display a Change a password option.

ExplainED

Regardless of which of these two methods you choose, you'll need to type in your old password in order to select a new one.

LinkED

As you can see in Figure 2-11, Ctrl+Alt+Delete will also let you lock the computer, switch users, or log off the computer.

Creating a password reset disk

If you ever forget the password for your account and you didn't create a password hint as a reminder (or you did but the hint fails to jog your memory), you can still access your account as long as you have a password reset disk. A password reset disk will let you bypass your old password and create a new one in its place, but in order to get around a forgotten password with a password reset disk, you have to create the disk in advance. If you wait until you need the password reset disk to make it, it will be too late.

You can create a password reset disk on a removable storage device like a floppy disk or USB flash drive. Since very few systems come with floppy disk drives these days, the flash drive option will be the best bet for most systems. The amount of data stored on a password reset disk is tiny, so you don't need a high-capacity flash drive to make one. In fact, the smaller, the better—you'll want to put the drive away for safekeeping, so you won't be able to use it for other things.

To create a password reset disk, follow these steps:

1. Log into the account you want to create the disk for, and plug your flash drive into a free USB port.

2. Then type `password reset` into the `Start` menu's search box, and select `Create a password reset disk` to start the Forgotten Password Wizard (Figure 2-12).

Figure 2-12. The Forgotten Password Wizard will help you make a password reset disk.

3. The wizard will ask you to confirm the storage device you want to use and ask you to type in your current password before creating a password reset disk for your account. It will usually select the correct storage device for you automatically, but if you have any other removable storage devices connected to your computer, you may need to choose your flash drive from the drop-down list.

After making your password reset disk, be sure to clearly label it as such and put it away in a safe place. It's important to protect your password reset disk from loss or theft, because anyone who finds it can use it to gain access to your account. A password reset disk can store information for only a single account; if you want to create one for more than one account, you'll need a separate storage device for each.

Once you've created the password reset disk for a particular account, you won't need to do it again. You can use it as many times as you need to, even if you change your password after making the disk.

Using a password reset disk

If you ever need to take advantage of your password reset disk, you'll be able to after you've typed in an incorrect password. When you return to the account login screen, you'll see a new link called `Reset password` beneath the password box (Figure 2-13).

Figure 2-13. After you type in the wrong password, a `Reset password` link will appear.

Insert your password reset disk, click the link to start the Password Reset Wizard (see Figure 2-14), and then follow the prompts to choose the storage device and create a new password for your account.

Figure 2-14. You can create a new password using the Password Reset Wizard.

Changing account options as an administrator

In the `User Accounts` window (shown earlier in Figure 2-10), you'll see several options, such as `Change your account name` and `Change your account type`, that have a shield icon next to them. This icon indicates that an administrator account is required to access the setting, so if you try to change it with a standard account, you'll be prompted to type in the password for an administrator account before you can do so.

LinkED

The feature that prompts you for an administrator password is called User Account Control, which you'll learn more about in Chapter 9.

49

If you want to change settings for an account that's not currently logged in, follow these steps:

1. Type `change accounts` into the `Start` menu's search box, and select `Make changes to accounts`. (You'll be prompted for an administrator password at this point if you're not already logged into an administrator account.)

2. Click the account you want to change, and the Change an Account window will appear listing all the settings you can change (Figure 2-15). These include changing the account name, the account type (from standard to administrator, or vice versa), setting up Parental Controls, and even deleting an account.

Figure 2-15. Administrators can make a variety of changes to other users' accounts.

Using Parental Controls

If any children will be using the computer, you may want to turn on Windows 7's Parental Controls, which give you a way to limit when and how the computer can be used. By turning on Parental Controls for a particular account, you'll be able to decide when that person can use the computer, whether they can play games (and if so, what kind), and designate certain programs as off-limits.

Note that you must use an administrator account to turn on Parental Controls, and you can apply Parental Controls only to users with standard accounts.

To set up Parental Controls, follow these steps:

1. Type `user parental` into the `Start` menu's search box, and choose `Set up parental controls for any user` to display the window shown in Figure 2-16.

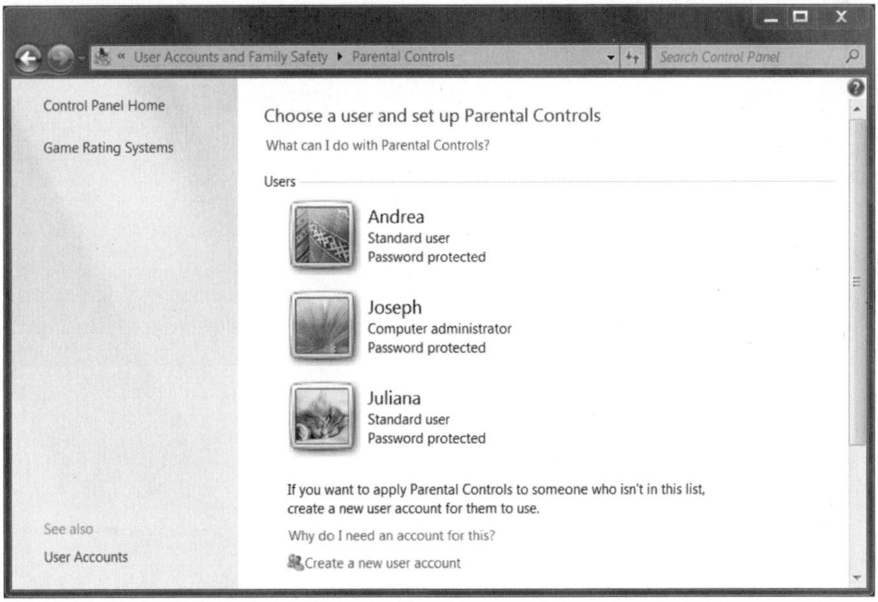

Figure 2-16. To control how a child is able to use the computer, set up Parental Controls for their account.

2. After you've selected the account you want to set up Parental Controls for, click the `On, enforce current settings` option. Now you can customize each of the items listed under `Windows Settings` (Figure 2-17).

ExplainED

You'll want to make sure the guest account is turned off before setting up Parental Controls. That's because you can't set up Parental Controls for the guest account (and remember, you can't password protect it either), so leaving it turned on gives kids a way to bypass your restrictions.

Figure 2-17. After you turn on parental controls for an account, you can configure individual settings.

3. Click `Time Limits`. A **grid** is displayed with the hours that are allowed and blocked.

By default, all hours are allowed (Figure 2-18). Use the mouse to click and drag over the grid to indicate the specific hours and days of the week you want to block. Note that you can configure the grid with noncontiguous blocks—such as to permit computer use between 3 and 5 p.m. and then again between 7 and 9 p.m. Clicking a box in the grid toggles the setting between block and allow.

4. Click OK when you're done with these settings to return to the Parental Controls settings for this account.

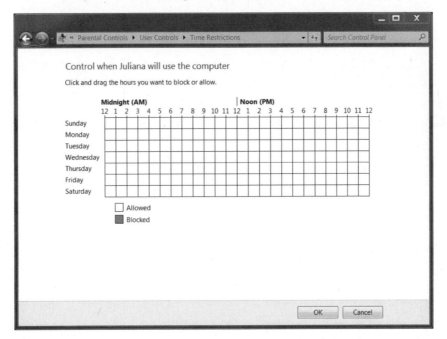

Figure 2-18. Time limits let you control when a child can use the computer.

5. Click Games.

    In addition to blocking access to games entirely, you can use the Set game ratings option to block games that have a particular Entertainment Software Rating Board (ESRB) rating, games that lack a rating, or those that contain certain kinds of undesirable content such as violence or drug references. You can also use the Block or Allow specific games option to disable access to any of the games installed on the computer.

6. Click OK when you're done (Figure 2-19).

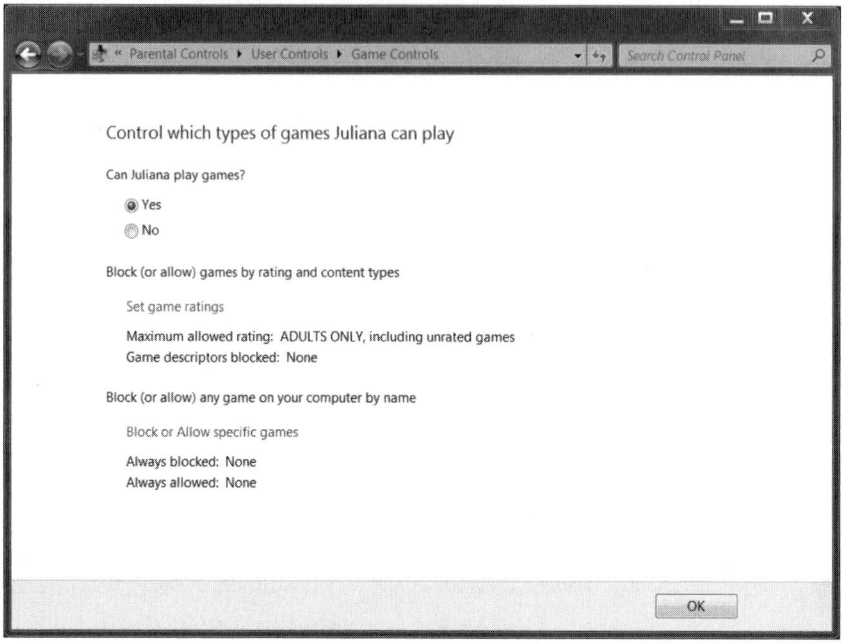

Figure 2-19. You can limit access to games by rating, content type, or name.

7. If you want to have control over not just games but other kinds of software as well (such as instant messaging or file-sharing programs), click the Allow and block specific programs option, and then click <account name> can only use the programs I allow.

8. Within a few moments, a list of all the programs available on the computer will appear. Select the box next to any program you want the account holder to be able to use. Then select the check box for each program you want to allow access to, and then click OK when you're done. (Figure 2-20).

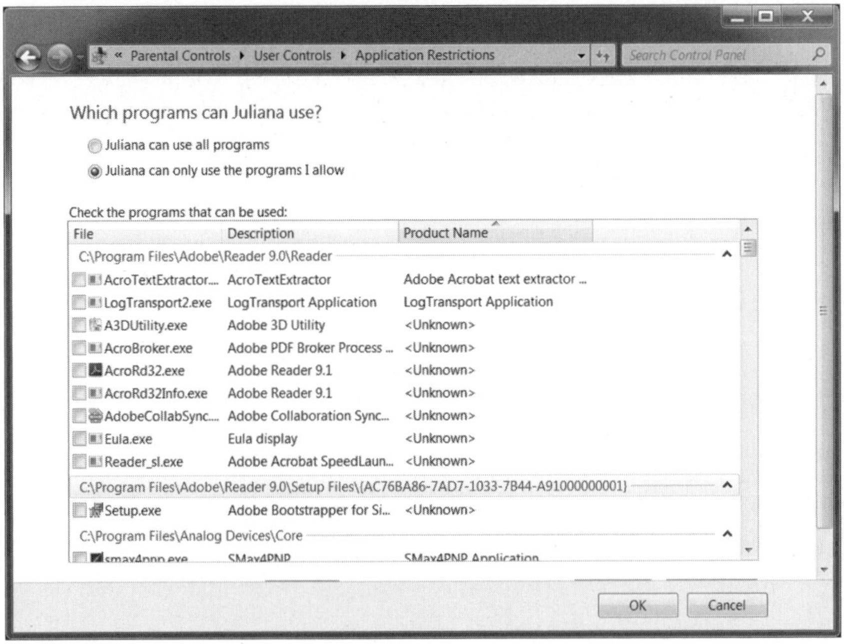

Figure 2-20. If you want to control more than just games, you can block access to all but selected programs.

When using the `Block or Allow specific games` option, the list of programs can be pretty extensive, so finding a specific program you want to allow may take some digging. Also, remember that when this option is selected, only the programs you selected will work.

Summary

Here's a review of what you've learned in this chapter:

- About Windows 7 account types
- How to create an account
- How to activate the guest account
- How to log off and switch between accounts
- How to create and change passwords
- How to create a password reset disk
- How to change account options as an administrator
- How to set up parental controls

Working with Files and Folders

Using a computer is all about working with information, so in this chapter you'll look at how Windows 7 stores and organizes it. You'll learn how to browse the contents of storage devices—for example, hard disks—that are connected to your system, and how account folders and public folders are used to store data files such as documents, pictures, video, music, and so on. You'll also explore how libraries can make organizing groups of related files easier, and how to use Windows 7's search feature to find files and other kinds of information on your system.

Browsing storage devices

A Windows 7 system can have various types of storage either built in or connected to it. These devices typically consist of hard disks, DVD or Blu-ray disc drives, and USB flash memory drives (sometimes called **memory sticks**).

To see all the storage devices available on your system, left-click the Start button, and then click Computer in the Start menu's right pane (or press Windows+E), as shown in Figure 3-1. This opens a **Windows Explorer window** (an important type of window that will make an appearance in one form or another many times over the course of this chapter).

Figure 3-1. To see what storage devices are available on your system, select Computer from the Start menu.

In the left-hand, or navigation, pane of the window, Computer will be highlighted. In the right-hand pane, you'll see a group of icons representing the storage devices available on the system. The devices will be organized by type (for example, hard disk drives, removable storage, and so forth), and you'll see the name and drive letter of each one. Depending on the view selected, you may also see how much capacity a storage device provides, and how much of that space is still available for use (see Figure 3-2). When a device's capacity bar is red, it means the device has less than 10 percent free space left.

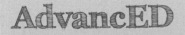

Figure 3-2. The `Computer` window shows the storage devices present on your system. (The specific drives on your system will not be identical to the ones shown here.)

AdvancED

If the navigation pane is missing, choose `Organize` ➤ `Layout` ➤ `Navigation pane` *to make it visible. If the right pane of the* `Computer` *window doesn't look like the one in Figure 3-2, click the down arrow to the right of the* `Change your view` *button and select* `Tiles view`*.*

You'll notice that one of the hard drive icons (typically the C: drive) sports a small Windows logo—this denotes the drive where Windows 7 is installed. Double-click this drive to see the folder structure Windows 7 sets up on it.

Operating system folders

The hard drive that Windows 7 is installed on contains three special folders: Program Files, Users, and Windows. (There's also a PerfLogs folder, which isn't important for our purposes.)

The **Program Files folder** stores files needed to run software programs, including the programs that come with Windows 7. When you install a new piece of software on your system, its files usually go into their own folder within the Program Files folder. You should avoid making any changes to this folder, because doing so may cause programs to malfunction.

The **Users folder** contains personal account folders used to store data files and operating system settings that belong to each user created on your system. This folder also stores data files shared among all system users. Although it won't necessarily be obvious, you'll interact with the Users folder frequently on a day-to-day basis as you load and save various files.

The **Windows folder** stores all the critical operating system files that Windows 7 needs to run. Except in very rare circumstances—and then only if you're an experienced user—you won't want to make any changes to this folder. Doing so could damage the operating system and possibly prevent your system from starting properly.

AdvancED

If your system had a prior version of Windows on it before you installed Windows 7, you may also see a folder called Windows.old, which contains files saved from the earlier version.

Account folders

Every user account in Windows 7 gets its own personal folder within the Users folder. For example, if your account name is Joseph, there will be a folder named Joseph in the Users folder. Inside each account's personal folder are a group of subfolders: Contacts, Desktop, Downloads, Favorites, Links, My Documents, My Music, My Pictures, My Videos, Saved Games, and Searches. You use these folders to store the personal files that you accumulate as you use your system. (There's an additional hidden folder called AppData that some programs use to store user-specific data, such as an e-mail program's mailbox file.)

Information stored in an account's personal folder is accessible only by that account holder. To browse the personal folder for your account (Figure 3-3), click the account name in the upper-right corner of the Start menu.

LinkED

Chapter 1 covered navigation using the Start *menu. Go and have a look if you need a refresher about any of the shortcuts that the* Start *menu provides.*

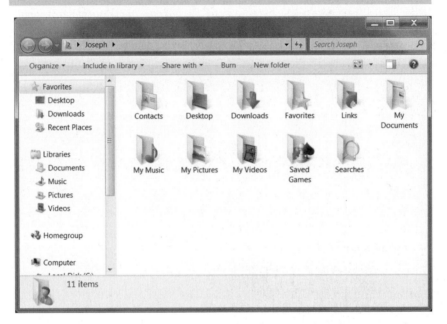

Figure 3-3. Click your account name in the Start menu to view the contents of your personal folder.

Public folder

In addition to each of the account-specific personal folders (and a folder for a guest account, which is visible only when the guest account has been enabled and someone has used it), the Users folder contains another folder called Public. Inside the Public folder are subfolders called Public Documents, Public Downloads, Public Music, Public Pictures, Public Recorded TV, and Public Videos.

The contents of the Public folder are automatically available to all accounts on the system (including the guest account). This makes it a good place to store files, such as a collection of family photos, that you want to share with other system users.

To view the contents of the Public folder, open the the aforementioned `Computer` window and navigate to \Users\Public (double-click `C:`, double-click `Users`, and then double-click `Public`) to display the `Windows Explorer` window shown in Figure 3-4.

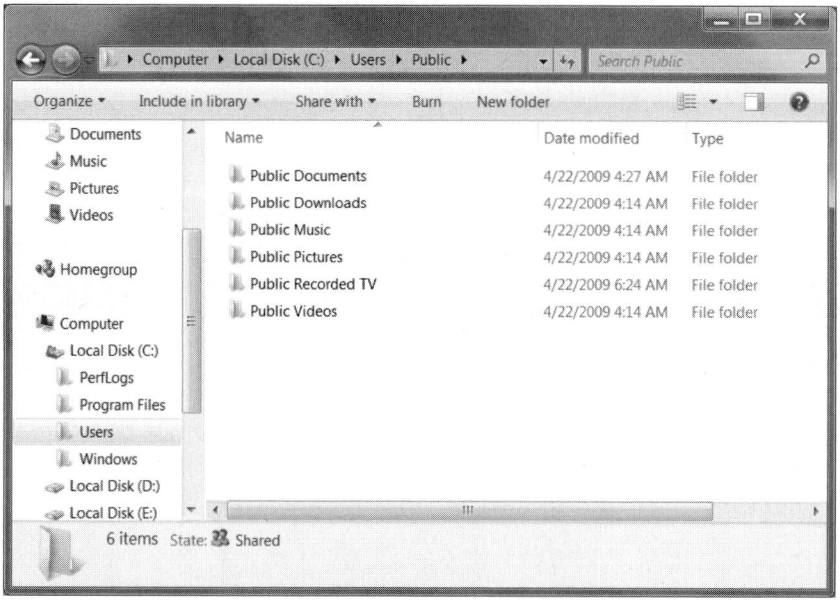

Figure 3-4. The Public folder is a place to save files when you want to share them with other system users.

As a rule, when you save files while using software programs, whether the programs come with Windows 7 or you installed them yourself, the default save folder will be one appropriate to the type of program. For example, a word processing program will automatically save files into the My Documents folder, while an image-editing program will automatically save files into the My Pictures folder.

Irrespective of where a program suggests you save a file, you're free to choose another location, such as one of the Public folders.

Using libraries

As you accumulate files over time, the same category of file may wind up being stored in several locations. For example, you may have some pictures saved in your My Pictures folder and others saved in Public Pictures, or you might have videos saved in the Public Videos folder, and additional videos saved in another folder on a second hard drive.

Having countless pictures, videos, or any other type of file strewn all over the system can make keeping track of them cumbersome. Fortunately, a Windows 7 feature called **libraries** can simplify access to similar kinds of files, even if they're stored in different places.

Whereas a folder is a physical place on a hard drive to store files, a library doesn't actually store any files. Instead, libraries track the location of files across multiple folders, which lets you access groups of files as if they were all stored in the same folder even when they're not.

Using standard libraries

Windows 7 provides four predefined libraries: Documents, Music, Pictures, and Video. Each library tracks two default storage locations for the file category: the account holder's personal folder and the public folder. For example, the Pictures library includes the My Pictures folder and the Public Pictures folder.

Even though libraries aren't physical file storage locations, they still work as if they were. When you open or save a file from within a program, the default open/save location will typically be the appropriate library for that kind of file (that is, the Pictures library for an image-editing program, or the Documents library for a word processing program).

So how can you save a file to a library if a library isn't a physical storage location? Whenever you save (or copy) a file to a library, it is automatically saved to the library's default save location. For the four default libraries mentioned earlier, the default save location is the user's personal folder (for example, My Pictures, My Documents, and so forth).

Viewing the contents of a library

To view libraries on your system, click Libraries in the navigation (left) pane of an open Explorer window. If none are open, click the Windows Explorer taskbar button (the one that looks like a group of folders, usually found second from the left after the Start button). Either method displays the Libraries window shown in Figure 3-5.

Figure 3-5. Windows 7 comes with four preconfigured libraries.

To view a specific library, double-click its name in the navigation pane. This expands the library to show the individual folders it contains, and displays the contents of the entire library in the content pane, as you can see in Figure 3-6.

ExplainED

Click a specific folder to see only the items in that folder.

Figure 3-6. Select a library in the navigation pane to show its contents in the content pane.

How a library's contents are displayed in the content pane depends on which library you're looking at. For example, by default the Pictures library displays thumbnail images (as shown in Figure 3-6), while the Documents library displays a list of filenames and details. You can customize how a library's contents are displayed by clicking the `Change your view` button (see Figure 3-7).

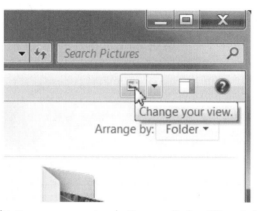

Figure 3-7. The `Change your view` button can display different-sized icons or additonal details about files and folders.

ExplainED

The `Change your view` *button is available in all* `Explorer` *windows, though the icon it displays and the view options it offers differ depending on what you're looking at.*

You can also sort a library's contents in many ways by clicking the drop-down menu next to `Arrange by`, as shown in Figure 3-8. The available sorting options depend on the library. For example, you can sort the Pictures library by the month or day a snapshot was taken, the Music library by song or artist, and the Documents library by author or file type (text file, spreadsheet, and so forth).

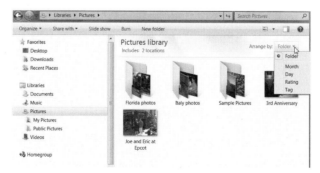

Figure 3-8. Click `Arrange by` to change how library contents are sorted.

Modifying a library

You're free to customize any of Windows 7's default libraries by adding new folders to them. For example, you might have a folder full of photos on a hard drive somewhere (other than the My Pictures or Public Pictures folder) that you want to add to the Pictures library.

To modify a library, follow these steps:

1. Right-click its name in the left pane and select `Properties`.

2. Click the `Include a folder` button to find another folder you want to add to the library, as shown in Figure 3-9.

3. To add additional folders, just click `Include a folder` again and repeat the process.

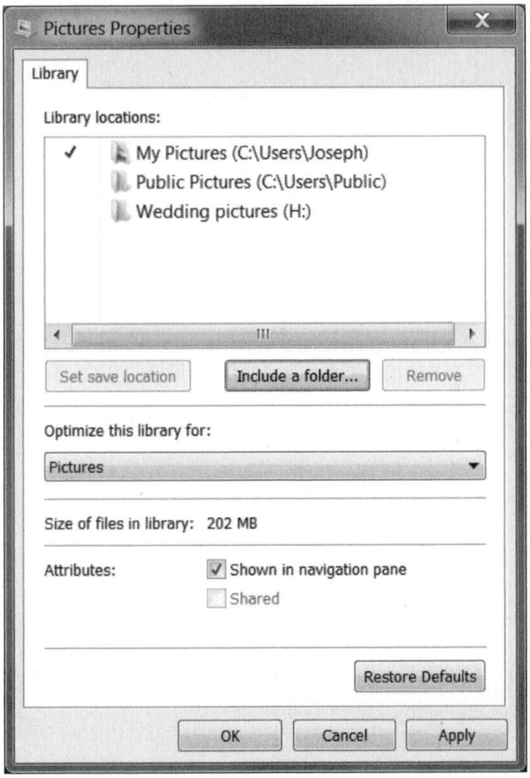

Figure 3-9. You can add   (or remove) folders from any of the default libraries.

4. Notice the check mark next to the My Pictures folder in Figure 3-9. This means the folder is the library's default save location. To change the default save location, highlight another folder and click the `Set save location` button.

5. To remove a folder from a library, highlight it and click `Remove`.

The `Optimize this library for` menu determines the sorting options that are available from the `Arrange by` menu. You can optimize the library for documents, music, pictures, videos, or for general items.

ExplainED

Adding a folder to a library doesn't change where the actual files are stored, and removing one from a library doesn't delete the folder from your hard drive.

You can also right-click a folder anywhere in Windows and select `Include in library` to add the folder to an existing library, as shown in Figure 3-10. Alternatively, you can create a new library for the folder, as described in the next section.

Figure 3-10. Right-click a folder anywhere in Windows and select `Include in library` to add it to an existing library, or create a new one.

AdvancED

A library can contain as many as 50 folders and can include folders that are already part of other libraries.

Creating a new library

Aside from customizing the standard Windows 7 libraries, you can also create new libraries of your own. Let's say you take an annual vacation and have a collection of photos from each year's trip stored within individual folders inside the Public Pictures folder. Although you can get to those vacation-related photos from the Pictures library, they'll be mixed in with numerous other photos that you'll have to wade through to reach them. If you create a new library just for the vacation snapshots, on the other hand, accessing them will be much easier.

To create a new library, follow these steps:

1. Right-click `Libraries` in the left pane.

2. Choose `New` ➤ `Library`, and then give your library a name by typing over the `New Library` label (see Figure 3-11).

Figure 3-11. To create a library, click `New` ➤ `Library` and give the library a name.

3. Now add folders to your new library by following the same process described earlier under "Modifying a library." The first folder you add to the library will become the default save location, so remember to adjust it if necessary.

AdvancED

Although the default Windows 7 libraries all pertain to a specific category of files (for example, documents), you can create libraries that include multiple file types, such as documents and pictures, or music and video.

Using Windows search

Libraries help you organize large groups of files stored in different places, but they don't do much to help you locate a particular file or folder you need. When you need a specific file, folder, program, setting, or other piece of information but don't know exactly where it is, Windows 7's search feature can help you find what you're looking for relatively quickly.

Understanding the index

Windows 7 helps improve the speed and efficiency of searches by automatically indexing the contents of much of your system in advance. The **index** is essentially a database of filenames, locations, and other characteristics that's updated regularly as the information on your computer changes. More often than not, the index will contain information you're searching for, and by consulting it, Windows 7 can locate items much more quickly than by searching through the actual files on the hard drive.

Consider this: if you misplaced your car keys somewhere around the house, you probably wouldn't start looking for them in odd places such as the shower or refrigerator. Instead, you'd concentrate on places where the keys would most likely be found—for instance, the nightstand drawer or the pocket of yesterday's pants.

The index in Windows 7 works in a similar way. Because indexing the entire contents of your hard drive would make the index file excessively large and slow down the speed of all searches, Windows 7 automatically indexes only the places that are most likely to contain the information you want, which is to say, the places where you actually save files. By default, Windows 7 indexes the contents of your personal account folder, the Public folder, and any folder that you add to a library, as well as some special areas such as the `Start` menu and your Internet Explorer browser history. On the other hand, Windows 7 doesn't index locations that contain program or operating system files, such as the Program Files and Windows operating system folders, because these aren't places where you normally store files.

LinkED

A bit later, you'll see how to search nonindexed locations, as well as how to have Windows index any folder of your choice.

AdvancED

Windows 7 doesn't index files that belong to other users on the computer (that is, files saved in an account folder other than your own). Therefore, someone else's files won't show up as part of your search results, or vice versa.

Searching from the Start menu

There are several ways to search for information in Windows 7, starting with, as you've previously seen, from the `Start` menu. Because the `Start` menu offers a comprehensive search of all the indexed areas of your system, it's the ideal place to search from when you want to cast the widest possible net. Via the `Start` menu, you can search not only for files and folders, but for things such as programs and Windows features too.

To conduct a search from the `Start` menu, just begin typing a search term (also known as a **keyword**) into the search box. You don't necessarily need to type in a whole word; Windows 7 will display any matches it finds (usually instantaneously or very nearly so) and update the list of results as you type.

For example, let's say you wanted to change your screen's resolution but don't remember where the setting is or even exactly how to describe it. By simply typing the word `screen` into the `Start` menu's search box, you'll get a list of results that contain that word or are somehow related to it. Among the results will be the specific item you were looking for, `Adjust screen resolution`, as shown in Figure 3-12.

Programs (1)

On-Screen Keyboard

Control Panel (32)

Change screen saver

Turn screen saver on or off

Set screen saver password

Adjust screen resolution

Change screen orientation

Adjust screen brightness

Use screen reader

Magnify portions of the screen using Magnifier

Display

View solutions to problems

Choose how to check for solutions

View message archive

Change window glass colors

See more results

screen   ×   Shut down   ▶

Figure 3-12. Typing a term (or part of one) into the `Start` menu's search box will get you a list of related results.

ExplainED

Because searches conducted from the `Start` menu can find files, folders, programs, and settings, they'll often result in matches from more than one category, depending on how specific the search term is. As shown in Figure 3-12, searching on the word `screen` finds the `On-Screen Keyboard` program along with numerous screen-related settings from `Control Panel`.

Searching from an Explorer window

Although the `Start` menu will often be a convenient place from which to conduct a search, it's not the only one, and sometimes it's not necessarily the best one. That's because every `Explorer` window has its own search box in the upper-right corner, which you can use to search a specific area of your system.

When you're looking for a file or folder (as opposed to a program or setting) and know the general location of what you're looking for, you can get a more targeted set of results by searching from an `Explorer` window focused on that specific location.

For example, when you open the Documents library from the `Start` menu by clicking the `Start` button and then `Documents`, the window's search box reads `Search Documents` next to the magnifying glass icon (see Figure 3-13). As a result, any search conducted here will limit its focus at least initially, on the portion of the index that pertains to the Documents library.

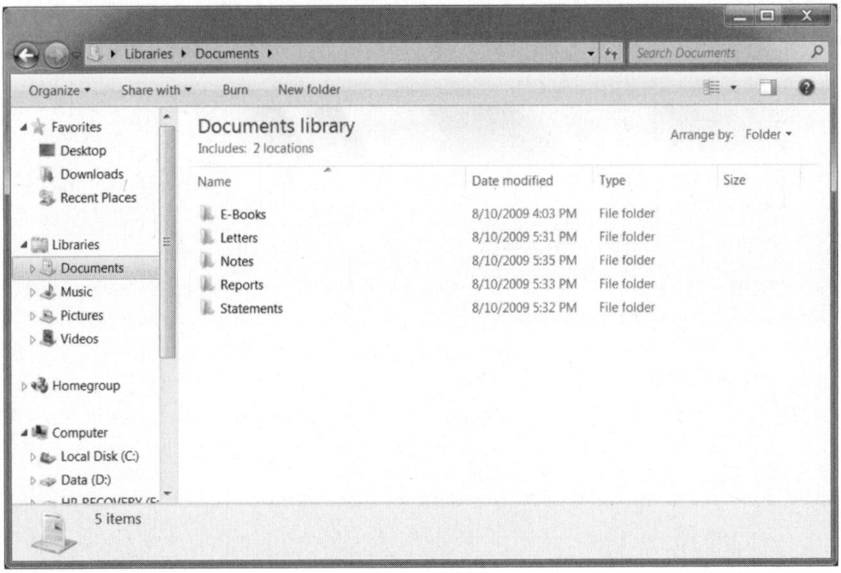

Figure 3-13: Each `Explorer` window contains a search box that you can use to search a specific area of your system.

Let's say we want to find a file named brown fox, and because it's a document as opposed to say, a picture or a video file, we know it's most likely in the Documents library. When we type brown fox into the Search Documents box, the results list a file by that name along with its location, size, and the last date modified, as shown in Figure 3-14.

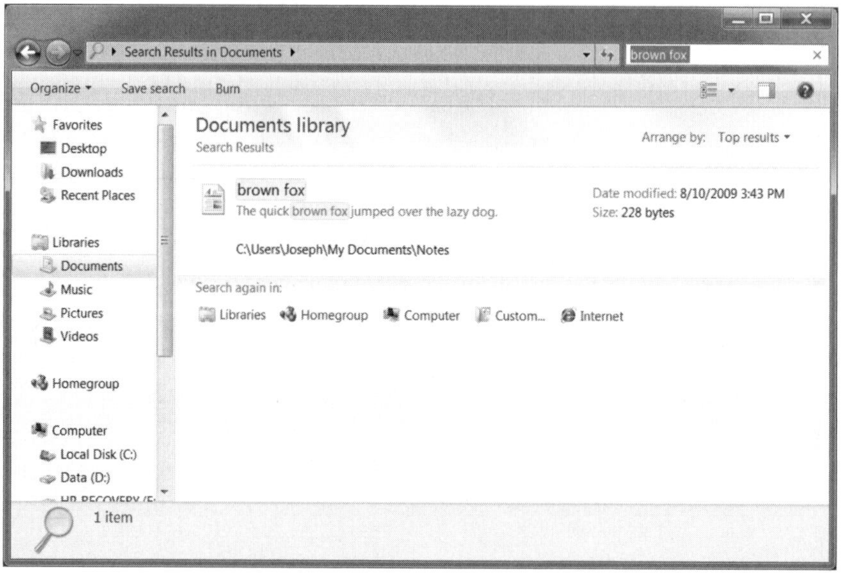

Figure 3-14: When you do a search, Windows 7 highlights any matches it finds.

Notice that in Figure 3-14, the words brown fox are highlighted twice within the search result. This is because for many types of documents, Windows 7 can search within the document text and not just the filename. In this case, the search term was a match for both the filename and the file text. If we search again for the term lazy dog, the same file comes up in the search results because the file text contains a match even though filename doesn't (see Figure 3-15).

Figure 3-15. In addition to filenames, Windows 7 can find search matches within the text of some types of documents.

AdvancED

Windows 7 can search the text within many common document types, including Microsoft Office and Adobe PDF files, but it won't necessarily be able to search inside every type of document file.

Expanding searches

If an initial search doesn't turn up any results (or perhaps just not the items you were looking for), you can easily expand it while keeping the same search term. Just scroll down to the bottom of the results list and under `Search again in` click the area you want to search (see Figure 3-16). Selecting `Libraries`, for example, will rerun the search across all libraries, while choosing `Homegroup` will search other systems that are part of your home network.

Search again in:

Libraries   Homegroup   Computer   Custom...   Internet

Figure 3-16. If an initial search doesn't produce the expected results, you can expand the search to cover other areas.

AdvancED

To search one or more specific locations on your system, choose the Custom option.

Using filters

In an ideal world, each search you do would lead you directly to the exact file or files you want. In practice, however, search terms can often be imprecise and therefore may produce a laundry list of results that you'll need to sift through to find the specific file or files you're looking for.

This is where **search filters** come in. Applying a filter to your search can give you more-targeted results by letting you find files not only by keyword or name, but also by other characteristics as well, such as date, type, size, and more. In a nutshell, filters provide a way to narrow search results, thus making it easier for you to zero in on what you want.

Search filters are available whenever you perform a search from Windows Explorer. The specific filters that are available vary depending on what kind of search you're doing. For example, when searching the Documents library, you can filter results by relevant properties such as the author or the file type (for example, Microsoft Word or Adobe Acrobat document). Similarly, when searching the Pictures library, you can filter by the date an image was taken or the tags used to describe it, and when searching for music, you can filter by characteristics such as genre or artist name.

To show how search filters work, we'll do a search within the Pictures library for a group of photos from a trip to Italy. After we find them, we'll use a filter to narrow the results to only the photos taken on a specific day. Follow these steps:

1. We'll begin our example by searching on the keyword `Italy`. As shown in Figure 3-17, the search results show a folder called Italy October 2008 along with pictures stored within, for a total of 183 items as reported in the lower-left corner (next to the magnifying glass).

Figure 3-17. A keyword search of the Pictures library, prior to adding a filter.

2. Now that we've located the correct group of photos, we want to pare down the search results so that they include only the snapshots taken on October 22. To do this, we'll use the `Date taken` filter. By clicking inside the search box again, we see an `Add a search filter option` with up to three filters listed underneath it (see Figure 3-18).

Figure 3-18. Filters are available when you perform a search from a `Windows Explorer` window.

AdvancED

If you want, you can choose a search filter as soon as you've finished typing in your keyword. You can also use search filters without using a keyword at all; just click anywhere in the search box.

3. After selecting a filter by clicking it, you must choose a value for it. In the case of the `Date taken` filter, you may scroll through a calendar to choose a particular year, month, and day, or you can opt for a verbal description of the time frame desired, such as `yesterday` or `last week`, as shown in Figure 3-19. For the purposes of this example, we'll select October 22, 2008.

Figure 3-19. After selecting a filter type, you must choose a value for it.

AdvancED

By holding down the mouse button and dragging after clicking a date, you can select a range of dates instead of just one day.

As soon as you choose a value for your filter, the search results update to reflect the new parameter. As you can see in Figure 3-20, the search results now list 33 items, and the highlighted photo indicates it was taken on 10/22/2008.

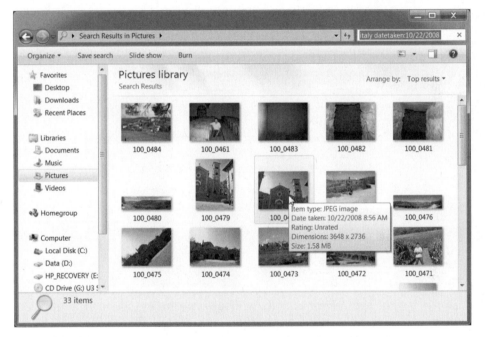

Figure 3-20. Picture search results after applying the `Date taken` filter

AdvancED

After you apply the first filter to a search, you can specify additional ones by clicking in the search box again and selecting another filter.

Saving searches

It's not uncommon to find yourself using the same keywords and filters to repeatedly perform searches. If you think you might need to run a particular search again in the future, you can save yourself some typing and clicking by saving your search for later use.

Saving searches saves the search parameters, not the search results. This means that when you run the search later, the results may be different depending on how files on your system have changed.

To save a search, click the `Save search` button found near the upper left of the results window, as shown in Figure 3-21.

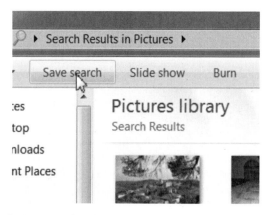

Figure 3-21. Saving a search makes it easier to access again later.

Windows 7 will give your search a default name combining the keyword and/or filters used, but you're free to change it to something more descriptive. Note that as shown in Figure 3-22, the search will be saved within the user's personal account folder, inside a subfolder called Searches.

AdvancED

Even if you don't save your searches, clicking a `Windows Explorer` *search box will display the last few searches you did.*

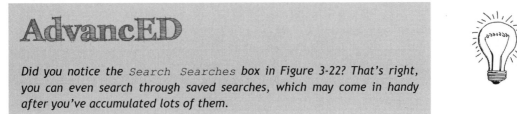

Figure 3-22. Any searches you save will be stored in the Searches folder of your account folder.

AdvancED

Did you notice the `Search Searches` *box in Figure 3-22? That's right, you can even search through saved searches, which may come in handy after you've accumulated lots of them.*

After you've saved a search, you can access it from your Searches folder. Saved searches will also appear in the list of `Favorites` found within the navigation pane of each `Windows Explorer` window, as shown in Figure 3-23.

Figure 3-23. Once saved, past searches can be easily accessed again via the `Favorites Favorites` list.

Searching nonindexed locations

As noted earlier, Windows 7 uses an index to improve the speed and efficiency of most searches. But there will likely be times when your search involves a location that's not included in the index, such as a folder that's not part of a library, an entire hard drive, or perhaps even the whole computer.

You conduct a search of a nonindexed location the same way you do an indexed one, though the process doesn't work quite the same way behind the scenes. For this example, we'll do a search of the C: drive, which contains the nonindexed folders Program Files and Windows.

ExplainED

Searching an external storage device such as a USB flash memory drive is an example of a searching a nonindexed location.

To search the C: drive, follow these steps:

1. Click the `Start` button, then `Computer`, and then the C: drive's icon in the `Explorer` window's navigation (left) pane.

2. Type a search term (in this case `brown fox`) into the `Search Local Disk (C:)` box (your C: drive may have a label other than Local Disk) and you'll see a yellow bar appear near the top of the window to warn that you're searching a nonindexed location and that searches might be slow as a result. Because you're searching outside the index, Windows 7 must look through all the files in the search location (which in this case is an entire hard drive) and will display a status bar at the top of the window to indicate the search's progress (see Figure 3-24).

Figure 3-24. Searches of nonindexed locations can take some time.

3. Whenever you see the warning bar about searching a nonindexed location, you can click anywhere on it to add that location to the index. When you do so, you'll see the menu shown in Figure 3-25.

Add to index...
Modify index locations...
Don't show this message again

Figure 3-25. Clicking on the warning message will let you add a location to the index.

4. You can add any location you want to the index, but it's best to add only locations that include important data or that you expect to search frequently. That's because adding too many locations to your index increases the size of the index file, which will in turn make all searches take much longer than necessary.

ExplainED

As a rule, you should avoid adding entire drives or any nondata folders to the index.

Changing index settings

You've seen how to add a storage location to the index while searching it. But if you have important folders that aren't part of the index, you can add them to the index in advance rather than waiting until you actually need to do a search.

To change the index settings, follow these steps:

1. Type `index` into the `Start` menu search box, and then choose `Indexing Options`. The `Indexing Options` window (Figure 3-26) shows you a list of locations currently being indexed.

2. To add or remove folders from the index, click the `Modify` button, and then click the small arrows next to each drive to expand the list of folders on your system. When you find an item you want to index, put a check in the box next to it, and it will be added to the `Summary of selected locations` list.

3. When you're finished, click `OK` and you'll see the new folder(s) listed within the `Indexing Options` window. Windows 7 will begin indexing the new data immediately, but how long the process takes depends on how many folders you add and how large they are. Also, Windows 7 slows down the indexing process if it detects that the computer is in use, in order to prevent your system performance from slowing down.

ExplainED

Remember, any folder that's part of a library is automatically indexed, so if you add a folder to a library, you don't need to add it to the index too.

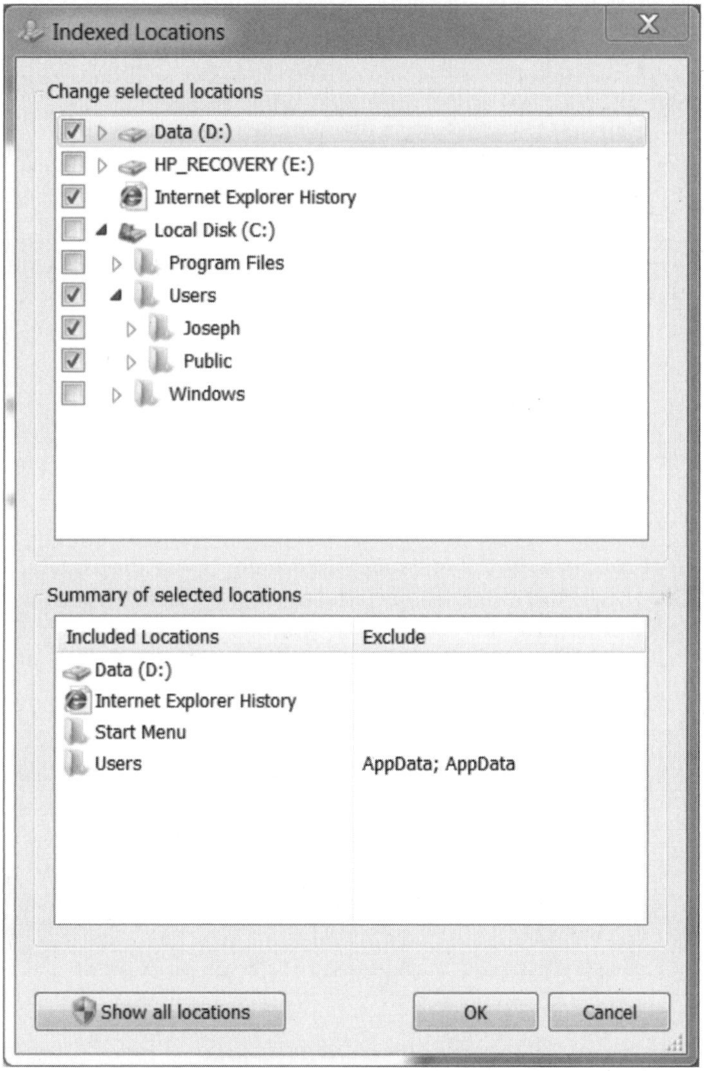

Figure 3-26. Put a check next to a folder or drive to add it to the index.

Summary

Here's a review of what you've learned in this chapter:

- How to browse the contents of storage devices connected to your system
- How operating system files, program files, user data, and shared data are each stored within their own special group of folders
- How Windows 7 uses libraries to organize different types of files
- How to customize or create your own libraries
- How the index makes searching quick and efficient
- How to search for programs, settings, files, and folders

Chapter 4

Personalizing Windows 7

Your favorite color is green, and you find pictures of a rainforest soothing. Your daughter likes pink. And purple. And some other colors you don't even know the names of. Your son is into video games, and what he likes is dark and scary. If you three share the same computer, good news! You can each have your own background pictures, windows colors, and sounds, with **personalization**.

Windows 7 looks great. When you start your computer, you're greeted with a colorful background and taskbar. One of the first things most people want to do when they start Windows is change how it looks. It looks nice out of the box, don't get us wrong, but there's so much more you'll want to do with it to make it really *you*. But personalizing Windows isn't just making it look pretty. It's also making it work the way you want it to and making it easy to get to the programs and features you use most.

In this chapter, we'll cover the following tasks to customize Windows for fun and to make it easier to use:

- Changing your desktop background
- Changing your other Windows colors
- Setting up your screen saver
- Making the screen easy to view
- Using or turning off sounds for Windows events
- Making the computer easier to use for people with visual, audio, or mobility accessibility needs
- Adjusting the mouse for your particular needs

Personalizing your login screen

The first place you see any kind of personalization in Windows 7 is your login screen. The login screen displays all the user accounts on your computer, as shown in Figure 4-1.

Figure 4-1. The first screen you see after Windows 7 starts up displays the user accounts on this computer.

When you click a username or tile, Windows asks you for your password, as shown in Figure 4-2.

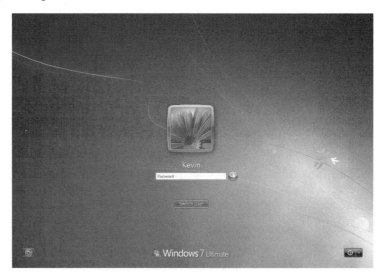

Figure 4-2. Each user sets their password and picture used for login through user accounts. The username and tile also appear at the top of the `Start` menu.

After you log in, you can change your user tile if you like:

1. Click the `Start` button, and in the `Start` menu's search box, type `account picture`. In the list that appears, click `Change your account picture`.

   The `Change Your Picture` window appears, as shown in Figure 4-3.

Figure 4-3. You can choose from a variety of pictures provided by Windows, or you can browse for other pictures on your computer.

2. If you see a picture you like, click the picture, and then click `Change Picture`.

   In a few moments, the window closes. To see how your new picture looks, you don't have to log off your user account and log on again.

3. Click the Windows `Start` button.

4. Your new picture appears on the `Start` menu, as shown in Figure 4-4.

Figure 4-4. Your new user account picture is shown on the Start menu.

But what if you want to use another picture from your computer that was not shown in the Change Your Picture window? You can select other pictures on your computer, such as pictures in your Picture library.

1. Click the Start button, and in the Start menu's search box, type account picture. In the list that appears, click Change your account picture.

   The Change Your Picture window appears.

2. Click Browse for more pictures.

3. An Open window appears, where you can navigate to the libraries or folders that contain other pictures on your computer.

   For example, the Documents library might not have any pictures, but you will find a Sample Pictures folder in the Pictures library, as shown in Figure 4-5.

Figure 4-5. Even if your computer is new, Windows 7 provides additional pictures in the Sample Pictures folder.

4. Locate the picture you want. For example, find the Koala picture shown in Figure 4-6.

Figure 4-6. When you locate the picture you want, select it and then click Open.

5. Select the picture, and then click `Open`.

In a few moments, Windows displays your `User Accounts` window, where you can see the new picture in place, as shown in Figure 4-7.

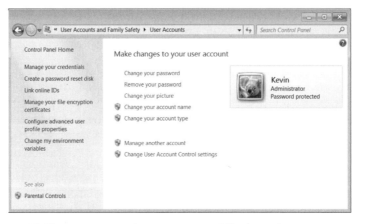

Figure 4-7. The user account picture was successfully changed.

Note that the Koala picture in the Sample Pictures folder was rectangular, but the account picture is square. Windows automatically crops the top and bottom or sides of rectangular pictures so they can be displayed in a square shape without stretching or distorting the picture.

ExplainED

*The starting point for all personalization is your user account, where almost all your personal settings and preferences are stored in a **profile**. This includes your own document and library folders, e-mail and Internet preferences, autofill, and other personalizations. If you have not already created your own user account, as described in Chapter 2, now is a good time to do so.*

If you already have a user account on your old computer, you can jumpstart your Windows 7 personalization with Windows Easy Transfer. Window Easy Transfer lives up to its name and is safe. It copies files and settings from your old computer to your new computer, without deleting anything from your old computer. To learn how to use Windows Easy Transfer, see Chapter 10.

Personalizing your desktop

The first things many people want to change or customize when they have a new computer are the colors and the desktop background. Others want to get right down to business and arrange the shortcuts to their favorite programs and features for easy access. There is no right or wrong order to what you customize first (other than you need to have your user account already set up).

We'll start with the big picture—like the one that covers your screen before you open any programs. That's called your **desktop background**. Windows offers lots of choices that make it easy to customize: you can use **themes**, which coordinate a desktop background with a matching window color, sounds, and screen saver. Or you can change each of these separately or even create your own themes.

You can change any of these settings on the `Personalization` window. The easiest way to get to the `Personalization` window is to right-click any place on the desktop, and then on the small menu that pops up click `Personalize`, as shown in Figure 4-8.

Can't find an open spot on the desktop to click because open windows cover everything? Hold down the Windows key and then press D. All your windows are minimized to the taskbar, giving you access to the desktop. Press Windows+D again if you want to restore the windows to an open state.

Figure 4-8. Access the `Personalization` window by right-clicking the desktop and then clicking `PersonalizePersonalize`.

93

The Personalization window, as shown in Figure 4-9, allows you to change almost all your visual preferences and many of your sound preferences. The currently selected theme will be highlighted, as the Aero theme called Architecture is in Figure 4-9.

Themes are listed in three groups:

- **My Themes**, which are any themes you create by specifying your own combination of desktop background pictures, window color, sounds, and screen saver. You can also click Get more themes online to download additional themes and desktop backgrounds.
- **Aero Themes**, which take advantage of Aero effects such as transparency.
- **Basic and High Contrast Themes**, which provide simpler desktop backgrounds and Windows colors or high-contrast themes to make the screen, windows, and text easier to view.

LinkED

High-contrast themes are just one of many Windows features that can make your computer easier to view. The section "Making your screen easier to view and read" later in this chapter describes in detail other visual features you can customize to suit your needs. Windows also provides the Ease of Access Center in the Control Panel to help you customize Windows for other accessibility needs. The section "Customizing Windows for visual, audio, mobility, or cognitive needs" later in this chapter describes the Ease of Access Center and how to use it.

When you first view this window, some of the theme groups may not be visible. If you do not see the Basic and High Contrast Themes set, scroll down.

Figure 4-9. The `Personalization` window allows you to change how your computer looks and sounds.

From the `Personalization` window, you can change many settings with just a few clicks.

Choosing a theme

The themes listed in the `Personalization` window display a preview of the desktop background pictures and the window color for each theme. Each Aero theme contains multiple pictures. When you select an Aero theme, the default is to show all the pictures in the theme as a slide show so that the picture changes to another picture within the theme every 30 minutes. This means you'll have a new desktop background every 30 minutes.

To choose a theme, scroll the themes list as needed, and then click a theme. Windows will automatically apply the theme you selected. The `Personalization` window stays open, so if you don't like the theme you just chose or you want to check the other themes, you can easily change it again.

Viewing or changing your desktop background

Themes provide a convenient way to set your desktop background, window color, and sounds all at once. But what if you don't want a slide show or want to change which pictures are in the slide show? Or, what if you want to use your own pictures? You can easily change just the desktop background:

1. In the `Personalization` window, click `Desktop Background`.

2. Select the picture or pictures you want to use in your background. Place the mouse pointer over a picture, and in a moment a check box appears. If the pictures you want to use are not displayed, select a different group from the `Picture location` drop-down list, or click `Browse` to navigate to a different folder on your computer or a shared folder on your network.

3. In the `Picture position` drop-down list, choose how you want the pictures positioned in the background. `Fill` is the default and works best for most pictures because it does not distort the picture to make it fit on the desktop and does not leave any blank areas at the top or the bottom. If you have pictures with proportions or shapes that don't match your screen dimensions, experiment with what looks best to you.

4. If you have selected more than one picture, you can also adjust the following slide show settings:

    •   In the `Change picture every` drop-down list, choose how often you want the pictures to change in the slide show.
    •   If you want the pictures to change randomly from among the pictures you selected for this desktop background, select `Shuffle`.
    •   If you want the selected pictures to change in the order they are displayed on the desktop background, deselect `Shuffle`.

5. When you are done setting your desktop background, click `Save changes`.

AdvancED

When you select or deselect pictures for your desktop, Windows does not copy, move, or delete the actual picture files.

If you use `Browse` to select pictures from a location that is not on your computer, such as a shared folder on a homegroup or home network location, the pictures can be displayed only when the location is online and available. If the location requires a username and password, the pictures may not be available the next time you use your computer.

To ensure that your selected pictures are always available, make sure the network location is always online and available and in a public folder that does not require a username and password. Or, copy the picture files from the network location to a local folder on your computer.

In `Picture location`, if you use `Browse` to navigate to a folder that contains a large number of pictures, it may take a while for Windows to retrieve and display the preview thumbnails of each picture.

If you choose `Fit` or `Center` in the `Picture position` drop-down list, the `Change background color` link appears below it so that you can select the color of the background that fills in the sides or top and bottom of the desktop when the proportions of the picture do not match the desktop.

AdvancED

The `Personalization` *windows includes a* `Window Color` *link. The color combinations provided by Windows themes work well for most people. If you are using a Windows 7 theme with Windows Aero, some of the colors, fonts, and sizes settings cannot be changed unless you are using the Windows 7 basic theme or a high-contrast theme. Changing the window color is not difficult or risky, but you'll find that the Windows 7 themes are easier and more satisfying.*

If you or the people you are setting the computer up for have special visual, audio, mobility, or cognitive needs, the Windows Ease of Access Center is a great resource for customizing the Windows experience. These features are for everybody, not just for what people traditionally label as disabilities. With age, hearing and vision decline; young or old, repetitive work or poor ergonomic conditions can affect mobility. Sometimes it's just easier if the computer provides feedback through one type of sensory input and tune out others. For example, a student may find it distracting to herself or others to hear Windows system sounds or see notifications popping up on the screen. For more information, see "How to customize Windows for visual, audio, mobility, or cognitive needs" later in this chapter.

Setting up your screen saver

A **screen saver** serves several purposes. As the name implies, it saves your screen. Computer and television screens can suffer from what is called **burn-in**. When the image on the screen does not change for a long time, the image can get imprinted so that every time you use the computer, there is a ghost of that image on the screen. (Older cathode ray tube monitors are more susceptible to burn-in. It happens less frequently with today's LCD desktop monitors, televisions, and laptop displays.) A screen saver prevents burn-in by keeping images moving on the screen so that nothing stays in one place too long. Screen savers can also help safeguard your privacy by hiding what is on your screen when you are away from your desk. If you are using a laptop computer, screen savers can work with your power management settings to reduce power use when your computer is on but inactive. Finally, a screen saver can be nice way to display a slide show of your favorite pictures.

The following steps describe how to use photos for your screen saver, but most of the steps apply to using one of the built-in animation screen savers as well:

1. Open the `Personalization` window if it is not already open from your previous personalization tasks. To open this page, right-click your desktop, and then click `Personalize`.

2. At the bottom of the page, click `Screen Saver`.

   The `Screen Saver Settings` dialog box appears, as shown in Figure 4-10.

Figure 4-10. The `Screen Saver Settings` dialog box `Screen Saver Settings` dialog box specifies which screen saver to use, how long to wait before it comes on, and whether to protect it with your password.

3. Click the drop-down list farthest to the left, like the one that displays (None) in Figure 4-10.

Windows includes several built-in screen savers, including a photo screen saver.

4. Click Photos, as shown in Figure 4-11.

Figure 4-11. Windows provides several built-in screen savers, including one to display your photos.

5. When you select Photos, Windows defaults to the Photos folder in your library. If you do not have any photos there or you want to use other photos, you can specify another folder to use.

6. Click Settings.

The `Photo Screen Saver Settings` dialog box appears, as shown in Figure 4-12.

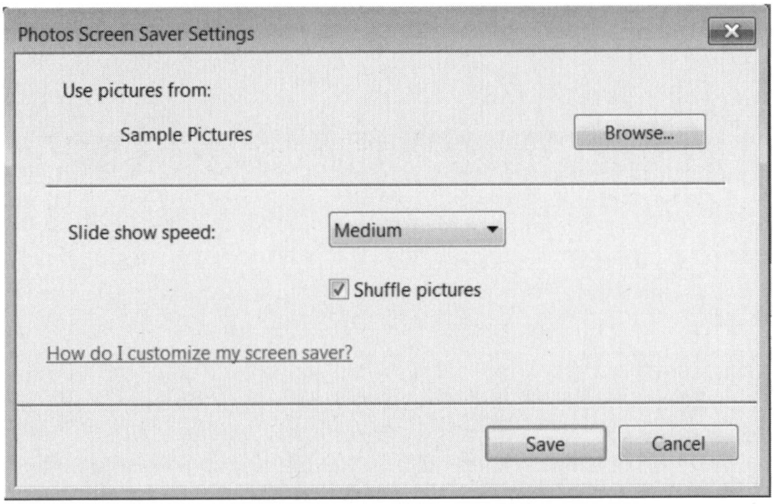

Figure 4-12. `Photos Screen Saver Settings` allows you to specify which folder to use pictures from and how you want them shown.

7. Click `Browse` to specify a different folder to get the pictures from.

8. Click `Slide show speed` to specify how fast to change the pictures: `Slow`, `Medium`, or `Fast`.

9. Select the `Shuffle pictures` check box if you want them displayed in a random order, or deselect this check box if you want them displayed in the order they are listed in the source folder. When you are done with these settings, click `Save`.

10. If you want to see what the screen saver will look like and how fast it changes, click `Preview`. The slide show will run for a bit and stop either when you move your mouse or, if you wait a few moments, by itself.

11. Select how long you want Windows to wait before it starts the screen saver and whether to require you to log on again when you stop the screen saver to resume using the computer.

12. When you are done, click `OK`.

ExplainED

As mentioned previously about selecting pictures for your desktop, if you use photos for your screen saver from a folder on another homegroup or home network computer, make sure the folder will be accessible all the time.

Making your screen easier to view and read

Changing the theme, desktop background, and colors that you see on the desktop makes Windows more enjoyable to look at, but sometimes the details on the screen or the text size may be difficult to view.

The high-contrast themes are often a good solution for many people who have difficulty seeing things on the computer screen. But some people may find they can make a few adjustments to their settings and still use one of the standard Aero themes.

Changing the size of text and items in Windows

You can change the size of text and objects on-screen without changing your screen resolution. You can set the size from small (100 percent or normal size) to medium (125 percent) or large (150 percent). This setting is easy to change, but each time you change, it you will need to restart your computer afterward to see the changes in effect.

To change the size of text and items on your screen, follow these steps:

1. Click the Windows `Start` button, and in the `Start` menu's search box, type `Display`.

2. In the results list, click `Display`.

   The `Display` window appears, as shown in Figure 4-13.

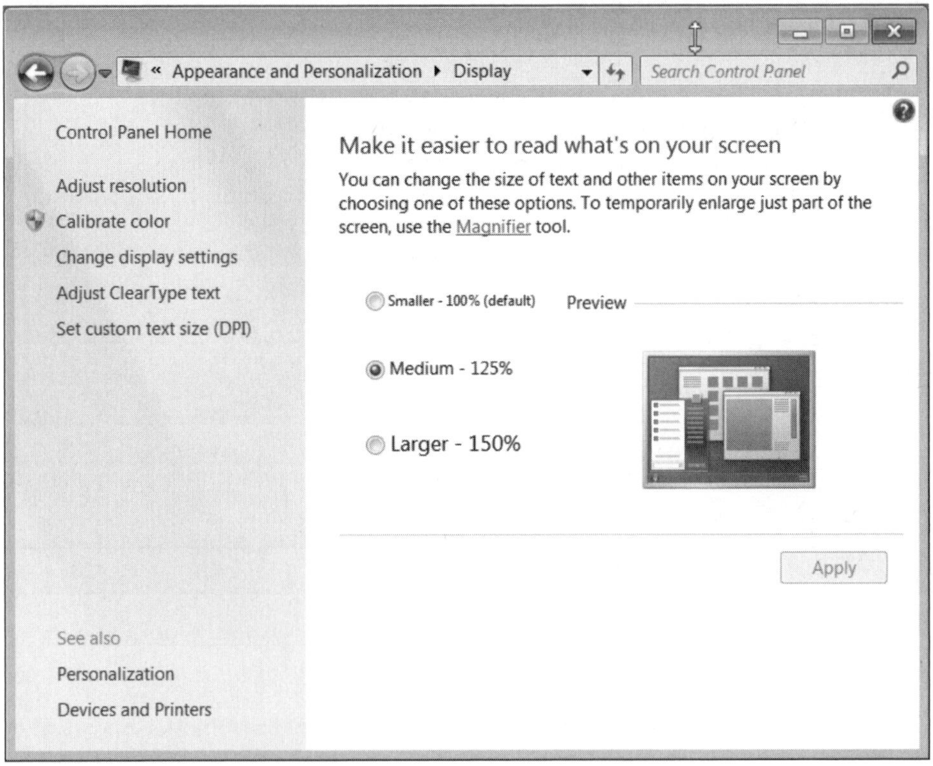

Figure 4-13. The `Display` window provides three preset sizes for the size of text and items on your screen.

3. Click a size to see an example in the `Preview` area.

4. Click `Apply` if you want Windows to make that change. You will need to restart your computer to see the new sizes put into effect.

AdvancED

Many programs provide a way to change the size of how things are displayed within the program window, separate from Windows size settings. Sometimes the feature is called **text size**, **magnification**, *or* **zoom**. *The most common places to check are the* View *menu, toolbars, or status bar, if available.*

For example, in Internet Explorer and Windows Live Mail, check the View *menu for the* Text Size *command. In Microsoft Office programs, such as Word, Excel, PowerPoint, and Visio, check the* View *menu or toolbar for the* Zoom *command.*

Your computer mouse may also provide a zoom feature. In Office programs or Internet Explorer, hold down the Ctrl key while moving the middle mouse wheel.

Changing your screen resolution

Screen resolution is the level of detail on your display. It is a measurement of how many pixels can fit across the width and height on your screen. **Pixels** are the smallest unit of measurement of the dots of color that make up the images on your screen. The higher the resolution, the finer the detail that can be shown on your display. With high resolutions like 1600×1200 pixels, the details are sharper, objects are smaller, and you can view more objects on your screen. At lower resolutions, such as 800×600, Windows displays fewer objects on your screen but they are larger. Compare Figures 4-14 and 4-15. For some people, high resolution may be too hard to see. At a lower resolution, objects are larger and easier to see, but you cannot fit as much on your screen.

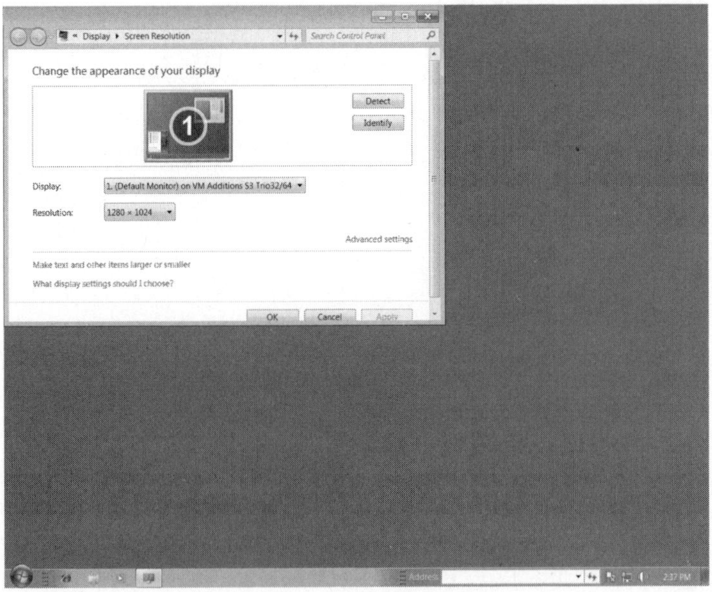

Figure 4-14. At a higher resolution like 1280×1024, objects are smaller, and you can fit more on your screen.

Figure 4-15. The Screen Resolution window, which took up only part of the screen at 1280×1024, is now too big to fit completely on the screen at 800×600.

105

Every monitor or laptop screen is designed to look best at a specific resolution. This is called the **optimum**, or **recommended**, resolution for the screen. When Windows is installed on your computer or you connect a monitor, it detects the type of monitor and automatically adjusts the screen to the recommended resolution. You can adjust the resolution to make it fit your needs.

To change your resolution, follow these steps:

1. Right-click your desktop background (in a blank spot where there are no program windows open), and then click Screen resolution.

2. In the Screen Resolution window, click the Resolution drop-down list. Figure 4-16 displays the resolutions available for this monitor.

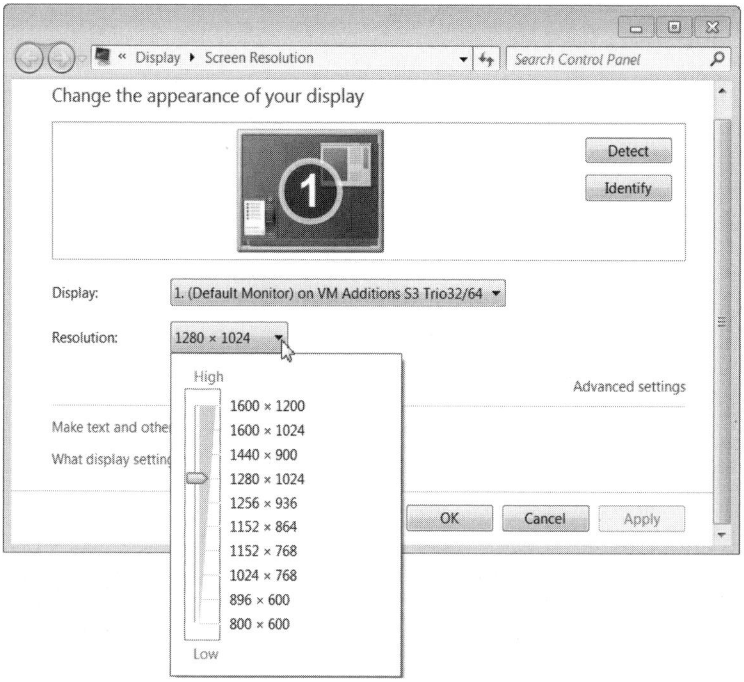

Figure 4-16. The screen resolutions available for this monitor

3. Drag the slider up or down. The preview will change in size and shape as you move the slider.

4. Click Apply to reset the resolution without closing the Screen Resolution window.

A dialog box may appear asking whether you want to keep these changes, as shown in Figure 4-17. This gives you a chance to try it without committing the changes.

Display Settings

Do you want to keep these display settings?

[Keep changes] [Revert]

Reverting to previous display settings in 15 seconds.

Figure 4-17. When you change your resolution, you have a chance to see what it will look like before committing to the new settings.

5. Click `Keep changes` if you like the new setting. Otherwise, let it revert.

   In some instances, if you select a resolution that is completely incompatible with your monitor or video card, Windows will display a warning message and not even attempt to apply the new resolution.

AdvancED

*Wide-screen monitors are becoming the norm for desktop PCs and are gaining popularity in laptop computers. The screen resolution list for your computer may include both wide-screen and regular width (sometimes called **normal aspect**) resolutions. As you move the slider up or down, compare the shape in the preview of your monitor. If you use a resolution that does not match the height and width ratio of your screen, it may not look right. You may end up with black bars on the top and bottom, part of the desktop off-screen, or all of it on-screen but squished together so everything seems unnaturally tall and skinny.*

AdvancED

If you connect your laptop computer to an external monitor or projector or if you have a desktop PC that has a video card that supports multiple monitors, the `Screen Resolution` *window provides additional settings and features. Each monitor has its own resolution settings, and you can drag the monitors around in the preview window to match the actual physical position of your monitors. This allows you to move your windows and mouse pointer smoothly between monitors. If your monitors are different sizes and you want to use them side-by-side, you may need to adjust the resolutions on one or both of them so that program windows appear about the same size on either screen.*

Cleaning up and organizing your desktop

You have this nice desktop background and a cool color scheme. But the desktop looks cluttered. There's a grid of little icons like tombstones in a cemetery. And they seem to be multiplying, even though you don't remember putting them there. Those are your **desktop icons**. Figure 4-18 shows a desktop that has become overgrown with desktop icons.

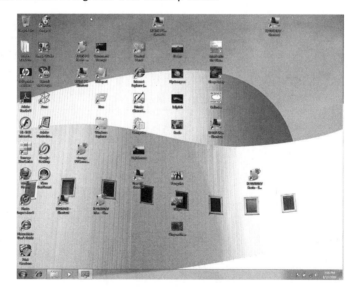

Figure 4-18. A desktop overrun with too many icons

Where did they come from, and why are they there? When you buy a new computer, the manufacturer often adds shortcuts to software that you can try or buy. Also, when you add new software or devices, the installation program asks whether you want to place a shortcut on the desktop. Fortunately, you can manage the icons in several ways:

- Organize the icons into tidy rows and columns
- Hide all desktop icons
- Delete individual icons you don't need
- Add a desktop toolbar

Tidying up your desktop icons

If you simply need to organize your icons into tidy rows and columns, you should follow these steps:

1. Right-click an empty area of your desktop.

2. On the menu that pops up, hover over View.

   Figure 4-19 shows the submenu that appears, with several commands for organizing and displaying your desktop icons.

Large icons	View ▶
● Medium icons	Sort by ▶
Small icons	Refresh
Auto arrange icons	Paste
✓ Align icons to grid	Paste shortcut
✓ Show desktop icons	Undo Copy Ctrl+Z
✓ Show desktop gadgets	New ▶
	Screen resolution
	Gadgets
	Personalize

Figure 4-19. When you right-click the desktop and click View, you can arrange, hide, or resize desktop icons.

3. Organize the icons as desired:

- To tidy up the icons, select Auto arrange icons or Align icons to grid, or both.
- Auto arrange icons is useful when you've dragged shortcuts to the desktop and they are scattered all over. Align icons to grid organizes the icons into uniform rows and columns.
- If you don't want to see any icons on your desktop, clear the Show desktop icons check box.

LinkED

Clearing Show desktop icons is useful when you have so many icons that they litter the nice desktop background you've chosen (like Figure 4-19) or it now takes you a long time to find the icons you want to click. If you like using the desktop as a container to hold all your favorite links and program icons, the section "Accessing your desktop with a toolbar" shows you how you can get to those links without showing them on the desktop.

Hiding or showing common Windows desktop icons

Windows includes some common desktop icons for Computer, User's Files, Recycle Bin, Control Panel, and Network that you can select to hide or display through the Desktop Icon Settings dialog box. By default, only the Recycle Bin is displayed.

1. Click the Start button, and in the Start menu's search box, type desktop icons.

2. In the list that appears, click Show or hide common icons on the desktop.

3. In the Desktop Icon Settings dialog box, shown in Figure 4-20, clear or select check boxes as needed.

Figure 4-20. You can hide or show Windows common desktop icons.

LinkED

You can also add a desktop toolbar to access desktop icons, even if you have hidden the icons on the desktop itself. This is covered in the "Accessing your desktop with a toolbar" section.

Deleting or moving desktop icons

If you like using the desktop to access programs, files, or folders but there are extra icons that you don't want or need, you can delete or move individual icons. As you've seen, you can also hide or show common desktop icons for things such as the Recycle Bin, Computer, Control Panel, User's Files, and Network.

Consider the following before deleting or moving desktop icons:

- Desktop icons can be **shortcuts** to open programs or files located elsewhere on your computer, or they can be actual files or folders located in the desktop folder.
- Deleting a shortcut icon does not delete a program or file or uninstall a program; it just removes the icon from the desktop.
- Deleting a folder or file icon actually deletes the folder or file. If you don't want the folder or file icon on your desktop, move it to one of your libraries, such as Documents.
- If you accidentally delete a file or folder, you may be able to retrieve it by pressing the key combination Ctrl+Z (Undo) or opening the Recycle Bin.

Figure 4-21 shows several types of desktop icons: a common desktop icon (`Recycle Bin`), a folder icon (`New folder`), a shortcut icon (`Adobe Photoshop`), and a picture file icon (`Lighthouse`). You can identify a shortcut icon by the arrow in the lower-left corner, like the `Adobe Photoshop` icon.

Figure 4-21. Examples of several types of desktop icons

To delete a desktop icon, follow these steps:

1. Right-click a desktop icon. A context menu appears, as shown in Figure 4-22.

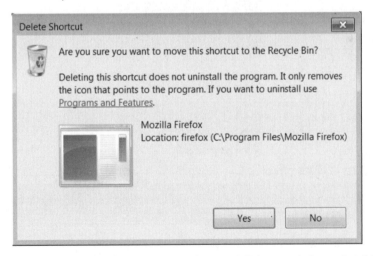

Figure 4-22. Desktop icon context menu allows you to delete an icon if you don't want it to appear on your desktop.

2. To delete a shortcut (an icon with an arrow in the lower-left corner), click Delete. A message similar to Figure 4-23 appears clarifying that this only deletes the shortcut and does not uninstall the program.

Figure 4-23. When you delete a program shortcut, Windows reminds you that this does not uninstall the program. This message is not displayed when you are deleting a browser shortcut to a website, because websites are not programs.

3. To permanently delete a folder or file, click `Delete`. A message similar to Figure 4-24 is displayed to confirm that you want to send the folder or file to the Recycle Bin.

Delete Folder

Are you sure you want to move this folder to the Recycle Bin?

ENGLISH
Date created: 8/1/2009 9:31 PM

Yes   No

Figure 4-24. When you delete a file or folder, Windows reminds you that this will place the item in the Recycle Bin.

4. To move a file or folder, click `Cut`, navigate to the folder you want to move it to (destination), and then click `Paste` in the destination folder.

Accessing your desktop with a toolbar

You can hide your desktop icons and still keep them handy for quick access:

1. Right-click the taskbar, click `Toolbars`, and then click `Desktop`, as shown in Figure 4-25.

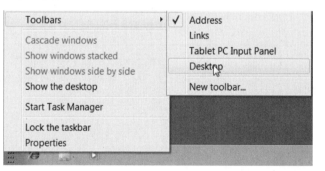

Figure 4-25. You can access the desktop icons from the taskbar by adding the desktop toolbar.

2. To access a desktop item from the taskbar, click the double angle brackets, as shown in Figure 4-26.

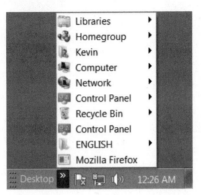

Figure 4-26. The desktop icons are now available from the desktop toolbar in the taskbar.

Customizing your computer sounds

Just as there are visual themes, Windows also provides **sound themes** for events that occur in Windows and other programs. These events include the sounds you hear when starting or exiting windows and when receiving new mail, warnings, and errors, to name a few. There quite a few things you can do with Windows sounds to suit your needs:

- Turn on or off the sound played at Windows startup
- Turn off Windows events sounds completely
- Change the sound scheme
- Change or turn off the sound assigned to a specific event
- Mute sounds

In this section, you'll learn how to use and change the Control Panel's sound and volume settings.

Changing system sounds

To change your system sounds, follow these steps:

1. Click the Windows `Start` button, and in the `Start` menu's search box, type `Sound`.

2. In the results list, click `Change system sounds`.

The Control Panel's Sound dialog box appears, displaying the Sounds tab, as shown in Figure 4-27.

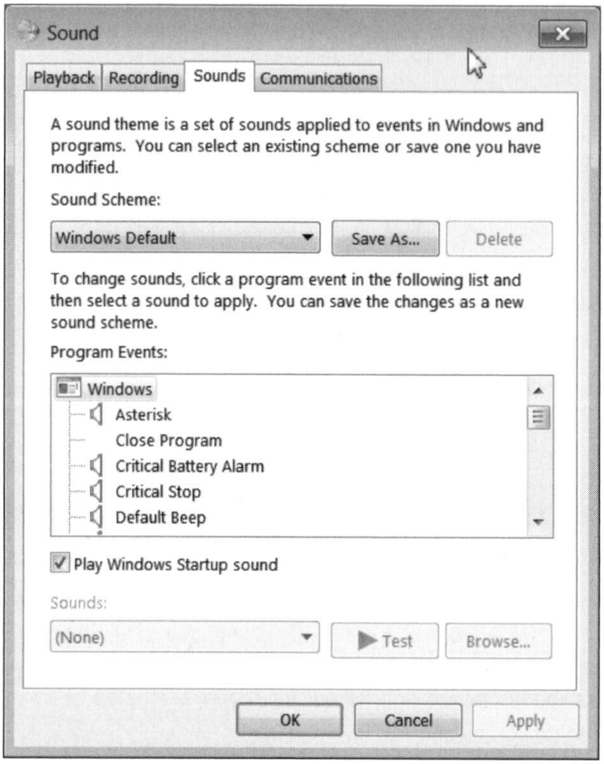

Figure 4-27. The Sound dialog box Sound dialog box in the Control Panel provides settings for changing Windows system sounds.

3. Change the settings if desired:

    *   To turn off the sound that is played when Windows starts, clear the Play Windows Startup sound check box.
    *   To turn off all Windows sounds for program events, click the Sound Scheme drop-down list, and then click No Sounds.
    *   To change the sound scheme, click the Sound Scheme drop-down list, and then click a different sound scheme.
    *   To listen to the sound for a specific program event, in the Program Events list click the event and then click Test.

- To change the sound for a specific event, in the `Program Events` list click the event, click the `Sounds` drop-down list, and then select the sound or select `(None)` at the top of the list if you don't want any sound for that event.
- To save all your changes without overriding the existing sound scheme your changes are based on, click `Save As` to create a new sound scheme.

LinkED

The Windows 7 Ease of Access Center provides a feature to use text or visual alternatives for sounds. To access settings for this feature, in the `Start` *menu's search box, type* `Sounds`, *and in the list that appears, click* `Replace sounds with visual cues`. *For more information about the Ease of Access Center, see "Customizing Windows for visual, audio, mobility, or cognitive needs" later in this chapter.*

Adjusting the volume or muting your computer

You can adjust the volume or mute all sounds from your computer, not just Windows system sounds. For example, you can adjust the speakers, headphones, music, videos, or any other application or device that is currently providing sound on your computer.

To adjust or mute the volume of devices and programs, follow these steps:

1. In the notification area at the bottom right of your screen, right-click the speaker icon, and then click `Open Volume Mixer`, as shown in Figure 4-28.

Figure 4-28. The Volume Mixer provides controls for the volume and muting of the audio devices and programs currently in use.

If the icon is not displayed in your taskbar, you can also click the `Start` menu and enter `Adjust Volume` in the `Start` menu's search box.

When the Volume Mixer opens, it displays at least one audio device that produces actual sounds such as speakers or headphones, as well as currently running programs that provide sounds such as System Sounds, Windows Media Player, or Windows Media Center.

2. You can adjust or mute the volume of any or all items. Each item can be changed individually, except `Device`. If you move the slider for the `Device` volume, all other sliders move with it. If you mute `Device`, all other items are muted:

   - To adjust the volume of an item, move its slider up or down.
   - To mute an item, click the speaker icon at the bottom.
   - To adjust the volume of all items at once, move the `Device` slider up or down.
   - To mute everything, click the speaker icon under the device. In Figure 4-29, all items are muted because the `Device` slider for `Speakers` is muted.

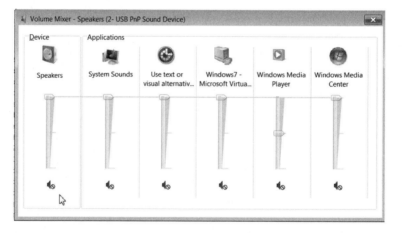

Figure 4-29. `Device` is a master control for the volume and muting of all the other mixer controls.

AdvancED

If you have a laptop computer, this has probably happened to you. You start up your laptop, and before you know it, Windows has announced itself to the world with the "Ta-da!" sound. Here's an easy, low-tech, cheap trick you can use without even turning on your laptop. Plug the sound leak with a dead headphone plug. The next time you throw away a pair of headphones, cut the plug off the end of the cord. Or, get a headphone Y-splitter jack that allows two sets of headphones to share one jack. Insert the plug into your laptop's headphone jack before you start your computer. Your computer thinks you are using headphones or external speakers, and it won't use your laptop's built-in speakers. Ta-da!

Customizing Windows for visual, audio, mobility, or cognitive needs

Windows 7's Ease of Access Center provides many features, settings, and programs to fit a wide variety of needs. These capabilities are designed to help you get the most out of your computer, through whatever means of input and interaction works best for you. There is no one-size-fits-all technique for visual, audio, mobility, or cognitive needs. The average age of the world's population is increasing, and with age, hearing, vision, mobility, and other abilities decline. So, many of the traditional definitions of disabilities are blurring.

The Ease of Access Center lists all the features that can make your computer easier to use. If you are not sure what you need, the Ease of Access Center also provides a great assessment tool to survey your needs and, based on your answers, recommends features and settings that will benefit you specifically. Any information gathered by Windows in this process is private and will not be shared or accessible to anybody else outside of your computer.

To open the Ease of Access Center, follow these steps:

1. Click the `Start` button, and in the `Start` menu's search box, type `Ease of Access`.

2. On the list that appears, click `Ease of AccessEase of Access`.

The Ease of Access Center window appears, as shown in Figure 4-30. In this window, you can directly apply many specific settings to make your computer easier to use, explore other settings, or answer a series of questions to help recommend features for you.

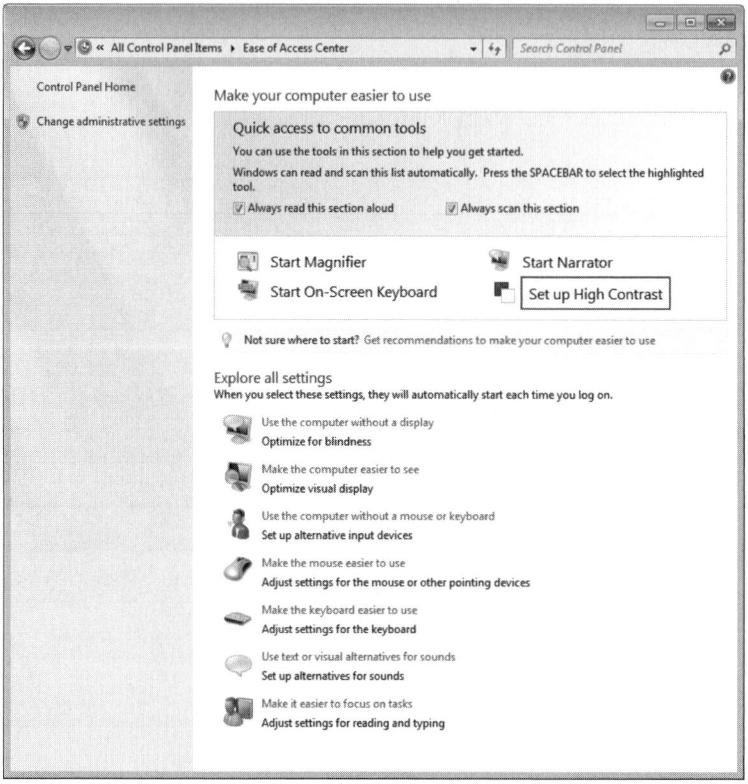

Figure 4-30. The Ease of Access Center provides many ways to view, explore, and apply a wide variety of tools and features to make your computer easier to use. This window is enabled for ease of use with a number of aids and needs.

3. If you don't know what you need or want some recommendations because you don't know what features Windows offers for your needs, click Get recommendations to make your computer easier to use. Again, the questions, answers, and recommendations are private. The results of the answers do not label, name, or group the user into a category but, rather, suggest the specific features and settings that may be of most benefit.

Customizing program preferences and personal information

Windows 7 provides many ways for you to customize which programs to use and how much personal preference information is saved on your computer and made available to programs and websites. PC stands for *personal computer*, right? So, almost every chapter in *Getting StartED with Windows 7* contains additional information about making your computer personal:

- Chapter 1 explains how customize your taskbar and `Start` menu for quick access to the programs you use most.
- Chapter 2 provides more information about personalizing your user accounts.
- Chapter 7 provides information about sharing and keeping private your libraries and documents across your home network.
- Chapter 8 includes information about bookmarking your favorite websites, saving and storing personal contact information in e-mail address books, choosing which programs to use for your favorite tasks such as browsing the Internet, reading e-mail, listening to music, viewing pictures and video, and writing and viewing documents.
- Chapter 9 includes information about personalizing your security settings, passwords, and identity information.
- Chapter 10 explains how to move personal settings including browser cookies and your personal files to your new computer.

Summary

Here's a review of what you've learned in this chapter:

- How to change the picture on your logon screen and the `Start` menu with user accounts
- How to select a theme, desktop background, colors, and screen saver with personalization
- How to change the size of text displayed on screen and the level of detail on the screen with screen resolution
- How to tidy up your desktop by arranging, removing, or hiding desktop icons

- How to adjust your Windows system sounds and volume with the `Sound` dialog box in the Control Panel and the Volume Mixer
- How to customize for visual, audio, mobility, and cognitive needs with the Ease of Access Center in the Control Panel

In the next chapter, you'll learn not to take it personally when your computer misbehaves and what you can do to bring it back in line.

Chapter 5

Fixing Problems from A to Ctrl+Z

If you never use your computer, you will never need to fix any computer problems. Don't let fears of wrecking your computer keep you from enjoying your computer. This book is here to help you feel comfortable and have some fun with Windows 7. And this chapter is here to help you when things go wrong, big or small. Windows 7 has many features to help you prevent problems as well as fix them. From troubleshooters to Windows Help and Support, they're easy to use. So you can spend less time worrying and more time enjoying.

Chapter 6 will show you how to protect and fix problems with data and files. In this chapter, you'll go through Windows 7 features that help you fix problems with your computer, Windows, software you've installed, and devices you have connected. You'll learn how to use Safe Mode, System Restore, and Advanced Recovery, fix smaller pesky problems at the document and program level, and use Windows Help and Support for...help.

Using Windows 7 to fix problems

Oops! You did something wrong. You lost something. Or so you think. The sooner you discover something is wrong, the easier it is to fix it. There is no panic button that will magically make everything right again. But a few Windows features and good practices will help a lot.

So let's say that one day your computer works fine, but the next day it is slow or some programs do not work right. There are several possible causes:

- A new program you installed
- A new device you added
- Changes or customizations you made through various Windows settings
- A virus or spyware infection on your computer

Windows 7 provides several features that can help you fix your computer. They can help you at every level—from Windows not starting right, to Windows starting but the computer not running as fast or as smoothly as before. Some of the most useful tools and features for fixing Windows problems are as follows:

- **Windows troubleshooters:** Windows provides troubleshooters to help you fix common problems. You can access these through the Help system, or they may pop up when Windows detects specific problems.
- **Programs and Features:** This Control Panel item enables you to uninstall, change, or repair programs or updates already installed on your computer.
- **Safe Mode:** When you start your computer in Safe Mode, Windows runs with the minimum number of drivers and settings so you can uninstall programs or devices or make other changes.

AdvancED

Drivers are small files that tell Windows and your device how to work with each other. Almost every device in or attached to your computer has some kind of driver. Some of these may not be necessary when your computer requires only a few basic functions—for example, when your computer is running in Safe Mode. By loading only the basic drivers for devices such as your keyboard, mouse, and video card, Safe Mode enables you to fix problems that are occurring when your computer is operating in a normal state with all of the drivers running.

- **System Restore:** If your computer worked fine a few days ago but started running poorly after installing some programs or devices, you may be able to fix it with System Restore. System Restore enables you to go back in time to a point when your computer was working properly, and restore your computer to the state it was in then. System Restore does not remove or delete document or content files created after the restore point. It is not a file or image backup, like the backup and restore features described in Chapter 6.
- **Backup and Restore:** If you perform regular backups of your system image and your files, you can restore the entire computer or just your files.

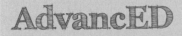

Chapter 6 describes how to set up a recurring backup plan so your computer files and computer images are backed up daily, weekly, monthly—whatever you choose. For most people, backing up your computer one or more times a week is safe and sufficient.

- **Recovery disc:** This is provided by the computer manufacturer, not Microsoft or Microsoft Windows. This recovery disc contains the complete Windows installation files, and resets your computer back to the settings and state it was in when it left the factory. This will erase all data on your computer, and you will need to reinstall all programs that you installed after you bought the computer.

AdvancED

Some computer manufacturers don't provide a DVD with all of the Windows installation files, and instead create a separate hidden partition on your hard drive and store the files there. To access the recovery disk (partition), you may need to have created a separate boot disc beforehand, or select a special command when you start your computer. If you don't receive a recovery disc with your new computer, contact your computer manufacturer. Upon request, some will send you a recovery disc, even if your computer already has a hidden recovery partition on the hard drive.

Using Windows Troubleshooters

Windows 7 provides **troubleshooters** to solve a wide variety of Windows, software, and hardware problems. When Windows detects a problem with Windows, a program, feature, or device, it will attempt to fix the problem or start a troubleshooter that might fix the problem.

If you have a problem and want to try a troubleshooter, there are several ways you can view a list of troubleshooters and types of problems they address. Windows often offers several ways to do the same thing, and that is true with accessing troubleshooters:

- **Opening the troubleshooter in Control Panel:** This method enables you to start with broad groupings and then work your way down through more-specific lists to one or more troubleshooters that seem to match your problem.

- **Accessing troubleshooters through Help and Support:** This method is more direct if you know which troubleshooter you are looking for, or you know of a problem and want Help and Support to search for troubleshooters that best match your problem.

Either method is just as good; the choice is a matter of preference. Explore both and use the method that works best for you.

Opening the troubleshooter in Control Panel

To open the troubleshooter in `Control Panel`, follow these steps:

1. Click the `Start` button, and in the `Start` menu's search box, type `Troubleshooting`. In the list that appears, under `Control Panel` click `Troubleshooting`. The `Control Panel` item `Troubleshooting` is displayed, as shown in Figure 5-1.

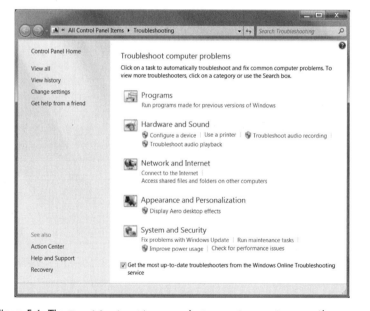

Figure 5-1. The `Troubleshooting` page in `Control Panel` groups the troubleshooters into categories such as `Programs` and `Hardware and Sound`, and lists the most common problems under each category.

2. Under a category, click a task that matches your problem. If you don't see a task that matches your problem, click a category name to view a larger list of problems in that category. For example, click `Programs`. Windows will check the Internet for new troubleshooters in addition to the ones already installed on your computer, and then display a list of problems in the `Programs` category, as shown in Figure 5-2. If you are not connected to the Internet, Windows 7 will just display the troubleshooters already installed on your computer.

Figure 5-2. Many troubleshooters are available to help with problems with programs.

3. Click a task to view a troubleshooter. If after viewing the first screen of the troubleshooter it does not appear to be what you want, you can click `Cancel`.

Accessing troubleshooters through Help and Support

To access troubleshooters through Help and Support, follow these steps:

1. Click the `Start` button, and then click `Help and Support`. `Windows Help and Support` is displayed, as shown in Figure 5-3.

Figure 5-3. `Windows Help and Support` includes help with using troubleshooters.

2. In the `Search Help` box, type `Troubleshooter` and then press the Enter key. A list of troubleshooting topics is displayed, as shown in Figure 5-4.

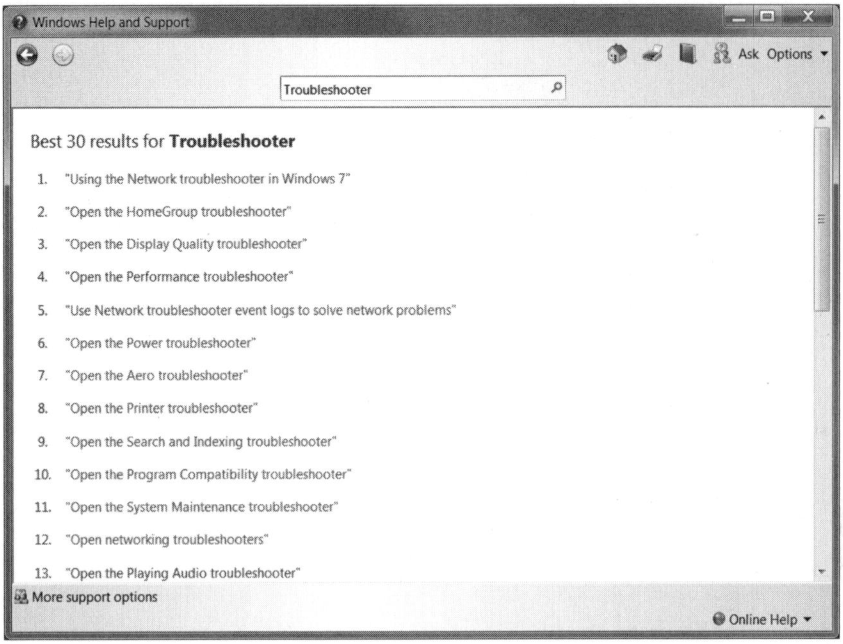

Figure 5-4. The search results for `Troubleshooter` in `Windows Help and Support` provide a longer list of troubleshooters than is displayed in the `Troubleshooting` page in `Control Panel` that was shown in Figure 5-1.

Using a troubleshooter to fix problems with hardware

A common problem people encounter with a new computer is that hardware or devices that worked with their old computer do not work on the new computer. You can use the Hardware and Devices troubleshooter to guide you through possible solutions.

To use the troubleshooter to identify and fix problems, follow these steps:

1. Scroll down the list of topics as described in the previous section, and click `Open the Hardware and Devices troubleshooter`. A Help topic describes the troubleshooter, as shown in Figure 5-5, and provides a link to open the troubleshooter itself.

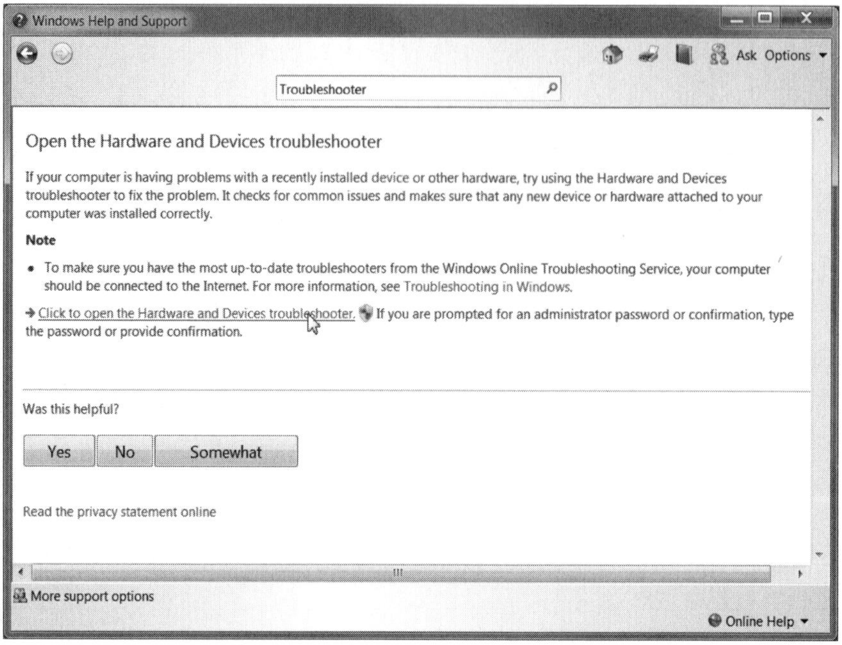

Figure 5-5. The Help topic describes the problems addressed by the Hardware and Devices troubleshooter, and provides a shortcut link to start the troubleshooter.

2. Click the link `Click to open the Hardware and Devices troubleshooter`. When you run this particular troubleshooter, it looks for problems with any hardware or devices on your computer. The troubleshooter will display a series of messages such as the following:

   - Detecting problems
   - Checking for missing driver
   - Resolving problems
   - Scanning for hardware change
   - Searching for device driver

If the troubleshooter detects that a device is disabled, it offers to enable it. In the example shown in Figure 5-6, the troubleshooter has detected that a wireless networking card on the computer is not enabled. The person using the computer had turned off wireless networking because the computer was already connected to the home network with a wired (Ethernet) connection.

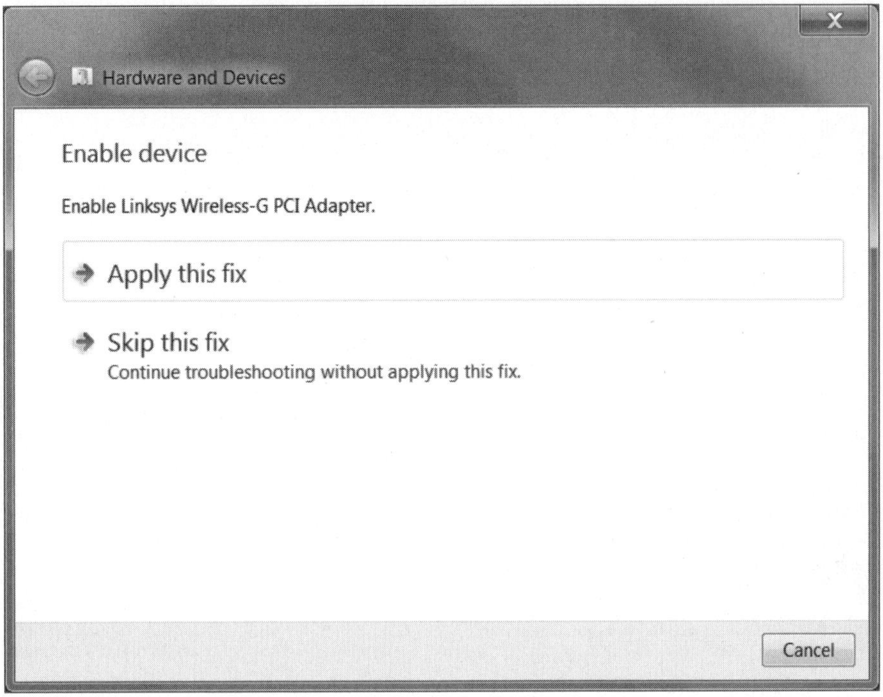

Figure 5-6. The Hardware and Devices troubleshooter detects a device connected to the computer that was not enabled.

3. `Apply` or `Skip` the fix as appropriate. The troubleshooter continues detecting problems and displays the next issue. In the example shown in Figure 5-7, the troubleshooter has detected a device that is missing a driver, and offers to install it.

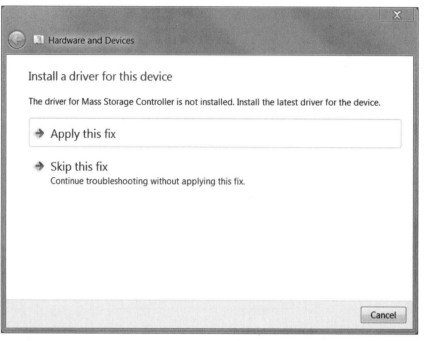

Figure 5-7. The troubleshooter detects another device that does not have a driver installed.

4. If the troubleshooter cannot find a driver, a message may be displayed in the notification area. Click the notification link for more details, and a message window is displayed, similar to Figure 5-8.

Figure 5-8. Clicking the notification message that the device did not install correctly displays a message with more details and a link to more help.

5. Click the link `What can I do if my device did not install properly??` to open a `Windows Help and Support` page similar to Figure 5-9 that provides more-specific things you can do.

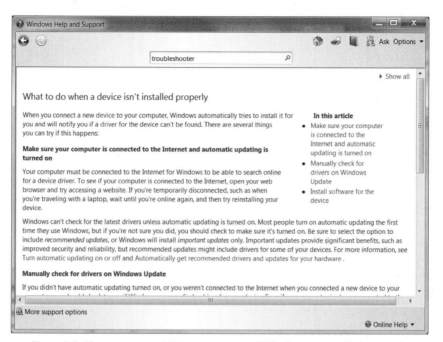

Figure 5-9. There are several things you can try if Windows cannot find a suitable driver for your device.

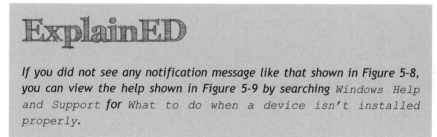

ExplainED

If you did not see any notification message like that shown in Figure 5-8, you can view the help shown in Figure 5-9 by searching `Windows Help and Support` *for* `What to do when a device isn't installed properly`*.*

Whether or not you click the notification messages for more information, the troubleshooter continues. When the troubleshooter has completed, it summarizes what was and was not fixed, as shown in Figure 5-10.

Figure 5-10. When the troubleshooter is done, it displays a report of issues, changes, and fixes.

The `Explore additional options` link displays a page with other places to look for possible solutions, as shown in Figure 5-11.

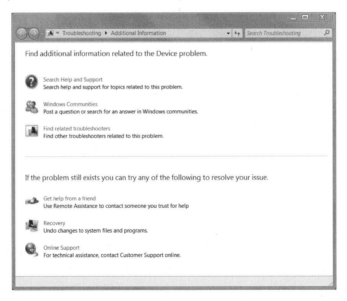

Figure 5-11. You can try these other links for suggestions on how to solve this problem. Windows Communities can be helpful because if other people have had a

similar problem with the same device, they may have found a solution and posted a message to share with others.

LinkED

One of the most common problems people encounter with a new version of Windows is that some older devices such as printers and scanners, and hardware such as sound or video cards, may not work because the drivers have not been updated to work with the newest version of Windows. Usually it is the responsibility of the hardware manufacturer, not Microsoft, to provide those updated drivers. Unfortunately, some drivers are never updated because the hardware is several years old and is no longer sold or manufactured.

"Updating device drivers" later in this chapter provides more details on finding and installing updated device drivers.

Using Programs and Features to fix problems

After you get a new computer or upgrade your existing computer to Windows 7, you may have many programs that you want to install. It is a good idea to install your programs one at a time, restarting your computer between each installation even if the installation program does not require it. If you have a lot of programs to install, spending a little extra time being cautious during installation will save a lot of time and aggravation later. Installing too much, too fast, can give your computer the equivalent of indigestion from eating too much that doesn't agree with you.

`Programs and Features` in `Control Panel` enables you to uninstall, change, or repair programs or updates already installed on your computer. If after installing a program or programs your computer doesn't work right, you can systematically remove your most recently installed programs until you have figured out which program is causing the problem and removed or repaired it.

LinkED

Programs and Features isn't just for fixing problems. It's also useful for removing programs you no longer use or for clearing disk space. Chapter 8 provides more information about adding and removing programs on your computer.

If you cannot start your computer, or it runs very poorly, you may want to start the computer in Safe Mode and then remove the programs while in Safe Mode. If you are not sure which programs are causing problems but have a good idea of when the problems started, you may want to use System Restore instead.

LinkED

Later in this chapter, "Running Windows 7 in Safe Mode" describes the trick to getting to Safe Mode when you start up your computer.

To remove a program, follow these steps:

1. Click the Start button, and in the Start menu's search box, type remove programs. In the list that appears, click Add or remove programs. The Programs and Features window is displayed, as shown in Figure 5-12.

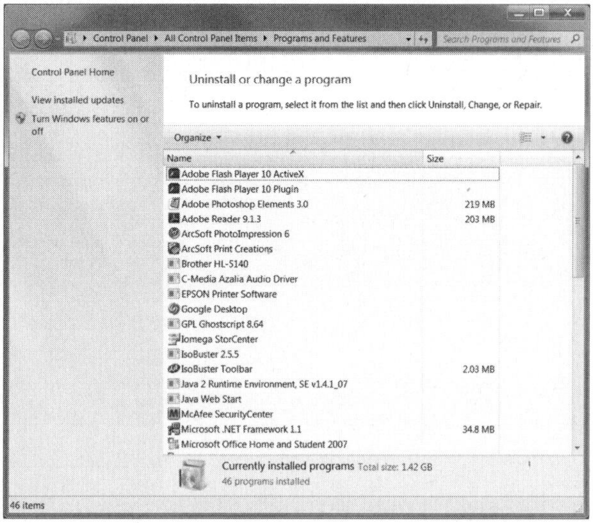

Figure 5-12. The `Programs and Features` window displays the programs that are installed on your computer.

2. Select the program you want to remove, and then click `Uninstall` in the toolbar above the list, as shown in Figure 5-13.

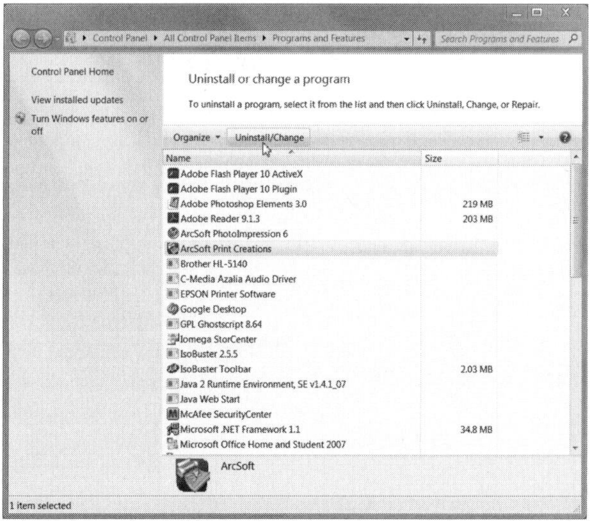

Figure 5-13. When you select a program in the list, the `Uninstall` button appears above the list. Some programs offer only `Uninstall`, and some may also offer `Change` or `Repair`.

When you click `Uninstall`, the program's *installation* program may start up even though you are *uninstalling*. The installation options for the program displayed in Figure 5-14 include `Modify` and `Repair`, in addition to `Remove` (uninstall). Sometimes you don't need to completely uninstall the program to fix a problem. You may want to try reinstalling the program if that option is available. In this program, you can reinstall with the `Repair` option.

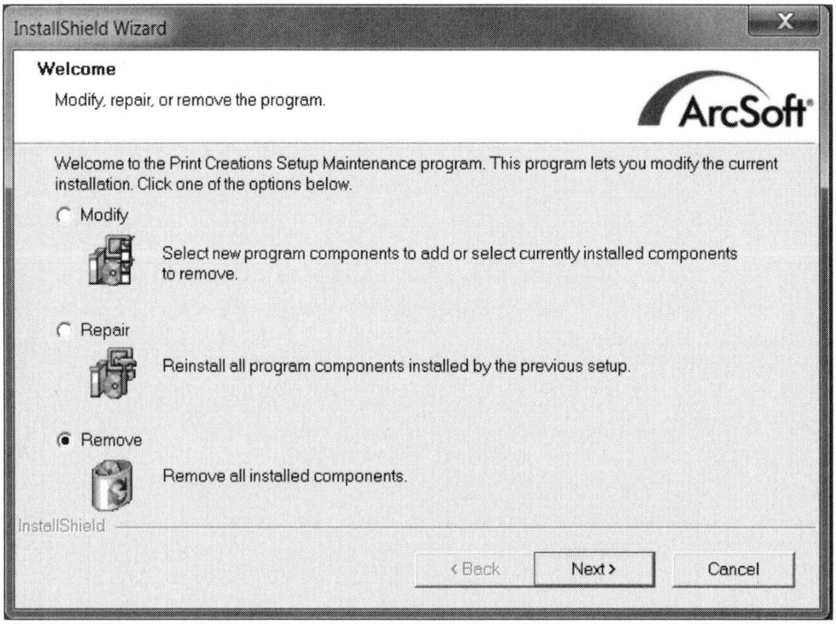

Figure 5-14. Some programs offer a repair or reinstallation option.

3. If you are having problems with a program that worked before on another computer, or that you think should run on this computer, try the repair or reinstallation option if available. Not all programs offer a repair option. Other programs may offer only an `Uninstall` option, as shown in Figure 5-15.

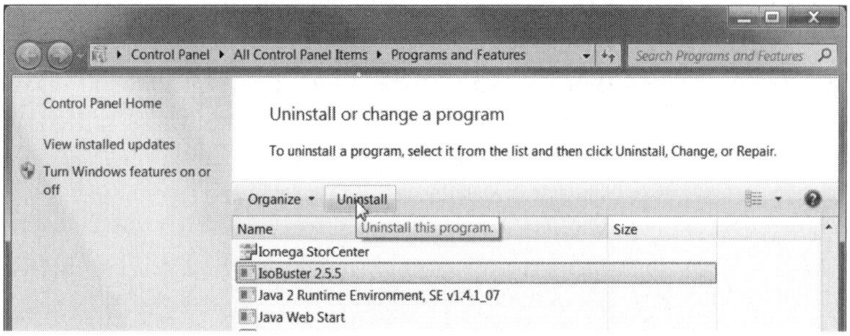

Figure 5-15. Some programs offer only an `Uninstall` option.

4. If the program offers only `Uninstall`, click the `Uninstall` button. Windows or the installation program may immediately start uninstalling the program, as shown in Figure 5-16, or may ask you to confirm that you really want to uninstall the program. The message and option displayed varies depending on how the software manufacturer designed the program.

Figure 5-16. The uninstall process may take several minutes, depending on the size and complexity of the program being removed.

5. When the repair or removal is complete, you may be asked to restart the computer. Even if you aren't asked to, it is a good idea to restart your computer anyway.

AdvancED

Many installation programs require that you restart the computer at the end of installation. If you are installing several programs at once, it may be tempting to wait to restart until you have installed all or several programs. Unfortunately, if you install multiple programs and then have problems after restarting your computer, you may not be able to tell which program is causing the problem. Then you'll have to uninstall all of the programs that you just installed.

To be safe, restart your computer whenever you install a major program, even if it is not required or suggested by the installation program. The same goes for uninstalling or repairing programs—restart the computer between uninstalls, repairs, and reinstallations.

Running Windows 7 in Safe Mode

Safe Mode starts Windows with a bare minimum of drivers and settings so you can uninstall programs or devices, run System Restore, or make other changes.

LinkED

You don't have to be in Safe Mode to use System Restore. "Using System Restore to fix problems" later in this chapter describes how to access System Restore as you would any other program from the Start menu.

To get into Safe Mode, you must run it when you first start or restart your computer, before the computer displays the Starting Windows screen with the Windows logo on the black background (see Figure 5-17).

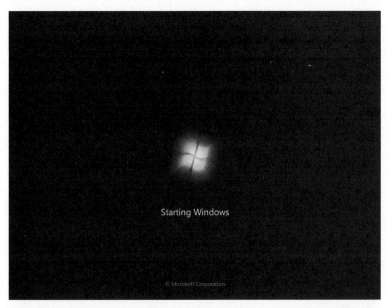

Figure 5-17. To start in Safe Mode, you must press F8 (usually repeatedly) before this `Starting Windows` screen is displayed. If this screen appears, you need to restart your computer and try again.

ExplainED

Each computer is different, so some computers get to the `Starting Windows` screen sooner than others. If you miss pressing F8 soon enough and your computer goes to the `Starting Windows` screen shown in Figure 5-17, restart your computer. Wait until the user login screen appears, click the down arrow on the red shut-down key at the bottom right of the screen, and then click `Restart`.

To access Safe Mode, follow these steps:

1. Start or restart your computer.

2. As soon as the screen starts displaying the BIOS information, press the F8 key repeatedly. If your computer displays a keyboard error message or beeps, or both, ignore it and keep pressing F8 until the `Advanced Boot Options` screen is displayed, as shown in Figure 5-18.

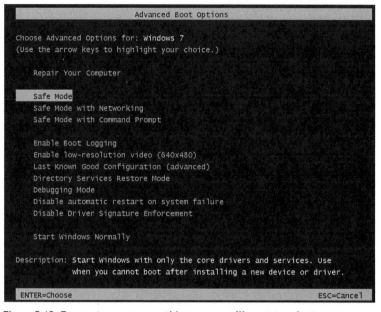

Figure 5-18. For most purposes, on this screen you'll want to select `Safe Mode`.

3.   Press the down arrow key on your keyboard to highlight `Safe Mode`, and then press Enter. Windows loads the minimum operating system features and drivers needed to run Windows in a very simple mode. As Windows loads drivers and files, the filenames roll down the screen, as shown in Figure 5-19.

```
                     Loading Windows Files
     Loaded: \Windows\system32\drivers\fltmgr.sys
     Loaded: \Windows\system32\drivers\fileinfo.sys
     Loaded: \Windows\System32\Drivers\Ntfs.sys
     Loaded: \Windows\System32\Drivers\msrpc.sys
     Loaded: \Windows\System32\Drivers\ksecdd.sys
     Loaded: \Windows\System32\Drivers\cng.sys
     Loaded: \Windows\System32\drivers\pcw.sys
     Loaded: \Windows\System32\Drivers\Fs_Rec.sys
     Loaded: \Windows\system32\drivers\ndis.sys
     Loaded: \Windows\system32\drivers\NETIO.SYS
```

Figure 5-19. It will take a few moments for Windows to load the files it needs to run in Safe Mode.

When Windows finishes loading the files, it opens in Safe Mode: you see a black screen with the words `Safe Mode` on each corner of the screen. `Windows Help and Support` automatically opens and displays a Help topic on using Safe Mode, as shown in Figure 5-20.

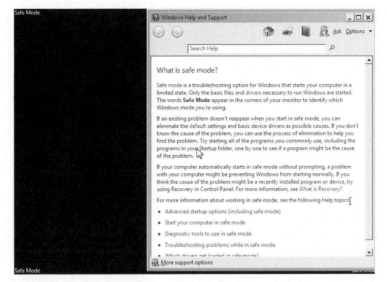

Figure 5-20. When Windows opens in Safe Mode, the screen isn't pretty but it is functional.

4. In the Help topic, click Troubleshooting problems while in safe mode. The troubleshooting page is displayed, as shown in Figure 5-21.

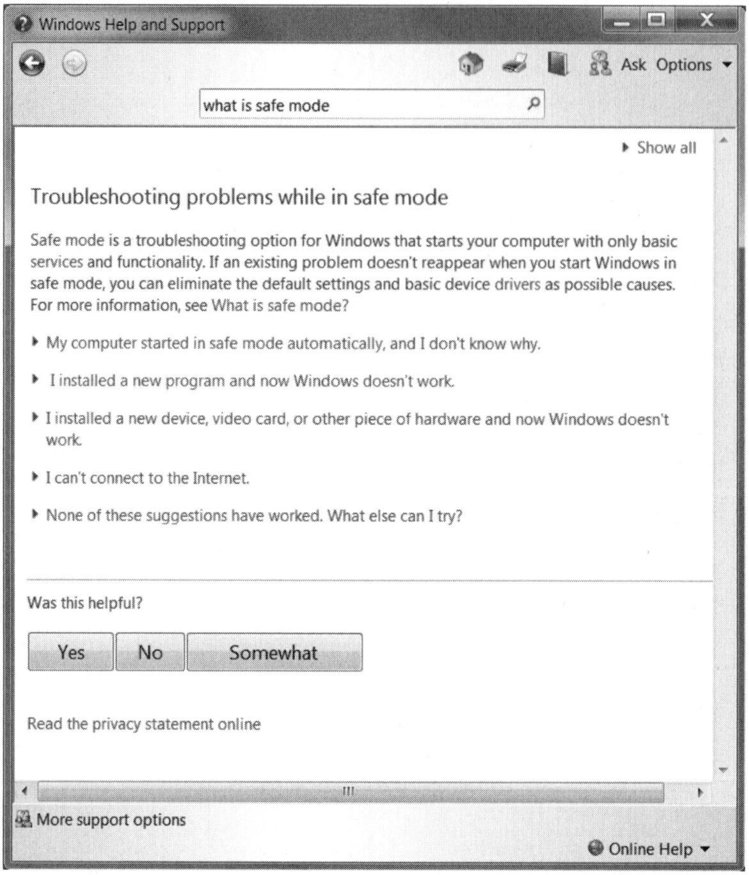

Figure 5-21. You can try several fixes while in Safe Mode.

5. If one of the problems listed matches what you are experiencing, click the link for possible solutions. If you are fairly certain that a program you recently installed is causing your problems, you can uninstall the program through `Programs and Features`, using the steps in "Using Programs and Features to fix problems."

AdvancED

The Safe Mode troubleshooter suggests using System Restore if Windows is not working correctly after you installed a program. Another option is to uninstall the program you suspect is causing the problem, instead of using System Restore.

System Restore is safe and reliable, but may take longer than uninstalling a suspect program. The more severe the problems, the better it is to use System Restore instead of uninstall. Sometimes it is easier to identify when your computer last worked okay and the problems started, than to pinpoint what program installation caused the problems. System Restore will usually be a better choice then.

System Restore does not identify what programs or settings are not running correctly, so it restores the settings and programs (good or bad) back to their state at the chosen restore point. You may not know which programs or settings are causing the problems either. After the System Restore is complete, you can carefully add programs back in and restore other settings.

Using System Restore to fix problems

If your computer worked fine a few days ago but started running poorly after installing some programs or devices, you may be able to fix it with **System Restore**. System Restore enables you to go back in time to a point when you know your computer was working properly, and restore your computer to the state it was in then.

System Restore automatically creates restore points every week as you use your computer, and whenever you install or remove programs or updates, or make other changes to Windows settings. These checkpoints are called **restore points**. They are a snapshot of the state of your Windows settings and programs at a specific point in time. You can also manually create your own restore points at any time.

AdvancED

For most people, the automatic restore points created by Windows are sufficient. However, some programs or setting changes may not automatically generate a restore point. Or you may be making changes that you think may be risky. In either case, you may want to manually create a restore point. To create a restore point, click the Start *button, and in the* Start *menu's search box, type* create a restore point. *In the list that appears, click* Create a restore point. *The* System Properties *dialog box appears. On the* System Protection *tab, click* Create *and follow the instructions on your screen.*

To restore your computer to an earlier point in time, follow these steps:

1. Click the Start button, and in the Start **menu's search box**, type recovery. In the list that appears, click Restore your computer to an earlier point in time. The Recovery window is displayed, as shown in Figure 5-22.

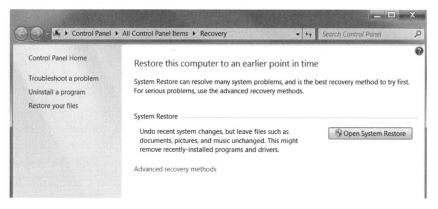

Figure 5-22. The Recovery window describes using System Restore to restore the computer to an ealier point in time when the computer was working normally.

2. Click Open System Restore. System Restore appears, as shown in Figure 5-23.

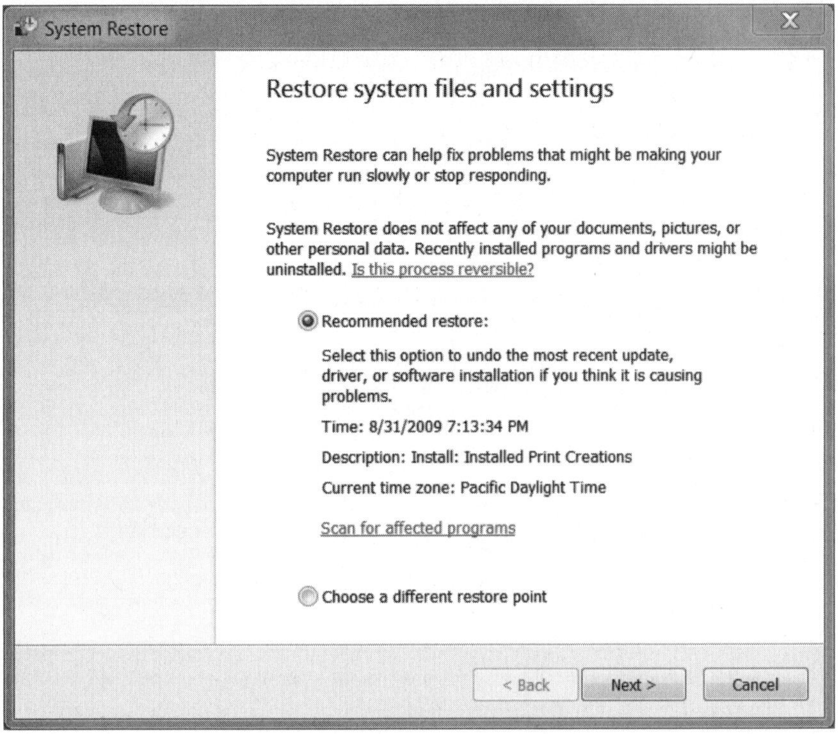

Figure 5-23. System Restore will recommend a recent restore point on the assumption that you just started experiencing problems. You can select another restore point if you think the problem started before or well after the suggested restore point.

When you access System Restore from Safe Mode, the page may vary slightly from Figure 5-23, in that it does not include the message that "Recently installed programs and drivers might be uninstalled."

3. Click Next if you want to use the recommended restore point, or select Choose a different restore point and then click Next. If you select this option, the next page will display a list of recent restore points, as shown in Figure 5-24. Select a restore point and then click Next.

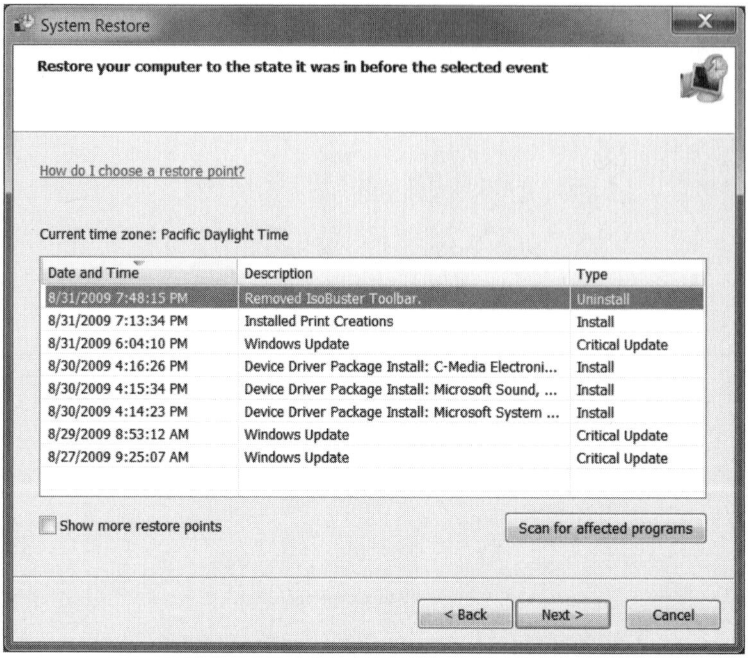

Figure 5-24. If you want to choose a restore point instead of accepting the recommended restore point, System Restore can display a list of recent restore points and associated events.

Figure 5-25 is an example of the screen System Restore will display to ask you to confirm your selection and prompt you to close any open programs.

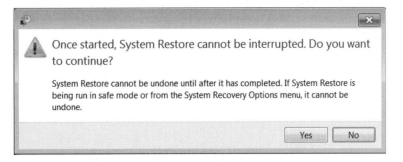

Figure 5-25. System Restore confirms your choice of restore point before starting the restore.

4. Click Finish. System Restore displays one more screen providing an opportunity to cancel System Restore, as shown in Figure 5-26.

Figure 5-26. This warning tells you not to interrupt System Restore, and that in some circumstances you cannot undo the restore afterward.

ExplainED

The warning about not being able to undo System Restore is not meant to scare you. If you are running System Restore from Safe Mode or from the `System Recovery Options` *menu, it usually means you were already in an unstable situation. You may not have any better or safer options except running System Restore.*

5. Click `Yes`. System Restore starts and displays the screens shown in Figures 5-27 and 5-28.

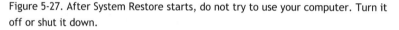

Figure 5-27. After System Restore starts, do not try to use your computer. Turn it off or shut it down.

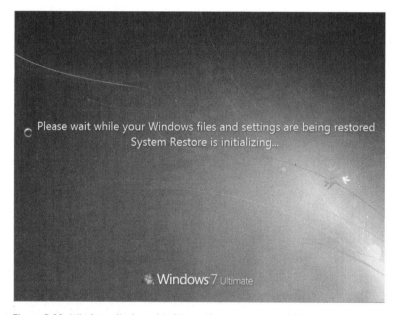

Figure 5-28. Windows displays this System Restore screen while performing the restore. System Restore will restart the computer when it is finished.

150

After Windows restarts and you log on, System Restore displays a message that it is complete, as shown in Figure 5-29.

System Restore

ⓘ System Restore completed successfully. The system has been restored to 8/30/2009 9:52:35 PM. Your documents have not been affected.

Close

Figure 5-29. System Restore completed successfully.

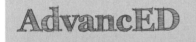

If you get a message that System Restore was not successful or did not complete, you may need to run System Restore again with a different restore point, or try a more advanced recovery option.

6. Check your computer to see whether it is now running correctly and the problems are gone. If you are still experiencing the same problems or new ones, run System Restore again and use an earlier restore point. If there are no earlier points available, or you've tried several restore points and none of them have fixed the problem, you may need to try Advanced Recovery. See the "Using Advanced Recovery" section.

Updating device drivers

The device manufacturers usually provide the drivers that enable your computer to work with printers and other devices that you attach to or install inside your computer. Microsoft may provide device drivers if they apply to a wide variety of products in a category.

Sometimes a new version of Windows leaves some older devices behind. If the device is several years old, the manufacturer may not have an updated driver available for Windows 7 right away. When you attach that device to your new Windows 7 machine, it may not work if it needs a new driver for Windows 7. Generally, almost all device drivers that worked in Windows Vista will work in Windows 7.

Examples of devices that may need updated drivers

This is not an exhaustive list, but gives you an idea of the wide variety of devices that may need updated drivers:

- Printers
- Scanners
- Web cams
- Wireless network cards and adapters
- Wireless routers
- USB switchers (for connecting a device to more than one computer at a time)
- USB multicard readers
- Digital cameras
- MP3 players
- External hard drives
- DVD drives
- Network-attached storage

ExplainED

A new computer with Windows 7 installed at the factory should have all the drivers for the devices and hardware that are installed in the computer. You should not have to update drivers on a Windows 7 computer when you take it out of the box. Sometimes the computer manufacturer or the store selling the computer bundles it with other external hardware such as multifunction printers. This added device might need updated drivers to run on Windows 7.

If you bought a Windows Vista computer with the promise of a free upgrade to Windows 7 when it became available, you may have to update some drivers after you install the Windows 7 upgrade. Check the manufacturer's website before upgrading to see whether there are additional drivers that you need to download.

You may discover that you need new drivers in the following ways:

- You use Windows Easy Transfer, and the Transfer Report lists devices that need updated drivers.
- You run the Devices and Printers troubleshooter, and it detects devices that need updated drivers.

- You attach a device to your computer, and the `Add New Hardware` wizard cannot find the right driver.
- A notification appears in the notification area of the taskbar.
- In `Devices and Printers` in `Control Panel`, or in `Device Manager`, one of the devices has a yellow warning icon.

When Windows detects that it needs a driver, it will check the drivers stored on the computer, or if you allow it, will look for drivers on the Internet. Sometimes all that is needed is the device installation disc.

Most devices that work on Windows Vista should work on Windows 7. But if you are moving from Windows XP (or older) to Windows 7, you are more likely to run into a few devices that don't work right away.

Getting the correct drivers to your computer can be the tricky part. After you have the updated drivers, installing the drivers on your computer usually is a cinch.

Locating updated drivers

Try any of the following to locate updated drivers:

- Install the device with the device's installation disc.
- Run the Devices and Printers troubleshooter. Sometimes the device just needs to be enabled. The troubleshooter can fix that. If the troubleshooter detects a missing or outdated driver, it can check your computer and the Internet for updated drivers.
- Go to the device manufacturer's website and check the support area for a downloads or drivers section. Look for updated device installation programs or drivers for Windows 7. If there is no Windows 7 device installation or driver listed, see if there is one for Windows Vista. Download and install the Windows Vista version.
- If the manufacturer doesn't have a Windows 7 driver but is working on one and hopes to release it soon, you could wait for the updated drivers.
- Search Internet user forums for drivers or other people with the same problem. For example, there didn't appear to be an updated driver for an older sound card on an older computer that was upgraded from Windows XP to Windows 7. Searching for `Sound Card Name drivers` produced a list of user websites where this particular sound card was discussed. Sifting through the messages posted on these sites provided several possible solutions:
- Download the Vista or Windows XP device installation program or drivers and install them using the Program Compatibility troubleshooter.

- Buy and install a new sound card that is compatible with Windows 7.
- In this example, installing the drivers through the Program Compatibility troubleshooter solved the problem.

Updating the drivers on your computer

Here are the steps for updating the drivers for a device on your computer:

1. Locate and install the device drivers from the device installation disc or a download from the Internet.

2. lick the `Start` button, and in the `Start` menu's search box, type `Device Manager`. In the list that appears, click `Device Manager`.

3. Locate the device with the yellow warning icon, right-click it, and then click `Update Driver`. Figure 5-30 displays a warning on a Mass Storage Controller device.

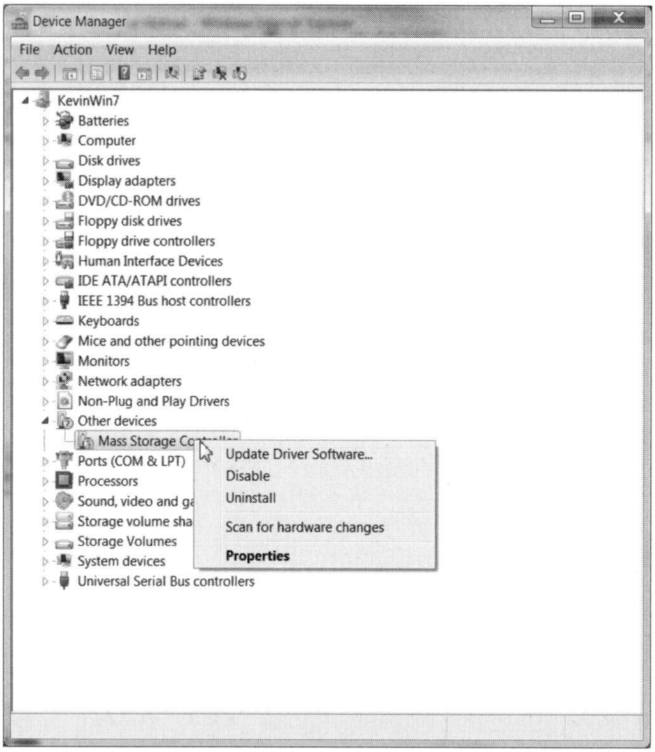

Figure 5-30. When you right-click a device, you can update the driver, disable the device, or uninstall the driver.

154

4. Click `Update Driver Software`. Windows asks where to search for the driver software, as shown in Figure 5-31.

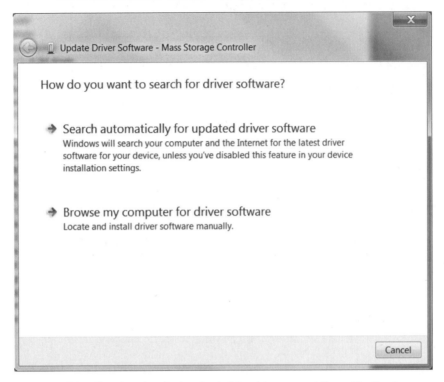

Figure 5-31. If you've already downloaded the drivers, you still need to direct Windows to the location on your computer.

5. Click `Browse my computer for driver software`. Figure 5-32 displays your options for finding the driver software.

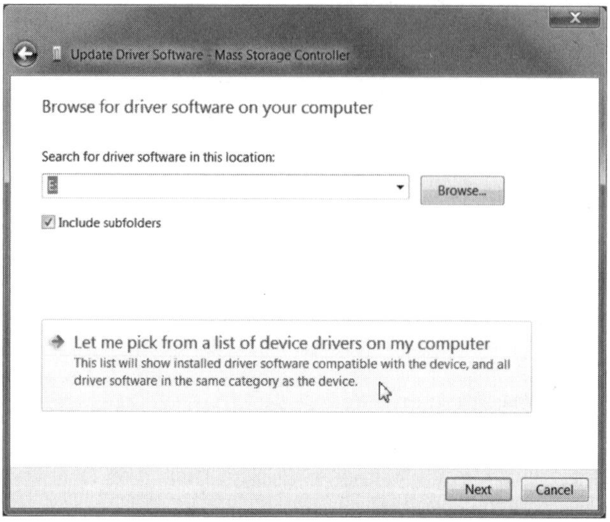

Figure 5-32. When drivers have been installed on the computer, sometimes all that is needed is to tell Windows where to find the driver for a device.

6.   Click Let me pick from a list of device drivers on my computer. A list of device types is displayed, as shown in Figure 5-33.

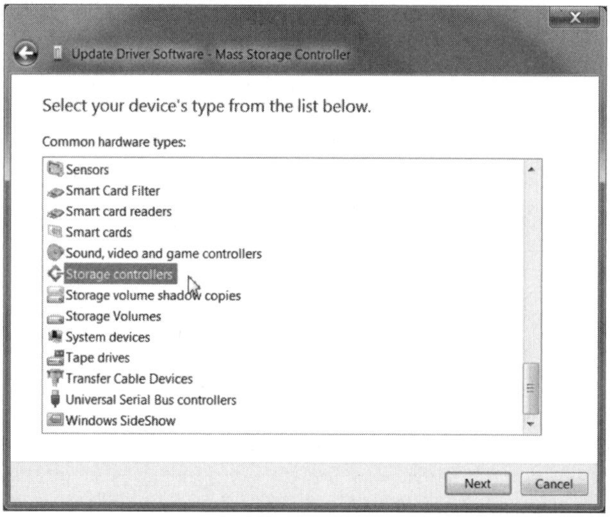

Figure 5-33. Scroll through a list of device types until you find one that matches your device.

7. Select the device type and then click Next. A list is displayed of the manufacturers of the type of device you selected, as shown in Figure 5-34.

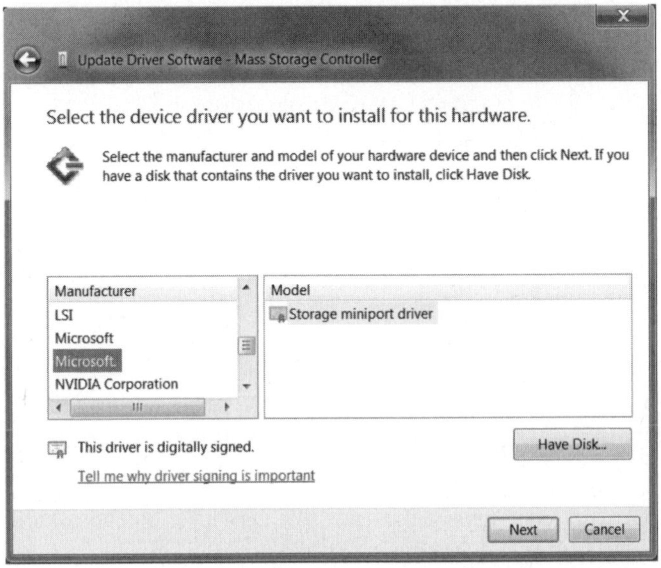

Figure 5-34. Click a manufacturer and then select a model from that manufacturer.

8. Select the Manufacturer and then a Model from that manufacturer, or click Have Disk if you have the device's installation disc or a driver disc.

9. Click Next. If you select a driver that Windows does not think is a good match, Windows will display a warning similar to Figure 5-35.

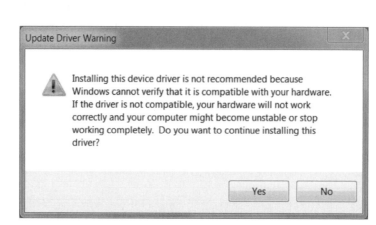

Figure 5-35. Installing the wrong driver could cause problems with your computer.

If you proceed anyway, Windows will try to install the driver software. If it is the wrong driver, the device may not even start, as shown in Figure 5-36. In this case, you may need more information to correctly identify the manufacturer and model, so you can download the right drivers.

Figure 5-36. If the wrong driver is installed, the device may not work.

If the correct driver is installed, you will get a notification in the taskbar that the installation was successful, as shown in Figure 5-37.

Figure 5-37. Successful device driver software installation

Using Advanced Recovery

Sometimes none of the previous methods can solve your problem. You've tried troubleshooters, uninstalling or updating device drivers, uninstalling programs, and System Restore.

There are two basic advanced recovery methods, both of which may cause you to lose data on your computer. Before you use any of these methods, it is very important that you completely back up all important files and documents to a location outside your computer, such as an external hard drive or network storage.

Before you can use one of these methods, you'll need a system image backup from before your problems started, or your Windows installation or recovery disc provided by your computer manufacturer.

Using a System image to recover

A **system image** is a backup of your entire hard drive. When you restore your system image, it is everything that was on the image. You cannot selectively restore parts of your system image. You must have created system image backups before you started experiencing problems. After you have problems, you cannot really make a good system image backup because it will still have the problems on it.

LinkED

For information about how to create a system image, see Chapter 6.

Using a recovery disc

The recovery disc is provided by the computer manufacturer, not Microsoft. This disc resets your computer back to the settings and state it was in when it left the factory. This will erase all of the data on your computer, and you will need to reinstall all programs that you installed after you bought the computer. Check your computer's documentation for information about disaster recovery and recovery discs. Some manufacturers provide a recovery disc that contains all of the Windows installation files, and some just provide a disc you can use to start the computer, and the actual Windows installation files are on a hidden section of your hard drive.

Whichever recovery method you choose, you should plan on it taking several hours. You may not need to attend to the computer directly during the whole time, but you will want to make sure that the computer is not turned off or needed during that time. Also, if you are using a laptop, make sure it is plugged in and not running off battery power. Otherwise, the laptop could run out of power before recovery is complete.

Carrying out an advanced recovery

To start an advanced recovery, follow these steps:

1. Click the `Start` button, and in the `Start` menu's search box, type `Recovery`. In the list that appears, under `Control Panel` click `Recovery`.

2. On the `Recovery` page, click `Advanced recovery methods`. The `Advanced Recovery Methods` page is displayed, as shown in Figure 5-38.

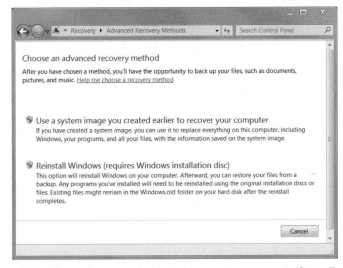

Figure 5-38. Advanced recovery is drastic because it means most, if not all, information on your hard drive is erased. No matter which method you use, be sure to back up files such as documents, pictures, music, or any other kind of document file that contains content or information.

3. Select a recovery method, or click `Help me choose a recovery method.`

4. Carefully read and follow the instructions on your screen.

LinkED

For information about how to back up all files, see Chapter 6.

Fixing things at the document level

A few Windows features are almost universal in any type of program and can get you out of a jam really quickly. Mistakes are usually pretty easy to fix, and working carefully can take the fear out of losing information from your documents.

Undoing

The Undo command, Ctrl+Z, is often available even if you don't see it listed on a menu in the program you are using. Typically, you will find it listed on the `Edit` menu. If you accidently cut, delete, or paste something in your program, press Ctrl+Z before you do anything else. Some programs offer multiple undos. For example, in Microsoft Office 2007 programs, you can undo and redo up to 100 actions. Some drawing and graphic programs may also offer multiple undos.

The Undo command can also come in handy when typing in or pasting into text boxes, web addresses in your browser, search boxes, and so forth. Some programs also redo. So if you undo something, and then decide that you didn't want to undo it after all, you can use the Redo command, Ctrl+Y. Not all programs that allow undo also allow redo.

Using Save As

If the Undo command is not available, or you didn't discover something was wrong until much later, another alternative is to immediately save the file you are working on with a new filename via the `File` ➤ `Save As` command. This saves all the changes you've made since your last save of this file in a new file, while keeping the original file unchanged under the original name.

Some programs offer a similar solution with a Revert command, which reverses all your changes since you opened this file in the current session. But with the Revert command, you will lose all changes made since the last time you saved this file.

Using the Save As command provides an opportunity to open both the new and old versions of the file and selectively add the changes from your new file back into the original.

Using autosave and saving regularly

If your program offers an autosave feature, turn it on (before your computer or program crashes). Occasionally, a program you are using crashes in the middle of your document, or the computer is shut down by a person or power outage before you have saved your latest changes. If the program has an autosave feature and you had it turned on before the accident, the next time you open the program or file that crashed, it will offer to open a recovered copy of the file.

Even with autosave or autorecovery, it is a good idea to save your files regularly as you work on them. How often you should save your document depends on how many changes you make as you work. If the power went out, how much of your latest work can you afford to lose? How drastic and risky are the changes you are making as you work on your file? The greater the number or severity of changes, the more frequently you should save your work.

Creating copies of the original

If you are going to be making a lot of changes and don't want to lose the original document, start with a copy of the file. As soon as you open the document, use the Save As command to make a copy of the file. Then work on the copy, not the original.

Saving your scraps

If possible, open a separate file or document to store information that you've removed from your document. As you delete or remove text or data, paste it into the scrap document. Later, if you decide you didn't want to remove the information after all, you can open your scrap document and retrieve it.

Getting help from within Windows

Windows 7 provides a lot of information onscreen as you use programs and features. If you do not understand a screen or window, look for underlined blue links indicating Help topics related to that page or screen.

For example, in the `Advanced Recovery Methods` window, each method is described (as shown previously in Figure 5-38).

If you need further help, you can click the link `Help me choose a recovery method` for a more detailed explanation of the features and options. The contents of these `Windows Help and Support` topics are shown in a separate window, so you don't lose your place in the window or feature you were using, as shown in Figure 5-39.

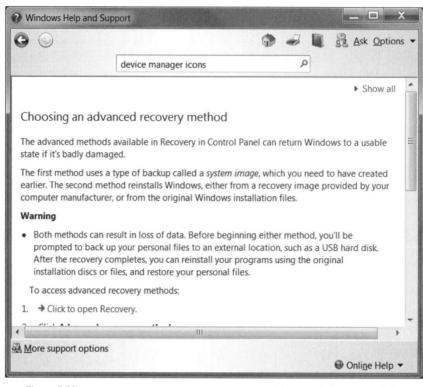

Figure 5-39. Windows Help and Support can provide more information if the screen you are viewing is not clear, or you just need to know more.

Accessing Help and Support

Windows Help and Support is not just for providing extra information about a particular window or feature. You can browse or search for information, just as you would on the Web. Much of the Help information is stored on your computer, but Help and Support also links to additional content on the Web.

To access Windows Help and Support, click the Start button and then click Help and Support. Windows Help and Support is displayed, as shown in Figure 5-40.

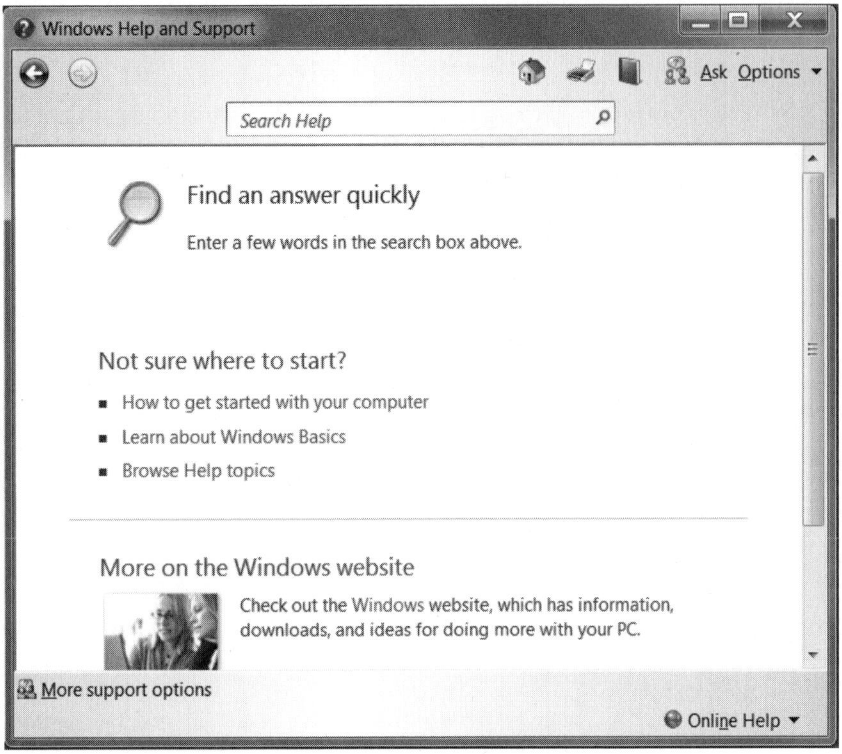

Figure 5-40. `Windows Help and Support` home page

Summary

An ounce of prevention is worth a pound of cure.
—Benjamin Franklin

Problems will happen with computers and sometimes are unavoidable. If you are prepared, you can minimize the damage and disruption caused by your computer not working right. Prevent problems before they happen, by keeping your data safe on your computer with regular backups, and automatic updates of antivirus, antispyware, and Windows.

Here's a review of what you've learned in this chapter:

- How to use Windows troubleshooters to identify problems and solutions
- How to use `Programs and Features` in `Control Panel` to fix problems
- How to Safe Mode to start Windows 7 with just basic functions so you can fix problems
- How to use System Restore to return your computer to a point in time when it was stable, before a specific problem started
- How to locate and update device drivers that are keeping your computer or attached hardware from working properly
- How to use Advanced Recovery, system image backups, and recovery discs to restore your entire computer or Windows
- How to fix things at the document level with the Undo command, autosave, and other good practices
- How to use Windows Help and Support for additional help

In addition, the following chapters will help you be prepared *before* catastrophe strikes:

- Chapter 6 provides complete steps for backing up your computer and your data.
- Chapter 9 includes information about personalizing your security settings, passwords, and identity information.
- Chapter 10 may be helpful as another way to back up and recover your settings and information from an old computer. Or you can transfer user settings and files from a badly behaving computer to another computer that already has a lot of the programs and devices installed and working.

Chapter 6

Protecting Your Data

Over time, your system will become home to all types of very important—even irreplaceable—personal data. Documents are just the beginning; consider years worth of digital family photos and home videos you never want to lose. Despite their reputation, computers generally provide reliable and trouble-free operation, but they do suffer from problems from time to time. In some cases, those problems can result in losing data and thus fond memories.

What could go wrong with your PC? It could be an equipment problem like the failure of a hard drive. Or, your system could become infected with a virus or other type of malicious software, or a routine software installation could go wrong, damaging Windows and perhaps even leaving your system unusable. You might even inadvertently delete or overwrite files or folders by mistake.

The bottom line is that it's absolutely crucial that you make regular backup copies of your data so you can get it back if something happens to the original data.

Fortunately, Windows 7 includes backup software that can ensure your important stuff isn't lost as the result of an unexpected system problem. Let's look at how it works and how to use it.

Backup types

Windows 7 provides two different but complementary ways to protect your data, called **file backup** and **system image backup**.

File backup

File backup is designed to protect personal data files, such as documents, photos, videos, music, and so forth. With file backup you can store as much or as little data as you like. You get to choose specific folders, drives, or libraries to make copies of, or you can let Windows decide for you. Similarly, if you ever need to restore data from a file backup, you can choose specific folders to restore—even individual files.

File backups don't make copies of Windows operating system files or program files, and restores must be done from within Windows. In the event of a complete system failure, if all you've done is a file backup, you must reinstall Windows and all your software before you restore that data.

System image backup

System image backup is designed to protect not just data files but the entire contents of a computer's hard drive. A system image backup consists of an exact replica of everything from the Windows operating system to its configuration settings to any programs you've installed, plus all personal data files.

You can use a system image backup to restore a computer to the precise condition it was in when the image was made, even if the Windows isn't working properly—or, in the event of a major problem, isn't working at all.

But system images are all-or-nothing backups. You can't pick and choose what to restore, and when you restore from a system image, anything already on the hard drive gets erased.

The most comprehensive way to protect your system and the data it contains is to do both file and system image backups, because this gives you the flexibility to restore anything from a single file to the entire hard drive in the event of a problem. You can have Windows 7 run both types of backup for you automatically according to a schedule, or you can run them manually whenever you want.

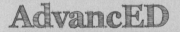

In addition to Windows 7's built-in backup feature, you can also buy (and sometimes even download for free) third-party backup programs that may provide more capabilities, such as the ability to password protect backups or greater control and flexibility over how and when backups are run. Such programs are often preinstalled on new computers or included with external hard drives.

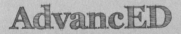

LinkED

Some services let you back up your important data to another location via the Internet. This is a good added level of protection in case your at-home backups are damaged or destroyed (such as by a fire or natural disaster). Two popular online backup services are Mozy (www.mozy.com) and Carbonite (www.carbonite.com).

Choosing a backup storage device

You can store Windows 7 backups to a variety of types of storage, including a system's internal hard drive, removable storage devices such as an external hard drive or flash memory drive, or writable DVDs.

Each type of storage has its own pros and cons, but for most people an external hard drive will be the best option. External hard drives can hold far more information than either flash drives or DVDs, so they usually have enough room to store large backups and multiple backups. Plus, unlike internal hard drives, the external kind can be easily disconnected from the system and stored for safekeeping if necessary (like in a safe or a fireproof box).

AdvancED

Whenever possible, it's a good idea to save your backups to an external hard drive with a storage capacity greater than your system's. For example, if your system came with a 500GB hard drive, your external hard drive should be 500GB or more. This will ensure that you always have as much backup space as you'll possibly need and can keep the backups for as long as possible.

AdvancED

If you're using the Professional or Ultimate version of Windows 7, you can also store backups on a network drive such as a network-attached storage (NAS) device.

The type of backup you do may dictate the kind of storage you need to use. For example, Windows 7 won't let you save a system image on a USB flash drive because they're generally much too small to store an entire image. As a result, you'd likely need quite a few of them to store a single image, which gets extremely expensive compared to DVDs. (Plus, you can't easily label them the way you can DVDs.) In addition, although you can save an image to a DVD (or, more likely, a set of them), the image can't be updated later like it can be when you save it on an external hard drive.

Creating automatic file and system image backups

To have Windows make file and system image backups on a regular basis, perform the following steps. Note that you must use an administrator account to create backups, change their configuration settings, or restore files from them:

1. Type `backup` in the `Start` menu's search box, and then choose `Backup and Restore` to display the window shown in Figure 6-1. If you've never done a backup before, you'll see a message saying `Windows Backup has not been set up`.

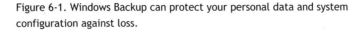

Figure 6-1. Windows Backup can protect your personal data and system configuration against loss.

2. Click Set up backup. Windows Backup will start up and ask you to choose a backup destination (Figure 6-2). Click a destination once to see what backup limitations it has, if any (such as not enough space, can't store a system image, and so on), or double-click a destination to select it and go to the next screen. If you want to use an external hard drive that you haven't connected yet, plug it in, wait a few minutes for Windows 7 to recognize and identify it, and then click Refresh to make it appear in the list.

Figure 6-2. Choose where you want your backups to be stored; external hard drives are usually the best option.

ExplainED

The `Save on a network` button will be available only with Windows 7 Professional or Ultimate.

3. To do the most comprehensive backup possible, select the `Let Windows choose` option (Figure 6-3), and go to the next screen.

Figure 6-3. Decide what kind of backups to do, or let Windows automatically choose for you.

AdvancED

When you let Windows choose what to back up, it automatically backs up files stored on the desktop and all the default folders—such as Desktop, Downloads, Favorites, Documents, Pictures, and so on—for every person with a user account on the system. Windows will also back up files saved in libraries and create a system image backup for you.

The `Let me choose` option will allow you to modify Windows 7's standard backup settings by dispensing with the system image backup and/or backing up additional locations besides the default ones. It's the option to use if you save important files in places other than standard user account folders or if you just want to back up a handful of specific folders.

4. Review your backup settings to make sure they're correct (Figure 6-4). Note that Windows automatically runs weekly backups on Sunday at 7 p.m. If you'd rather do them on a different day or time or do them more or less frequently (such as daily or monthly), click `Change schedule`. Once your choices have been made, click `Save settings and run backup`.

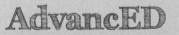

Figure 6-4. Verify that the settings and schedule are correct before running your first backup.

AdvancED

Any files that have been added or changed in the backed-up locations since the last backup will automatically be included in the next scheduled backup. Scheduling backups more frequently—daily rather than weekly, for example—will minimize the chance of losing files that were added or changed in between backups. When doing daily backups, however, it's a good idea to schedule backups at times a system is unlikely to be used because your system may run slowly while a backup is in progress. (If you don't shut your system off at night, scheduling backups around midnight is a good option.)

Regardless of the backup schedule, Windows will run an initial backup immediately and display a green `Backup in Progress` bar (to see what percentage of the backup is complete or stop a backup in progress, click `View Details`). After the first backup is finished (it can take as long as several hours depending on how much is being backed up), the `Backup and Restore` window (Figure 6-5) will indicate the details of the backup, when the last backup was done, and when the next one is due.

You can click `Back up now` to run a backup manually any time in between scheduled backups. To change what is backed up, where the backup is saved, or when it occurs, click `Change settings`.

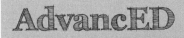

Figure 6-5. After your first backup completes, the `Backup and Restore` window will let you view or change backup settings.

AdvancED

Windows automatically manages the amount of disk space it uses for both file and system image backups, saving older backups until they must be deleted to make room for newer ones. Clicking `Manage space` will let you view or adjust how backup disk space is used or delete individual file backups to free up space for other uses.

Creating a system image manually

The term *system image* is something of a misnomer, because it doesn't necessarily back up the entire contents of a system. The system images that Windows 7 creates automatically only saves the contents of a hard drive or hard drive partition (portions of a hard drive that function independently and have their own drive letters) that Windows needs in order to run.

If a system has multiple hard drives or one drive divided into multiple partitions, those extra drives or partitions aren't included in the system image when you configure Windows 7 to automatically create backups as outlined earlier.

If you want a system image that includes extra hard drives or partitions—let's say you have Windows on the C: drive but also save files onto a D: or E: drive—you must create the image manually by performing the following steps:

1. In the `Backup and Restore` window shown in Figure 6-5 (type `backup` into the `Start` menu's search box, and then choose `Backup and Restore`), click `Create a system image`, choose where you want to save the system image (Figure 6-6), and then go to the next screen.

ExplainED

As with automatic backups, an external hard disk is usually the preferred storage destination for manual system images, because saving an image to DVDs can consume several—maybe even dozens—of discs.

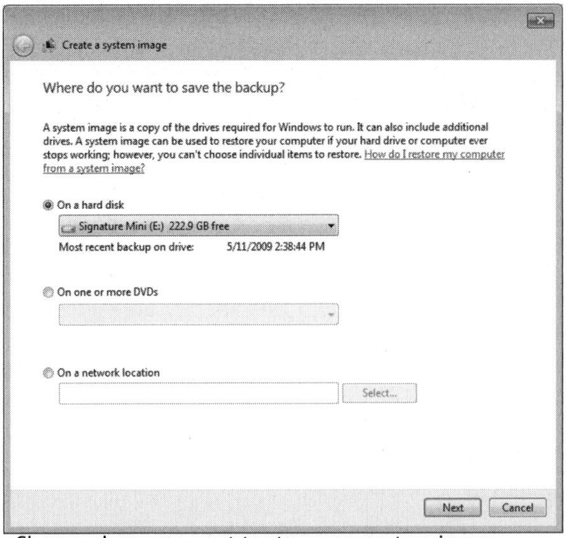

Figure 6-6. Choose where you want to store your system image.

2. Select the check boxes for the extra drives you want the system image
    to include (Figure 6-7), and then go to the next screen.

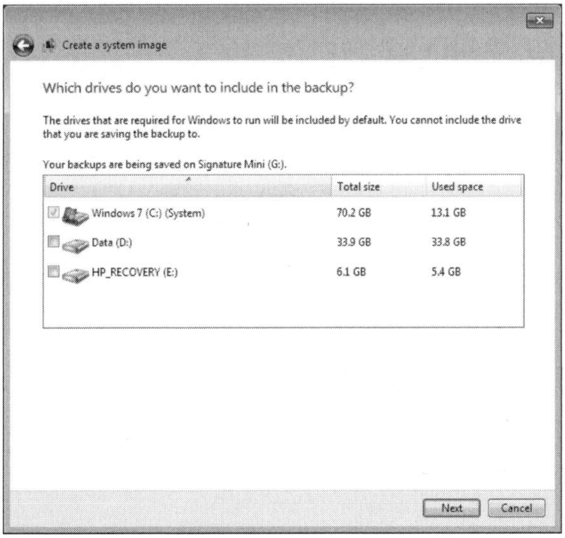

Figure 6-7. Select all the drives you want the system image to include.

3. Confirm the drives that will be part of the system image, and click `Start backup` (Figure 6-8).

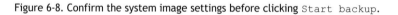

Figure 6-8. Confirm the system image settings before clicking `Start backup`.

AdvancED

When saving a manual system image to a hard drive, note the warning that *existing system images for this machine might be overwritten*. This means that if your drive is running low on space, an older image may need to be erased to make room for the newest one.

LinkED

After your manual system image is complete, Windows 7 will ask you whether you want to set up a system repair disc, a process outlined next.

Creating a system repair disc

Sometimes—ideally rarely—a system suffers a hard drive crash or a similar catastrophic problem that's so severe it keeps Windows from loading correctly. If this happens, a system repair disc will not only allow you to let you start your system and access repair options but will also let you restore your system to proper working order using a system image backup. (In Figure 6-4 you may have noticed a message warning that a system repair disc might be required to restore a system image.)

To create a system repair disc, perform the following steps:

1. Insert a blank CD or DVD into the CD/DVD drive, type `repair` in the `Start` menu's search box, and select `Create a system repair disc`.

2. Make sure the correct drive is listed, and then click `Create disc` (Figure 6-9).

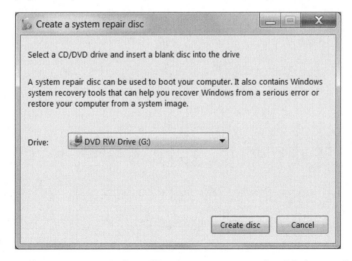

Figure 6-9. A system repair disc will start your computer when Windows can't load.

ExplainED

A system repair disc works the same way whether you use a CD or DVD. Use a CD if possible—they're cheaper.

Restoring data from backups

Once your system and its personal data are safely backed up, Windows gives you the option to restore individual files or folders, groups of files or folders, or your entire hard drive.

Restoring from a file backup

To restore personal data files, make sure the drive that contains your backup is connected, and perform the following steps:

1. In the `Backup and Restore` window, click `Restore my files`. If you want to restore only specific files, click `Browse for files`; to restore entire folders, click `Browse for folders` (Figure 6-10).

AdvancED

If you're administrator and want to restore another user's files rather than your own, in the `Backup and Restore` *window click* `Restore all user's files` *instead of* `Restore my files`. *The process of selecting what to restore will be the same as outlined in the following steps.*

AdvancED

If you're restoring data to a different computer than the one you backed up from, select `Select another backup to restore files from`. *Windows 7 will display any available backups you can restore from.*

Figure 6-10. Browse for files or folders or search for specific items to restore.

AdvancED

Windows automatically restores files from the most recent backup, so click `Choose a different date` *if you want to restore from an older one. If you're looking for a particular file or folder to restore, you can find it quickly by clicking the* `Search` *button and then typing all or some of the file/folder name.*

2. Click a backup name (`Joseph's backup` in this example) in the left pane to browse the contents of the backup in the right pane. When you find the file or folder you want to restore, highlight it and click either the `Add files` or `Add folder` button (Figure 6-11). The button that appears will depend on whether you're browsing for files or folders.

181

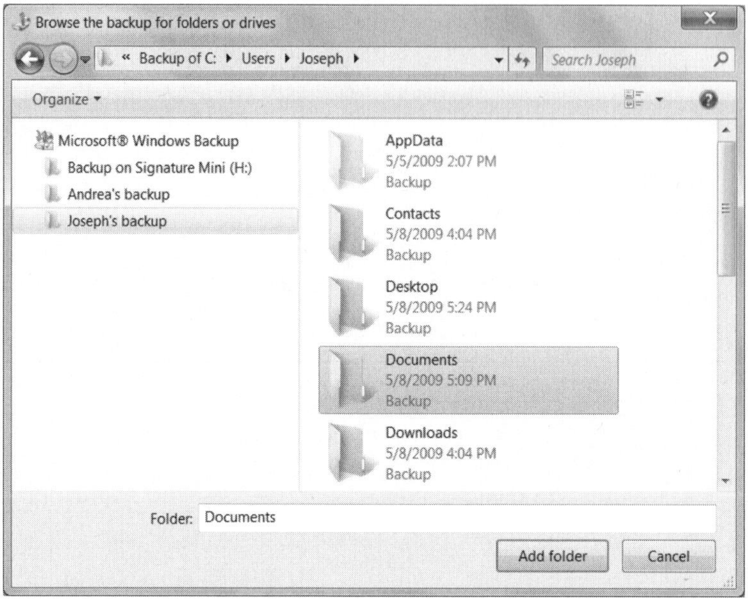

Figure 6-11. When you find an item you want to restore, click Add folder (Add folder (or Add files).

AdvancED

After you select a file or folder to restore, you'll return to the window shown in Figure 6-10. From there, browse again to select additional items to restore (you can restore files and folders at the same time). While browsing, you can select multiple files in the same folder (by holding down Ctrl while clicking to select), but you can select only one folder at a time.

3. Once you've selected all the items you want to restore, go to the next screen (Figure 6-12). Files are restored to their original location by default, but if you want to restore them somewhere else, click In the following location, and use the Browse button to choose one.

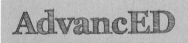

Figure 6-12. Choose where you want restored files to go.

AdvancED

Selecting a new location can be useful if you want to restore files to portable storage such as a USB flash drive so that you can transfer them to another computer, or if you still have the original version of the files on your system and want to restore from a backup without disturbing them.

4. Click `Restore` to begin the restore process. If any restored files will overwrite existing versions, a window will appear giving you the option to keep one version or the other (or save a copy of both by giving the file you're restoring a new name).

Restoring previous versions of a file

Normally you restore a file or folder from a backup because the original has been damaged or erased. But there may be times when you want to restore an intact file from backup. For example, if you edit a document or a photo and inadvertently save a change or if you do it intentionally but later decide that it was a mistake, then your file is still there, but it's not the version you want.

When this happens, you can restore the file from a backup using the procedure described earlier, but there's also another method that may be more convenient. When you right-click a file or folder anywhere in Windows, you'll see an option labeled `Restore previous versions`. Select it, and Windows will display a list of older versions of the file that were saved as a result of recent backups or system restore points (Figure 6-13).

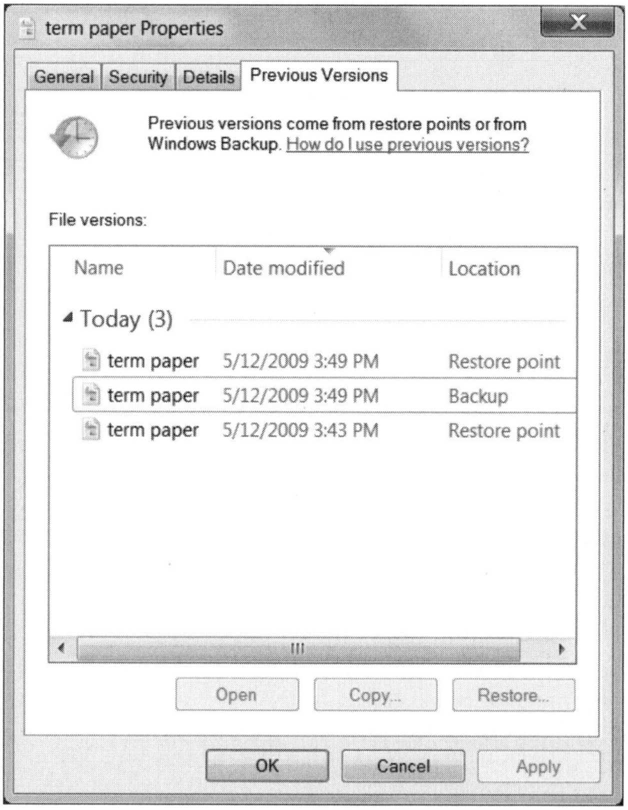

Figure 6-13. `Restore previous versions` can be a convenient way to get back older versions of files.

Highlight a previous version of a file, and click `Restore` to replace the current version of the file with the previous one. (A confirmation window will warn you that this action can't be undone.) If a file's previous version is the result of a restore point rather than a backup, then in addition to restoring the file, you can also click `Open` to view the file or `Copy` to save a copy to another folder.

Restoring a system image when Windows won't start

When your Windows 7 system starts having problems—especially after installing a piece of hardware or software—you can use the system restore feature to load a previously saved system configuration (restore point), which will often be enough to fix the problem.

LinkED

For more on the system restore feature and restore points, see Chapter 5.

However, should your system suffer from a catastrophic problem that prevents Windows from running—the hard drive fails, for example—you can restore your system to its previously working condition by restoring a system image (once you've replaced the hard drive, of course).

Restoring a system image when Windows isn't installed on the system requires a system repair disc. Before attempting to restore a system image, make sure system repair disc is in the drive and that the storage device containing the image is powered up and connected to the system (or if your system image is saved on DVDs, check that you have them handy).

ExplainED

Remember that restoring from a system image returns a system to the condition it was in when the image was made, not when the problem occurred. Therefore, you'll lose any programs that were installed or data files that were added or changed between the time the image was created and the problem occurred.

AdvancED

Can't find your system repair disc or forgot to make one? System repair discs aren't computer-specific, so if you have another Windows 7 system— or know someone who does—you can use it to make one belatedly.

1. Turn the system on and immediately watch the screen for a message telling you which specific key to press (Esc and F12 are commonly used) to start the system from the CD/DVD drive or display a "boot menu" that will let you choose the CD/DVD drive from a list of storage devices.

   This message will be visible only for a few seconds, so timing is important. If you don't press the appropriate key fast enough, the system will try to boot Windows normally and eventually freeze up (assuming that was the problem). If that happens, just turn the system off and try step 1 again.

2. After pressing the key necessary to start the system from the CD/DVD drive, watch the screen closely, because many systems may prompt you to `press any key` to confirm you actually want to load the disc in the drive.

If the system repair disc loads successfully, within a minute or two you'll see the screen shown in Figure 6-14.

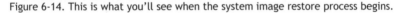

Figure 6-14. This is what you'll see when the system image restore process begins.

3. Confirm the keyboard type shown is correct (the right one is usually chosen for you), and then go to the next screen.

ExplainED

If you need to restore a system image stored on a set of DVDs, remove the system repair disc from the drive, and replace it with the last DVD in your backup set before you proceed to the next step.

4. Choose the `Restore your computer using a system image you created earlier` option, and then go to the next screen.

5. Windows will now look for available system images and automatically select the most recent one it can find (Figure 6-15). This is almost always the best one to use, but if you'd rather use a different one, choose `Select a system image`, and pick the image you want from the menu.

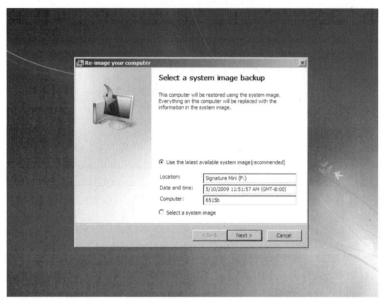

Figure 6-15. Windows will automatically select the most recent system image for you, or you can choose a different one.

AdvancED

To use a system image that was saved on a network (only an option with Windows 7 Professional or Ultimate), after choosing `Select a system image`, *click the* `Advanced` *button, and then click* `Search` *for a system image on the network.*

6. After selecting your system image, you can choose additional restore options. If you let Windows create your system image automatically, you'll see an option labeled `Format and repartition discs`, which is turned off by default. This option will delete anything already on the disc, so you should choose it only when you're restoring to a completely empty hard drive.

    If you created your system image manually, you'll see an additional option labeled `Only restore system drives, also turned off by default` (Figure 6-16). Selecting this option will only restore the drive that contains Windows and skip any others that are part of the image. Unless there are separate hard drives that you don't want to restore, you'll want to keep this option turned off.

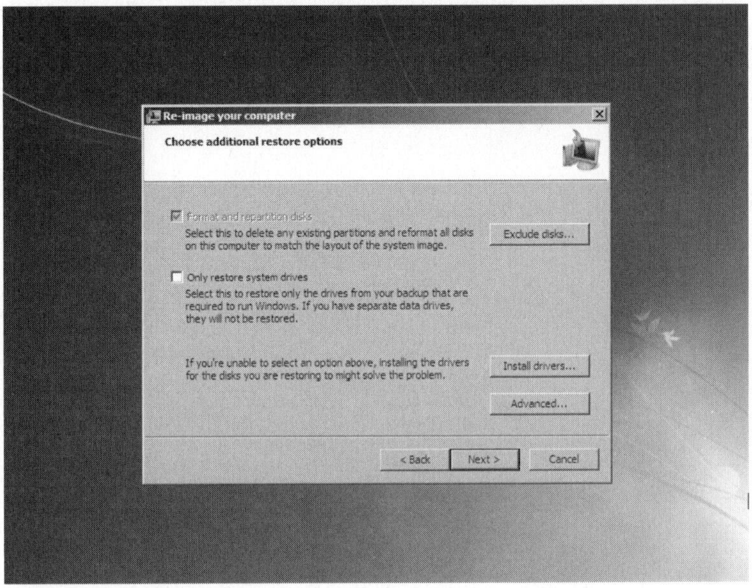

Figure 6-16. After selecting your system image, you can specify other options depending on how your image was created.

7. Verify that you've chosen the right system image to restore, and click Finish (Figure 6-17). A final confirmation window will appear, and when you click Yes, the restore process will begin.

Figure 6-17. Verify the details of the restore before you click Finish.

Depending on the size of your system image, it may take a while for the restore process to complete—perhaps an hour or longer. (If you're restoring an image from DVDs, you'll need to stick around to feed them into the PC.) When it's finished, the system will restart automatically and should be working properly.

ExplainED

Remember that restoring from a system image returns your system to the condition it was in when the image was made, so at this point you may need to reinstall some programs.

If your system came with Windows 7 installed, it may have included a set of **recovery**, or **restore**, discs. (If you didn't receive such discs, there's probably a program installed that will make them for you.) It's important to note that these manufacturer-provided discs are designed to return your system to its original condition—that is, the way it came out of the box. Unlike a Windows 7 system image, these discs can't restore the software and data you've added to your PC, and they'll actually erase everything already on your system, so don't use them without backing up your system first.

Summary

Here's a review of what you've learned in this chapter:

- The type of data backups Windows 7 can do
- The kinds of storage devices you can back up to
- How to configure automatic backups
- How to create a system image manually
- How to restore files and folders
- How to recover previous versions of files
- How to restore a system from an image

Chapter 7

Creating a Home Network

In this chapter, you will learn about Windows 7 home networking. You'll learn how to use the Network and Sharing Center and other Windows features to connect to the Internet, connect your computers to a home network, use HomeGroup, share printers and libraries, and protect your network.

Whether you have one computer or five, one of the first things you'll want to do is connect to the Internet. An Internet connection isn't just for e-mail or surfing the Web. Windows also depends on an Internet connection to activate your copy of Windows—which you may have already done the first time you started Windows 7—and to get the latest Windows updates.

LinkED

Chapter 9 covers Windows updates and how to apply them to your copy of Windows 7.

Checking your current network connections

Windows 7 provides a handy place to manage your network settings and tasks: the **Network and Sharing Center**. Even if you have not set up a home network, you can get a quick look at what kinds of network connections are already in place. For example, you may have already connected your computer to a digital subscriber line (DSL) or cable modem to connect to the Internet. The first time you start a new computer, it looks for Internet or network connections, and attempts to configure them for you. If you don't have a network, the Network and Sharing Center is where you can set it up.

To check your current connections, go to the Network and Sharing Center:

1. Click the Windows `Start` button, and in the `Start` menu's search box, type `Network`.

2. In the results list, under `Control Panel`, click `Network and Sharing Center`. The Network and Sharing Center appears, as shown in Figure 7-1.

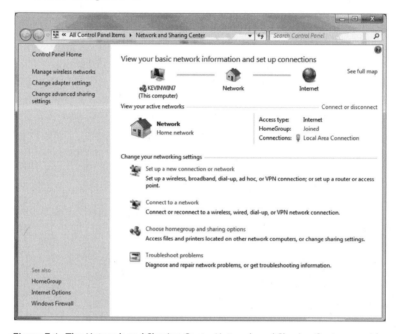

Figure 7-1. The Network and Sharing CenterNetwork and Sharing Center provides a snapshot of your current connections, and links for connecting or changing network settings.

In Figure 7-1, the diagram under `View your basic network information and set up connections` shows a computer connected through a network to the Internet. This page doesn't really tell you whether the network uses just a broadband modem or whether there is also a router. Normally, the first time you start your computer, Windows looks for a wired or wireless network connection, and prompts you for information to connect to it. However, if you did not set up an Internet connection, your basic connection may be similar to that shown in Figure 7-2.

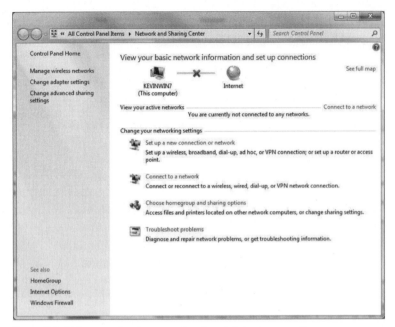

Figure 7-2. This computer has no network or Internet connection.

Connecting to the Internet

To connect to the Internet, you need Internet access, usually via DSL or cable and a broadband modem, or via dial-up access through a phone line. If you want to share that Internet access with more than one computer, or you want your computers to share libraries or printers on a network, you will need a router.

Usually the broadband modem and the router are two separate devices, but some cable or phone companies also offer a combination modem/router, or can suggest models you can buy that work with their system.

The **router** takes the Internet access from your modem and then provides that access to each computer connected to the router. Your computers can connect to the router through a wired connection (also known as an **Ethernet connection**) or a wireless connection (sometimes referred to as **Wi-Fi**).

For wireless connections, you need a wireless router and a wireless card on the computer. Wireless routers also include Ethernet jacks so you can use a wired connection to your computer. Figure 7-3 shows the network components that link two computers to a network and the Internet.

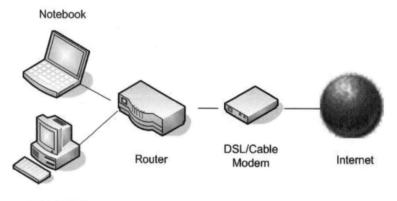

Figure 7-3. Two computers sharing an Internet connection through a router

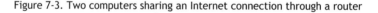

The most popular choices for connecting computers in a home network are wired and wireless. In addition, two other wired options use the existing electrical or phone wiring in your house: HomePNA and power line.

Connecting through a wireless network

One of the neat things about a wireless network is that it enables you to use your computer almost any place in the house without having to run long lengths of wires or drill holes through your walls. You can also connect other devices to your wireless network, such as wireless network printers. You can even have your laptop on, move around your house from room to room, and still stay connected.

In many cases, the only extra equipment you need to buy for a wireless network is a wireless router. Almost all new laptop computers have wireless cards built in. You can also use desktop PCs on a wireless network. Though desktop PCs usually don't have wireless cards built in, you can easily install one or plug in an external Universal Serial Bus (USB) wireless adapter. A USB wireless adapter can be used with laptop computers as well. If you do need to add a wireless adapter or card, be sure to run the installation program provided by the wireless device manufacturer. If your computer comes with a wireless card already built in, the drivers and software to use it should already be installed.

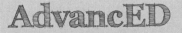

There are several different standards for wireless networks. Their long technical names are 802.11b, 802.11g, and 802.11n. Sometimes they are referred to as wireless B, wireless G, and wireless N. There is another standard, 802.11a, but it is rarely used or found in home wireless equipment.

Wireless B is the oldest of the three, and the slowest. Under the best conditions, the network speed is up to 11 megabits per second (Mbps). It has a weaker signal and uses a radio frequency that is prone to interference by cordless phones and microwave ovens. Wireless G is faster, up to 54Mbps, but uses the same radio frequency as wireless B and is still susceptible to interference. Wireless routers and cards that work with wireless G will also work with wireless B, but not the other way around. If you do use a computer with only wireless B on a wireless G network, it will slow down the entire wireless G network to the slower 11Mbps of wireless B. Most new computers with built-in wireless use wireless G, as do most new wireless routers.

Wireless N, or Draft-N, is the latest generation, but it is not a formally approved standard. It promises much faster speeds, greater distance, and less interference. The major wireless manufacturers have different implementations of the wireless N technology, so a wireless N router from one manufacturer may not work with a wireless N card from another manufacturer. Though wireless N offers much higher potential speeds of 100Mbps or more, and possibly up to 600Mbps, the hardware costs are much higher too.

The bottom line is that today, 802.11g is the most commonly used standard and is the most compatible between brands. It is also backward compatible with 802.11b. You cannot go wrong using 802.11g routers and cards together.

The Network and Sharing Center provides a wizard to walk you through connecting to a wireless network. Before you connect, review the following list to make sure everything else is ready:

- Your wireless router is turned on and is connected to your broadband modem.
- Your computer has a wireless card that is turned on.
- The computer and the wireless router do not have too many walls or too much distance between them.

AdvancED

If you are setting up the wireless router for the first time, check the documentation provided with the router. For the initial router setup, you may want to connect the router directly to the computer with an Ethernet cable, and complete the router setup before attempting to set up a wireless connection.

When setting up a wireless router, always set an encryption password to prevent unwanted guests from tapping into your network, hacking into your computers, or intercepting data wirelessly between your computer and your router or the Internet. There are several standards for wireless encryption, with very similar sounding acronyms: Wired Equivalent Privacy (WEP), Wi-Fi Protected Access (WPA, and WPA2). WEP is the oldest and the least secure and is not recommended. WPA2 is the most secure and highly recommended. Your wireless router manual and online setup will show you how to set the encryption for your model of router.

It is illegal to tap into somebody else's private wireless network without their permission, even if all you want to do is use it for a free Wi-Fi connection.

To connect to a wireless network, follow these steps:

1. Make sure your broadband modem is on, click the `Start` button, and then type `Network` in the `Start` menu's search box.

2. Click `Network and Sharing Center`.

3. Click `Set up a new connection or network`.

4. Click `Connect to the Internet` and then click `Next`.

5. Click `Wireless`. Windows will detect any nearby wireless networks and list them. If you live in a densely populated area, you may see other wireless networks listed besides your own. Figure 7-4 lists two possible wireless networks. The green bars indicate their signal strength. The more green bars, the stronger the signal.

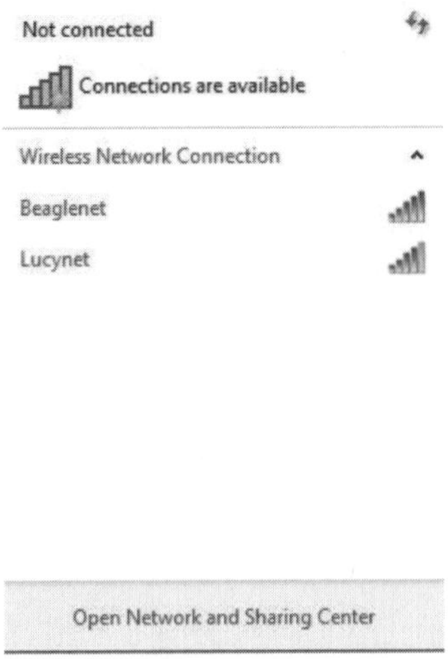

Figure 7-4. Viewing available networksavailable networks

6. Click your wireless network and then click `Connect`.

7. If you set up security protection when you previously installed your wireless router, you will be prompted for a network security key. Type the network security key and then click `OK`. If you do not remember your network security key, check the documentation that came with your wireless router on how to reset the security key.

When your computer is successfully connected to the Internet, your connection will be similar to Figure 7-5.

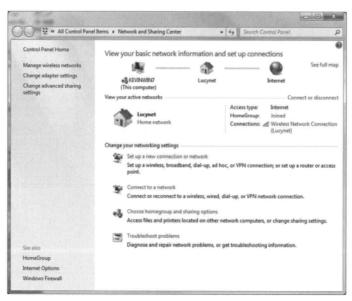

Figure 7-5. A successful wireless network connection

Connecting through a wired network

A wired network requires a separate network cable from your router to each computer. If you are adding a wired network to an existing house, that means running a hundred or more feet of network cable, possibly through your attic, through a crawl space, outside your house, or through walls. Sometimes you make this less noticeable by bringing the cable through the ceiling or floor of a closet, and then running it openly on the floor along a wall.

AdvancED

Some newer homes are constructed with the wiring built in, just like your electrical lines and phone lines. In fact, the type of cable used for this, called Cat5e, is also used for telephone wiring. The Cat5e cable contains eight color-coded wires, and electricians use different combinations of these wires depending on whether they are for your phone or your computer network. If you are fortunate enough to already have this network wiring prewired, hooking up your computer is a snap—connect your router to a central location where all of the room cables come together, and then hook up your computer to a jack in one of the rooms.

Almost all computers, laptop or desktop, have an Ethernet jack (also known as RJ-45), so you rarely have to add anything to the computer except the cable. The network cable can be quite expensive if you buy premeasured lengths with the jacks on both ends ready to connect. But if you are running long lengths of network cable throughout your house, it will be worth your time to learn how to make your own cables. The Cat5e cable is available in bulk at most home improvement centers in rolls from 50 to 100 feet. To complete the cable, you'll need plastic jacks and a special crimping tool to hold the wires in the jacks. For the price of two precut 25-foot lengths of network cable, you can almost pay for a 500-foot roll, the jacks, and the crimping tool.

For a wired network, you can use either a wired-only router or a wireless router. Wireless routers usually have about four jacks for wired connections, as well as the wireless connections.

Because most people do not have houses already wired for computer networks, a wired network may seem like a lot of extra work. However, there are several reasons for using a wired network or connection:

- A wired network is usually much faster than a wireless network. Depending on the router and network switch (if used), wired networks can run at 10, 100, or 1000Mbps. The common speed for most wired home networks has been 100Mbps, or almost twice as fast as the 802.11g wireless network's 54Mbps.
- Wired networks are not affected by interference from other devices in the house. If you work from home and connect to your work through a virtual private network (VPN), a wireless network connection may occasionally drop your connections long enough that you have to reconnect to your VPN.
- If you download or upload lots of files or large files, a wired connection is much more reliable because it has twice the speed of, and almost never drops connections like, a wireless network. And if you play online games with your PC, Xbox, or PlayStation, the speed and reliability of the wired connection may give you a slight competitive advantage.

AdvancED

Many newer computers support 1000Mbps (also called 1-gigabit) network connections, and many wired and wireless routers are available that support this faster speed on the wired connection. If shopping for routers or switches that support 1000GB speeds, look for labels or specifications such as 10/100/1000 or Gigabit router or switch. Don't worry about whether computers and networks will work with each other if they have different speeds. They'll automatically adjust to each other to use the highest common speed that they both can use.

After you have all of the network wires and outlets in place in your house, connecting to a wired network is even simpler than a wireless network. When you connect a network cable to your computer, Windows automatically detects the network and connects to it. You will not be prompted for a network security code, because it is assumed that anybody who has physical access to connect your router and a computer with an Ethernet cable must be trustworthy.

To connect to the Internet through a wired connection, follow these steps:

1. Turn on your broadband modem.

ExplainED

Broadband modems are intended to always be on and connected to the Internet. Generally, you do not turn off your modem unless you are having problems and want to reset it by turning the power on and off.

2. Connect your broadband modem to your router. Usually this connection is an Ethernet cable. Sometimes you may have the option of using a USB cable instead. If you have a choice, always use the Ethernet connection; it's more reliable.

3. Connect the computer to the router, with an Ethernet cable.

4. Click the Start button, and then type Network in the Start menu's search box.

5. **Click** `Network and Sharing Center`.

If all of the wires are connected correctly between the modem, router, or network switch and the computer, your connection should look similar to Figure 7-6.

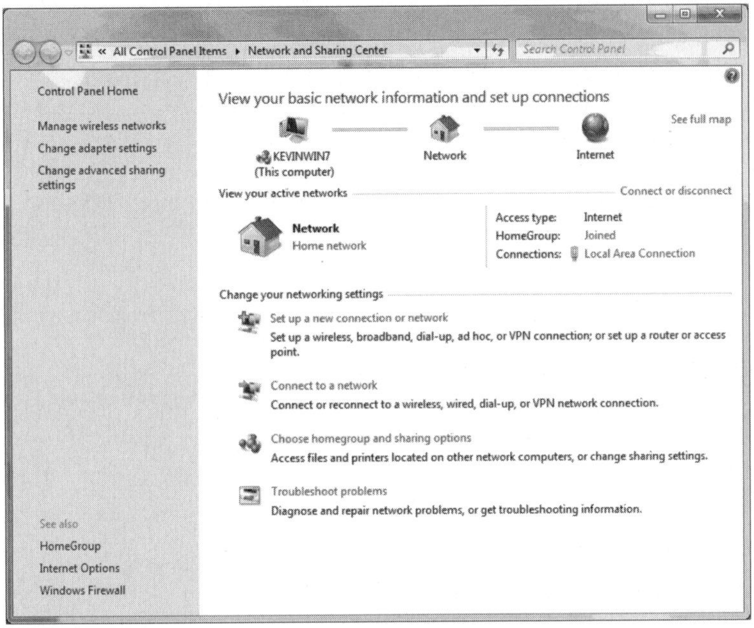

Figure 7-6. The network diagram shows a working network connection between the computer and the Internet. It lists the connection type as a Local Area Connection.

If the connection is not working, your connection may look similar to Figure 7-7 or Figure 7-8.

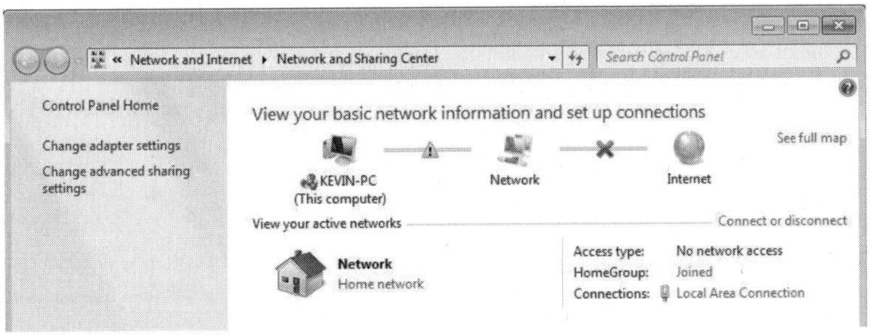

Figure 7-7. A previous local area connection is broken, and there is no network access.

203

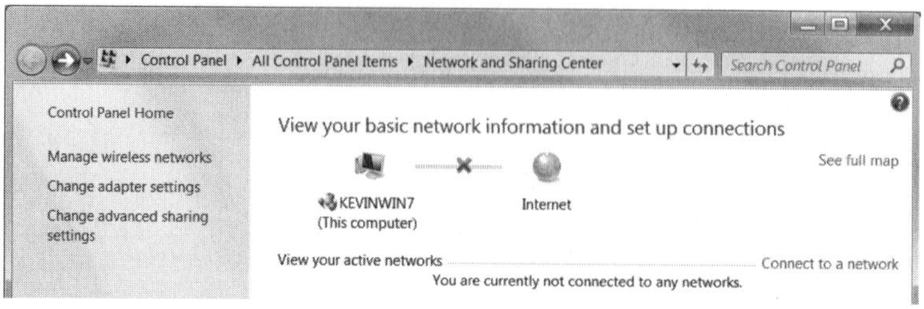

Figure 7-8. Windows did not detect any wired or wireless networks, or there previously was one that is now broken.

If your network information is similar to one of the examples in Figures 7-7 or 7-8, you can check the following:

- Are all of the cables connected—from the cable coming into the house to the modem, from the modem to the router, and from the router to your computer?

- Is your broadband modem on? Is the router on? On most modems and routers, small, green LED lights indicate that the connections are working. If there are no lights, your modem power may be off. If there are yellow or red lights, there is a problem at the device. If all the lights are green but the connection is still not working, one of your cable connections may be faulty. Try plugging and unplugging each cable, or replacing each cable with another cable, to see whether you can isolate a defective cable or connection.

- Sometimes you may need to reset the modem or router by turning it off for a minute or so and then turning it back on. Check the documentation for the modem or router.

- Contact your cable or DSL provider to make sure their network is working. Occasionally their networks go offline because of problems or for regular maintenance. Usually these providers try to schedule maintenance for the least busy times of the week, such as very late night or early morning.

Generally, after you've connected all of the cables from your modem to your router to your computer, that's all you need to do for a wired network connection.

Connecting through a power line or phone line network

Though not as common as Ethernet or wireless networks, power line and phone line (HomePNA) networks are alternative options. A power line network uses the electrical wiring in your house to carry network data between computers. A HomePNA network (not to be confused with phone dial-up or DSL) uses the existing phone wiring and jacks to connect your computers. One of the advantages of either of these systems is that they require no new wiring in your house, and the adapters to connect your computers to the network are fairly inexpensive—comparable in cost to the adapters and equipment used for wireless networks. The network speeds vary, but are comparable to wired and wireless network speeds.

Some networking equipment manufacturers offer systems that can use a combination of power line or HomePNA networks with wireless networks.

LinkED

For more information on these types of networks and manufacturers of equipment, search the Web for `power line` *or* `HomePNA`.

Connecting to a homegroup

Windows 7 introduces **homegroups** as an easy way to share files and printers with other computers in a home network. The HomeGroup feature is available only on Windows 7 computers and works only with other computers that are running Windows 7. If you have other computers on your home network running Windows Vista or Windows XP, you can still share files and printers by using the File and Printer Sharing features in those systems.

When you first start a computer running Windows 7, it will automatically create a homegroup if it doesn't detect one already in place on your home network. If a homegroup already exists, Windows 7 will prompt you to join that homegroup.

The purpose of joining a homegroup is to share files and printers among Windows 7 computers in a home network.

There are many options for sharing in a homegroup. You can specify whether to join the computer to the homegroup, but users must specify what they want to share from their libraries and printers: pictures, music, videos, documents, and printers.

Creating a homegroup

A homegroup is created the first time you start the first Windows 7 computer on your home network. After the homegroup is created, when you add other Windows 7 computers to your home network and go to the HomeGroup settings, you will be prompted to join the homegroup created by the first Windows 7 computer.

To create a homegroup for the first Windows 7 computer on your home network, follow these steps:

1. Click the `Start` button, and then type `homegroup` in the `Start` menu's search box.

2. Click `HomeGroup`. If this is the first Windows 7 computer on your home network, you will be prompted to create a homegroup, as shown in Figure 7-9.

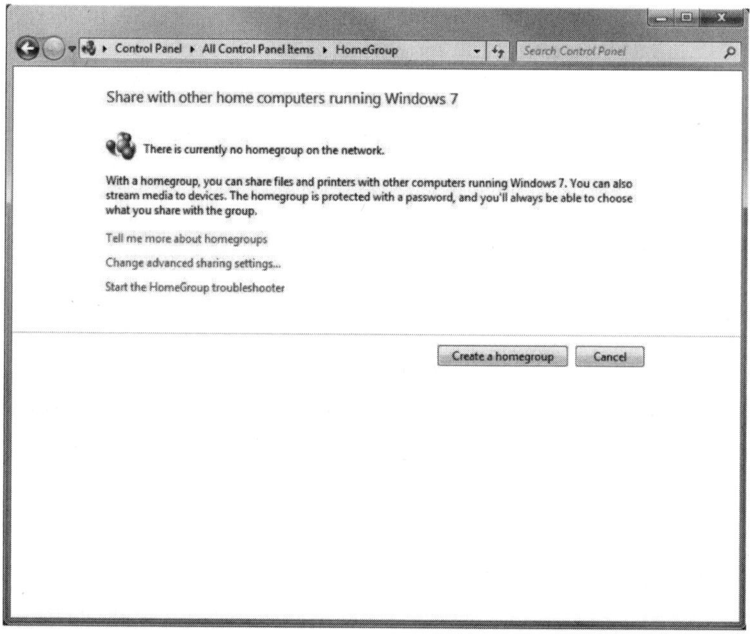

Figure 7-9. Windows can guide you through setting up a homegroup.

3. Click `Create a homegroup`. The next screen prompts you to choose what you'd like to share with other computers in your homegroup, as shown in Figure 7-10. Most items are preselected, except for Documents, which tend to be more private or individual. You may want to select Documents if you regularly work on many of your documents from more than one computer in your homegroup.

    The settings for what you select to share apply only to the current user. Each user must specify their settings by logging on to the computer under his or her own account.

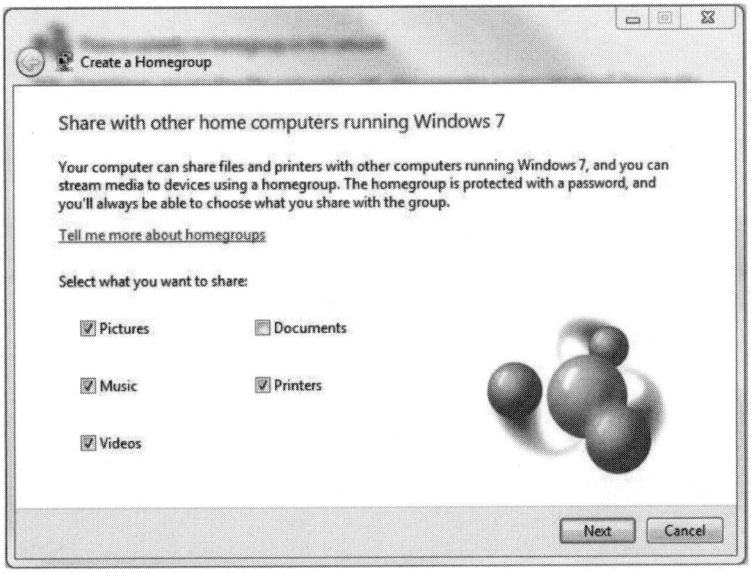

Figure 7-10. When you create a homegroup, you can specify what you want to share from your computer with other computers in the homegroup.

4. Select or clear the check boxes to specify what to share and then click `Next`. In the next screen, as shown in Figure 7-11, Windows displays the password for your homegroup. You will need to type this password on each computer in your home network to join the homegroup.

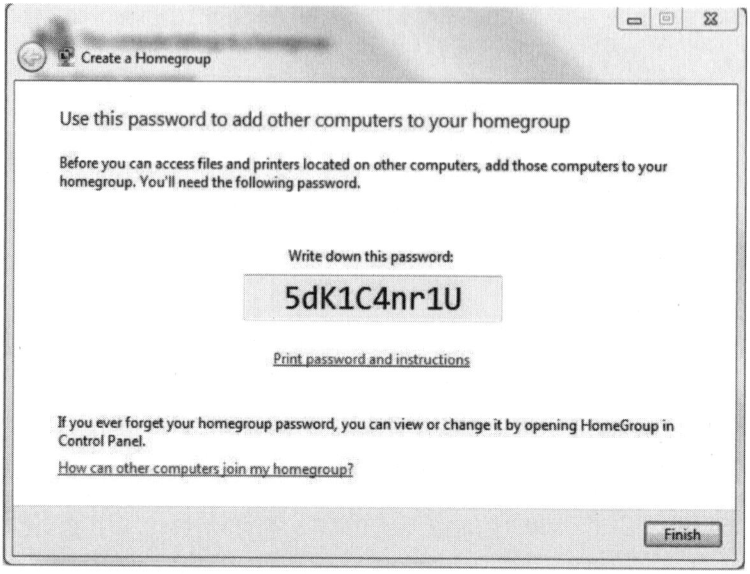

Figure 7-11. Windows generates a homegroup password password that other Windows 7 computers in your home network will need to join the homegroup.

5. Follow the instructions on your screen and then click `Finish`.

After you have set up the first computer in a homegroup, when you add other Windows 7 computers to your home network, they will detect the homegroup and offer to join it.

AdvancED

In previous versions of Windows, membership in a home network was through workgroups. Like homegroups, workgroups provided file and printer sharing, but not as easily or smoothly.

You can have more than one workgroup in a home network, though each computer can belong to only one workgroup at a time. Windows and other programs or devices that access home networks often used the workgroup name Workgroup or MSHOME. Or you could create a workgroup with a name of your own choosing. Sometimes people had problems sharing files or printers in a home network because the computers were using different workgroup names. If you wanted to share through a workgroup, you had to add all of the computers to the same workgroup. On each computer that you changed the workgroup name, you had to restart the computer so that it could join the new workgroup.

In Windows 7, there is only one homegroup in a home network. You don't have to worry about which name to specify because all the computers in a home network use the same homegroup. To add a computer to a workgroup, you just need to provide the homegroup password created for the first homegroup computer, and then specify what you want to share from each computer.

Joining a homegroup

To join a Windows 7 computer to the homegroup, follow these steps:

1. Click the `Start` button, and then type `homegroup` in the `Start` menu's search box.

2. Click `HomeGroup`. Windows detects that another computer has already created a homegroup and offers to join the homegroup, as shown in Figure 7-12.

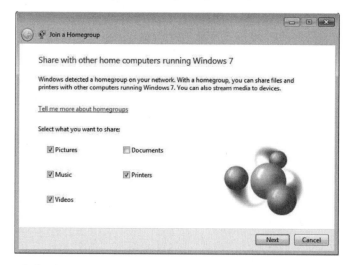

Figure 7-12. Windows notifies you that another computer has already created a homegroup that you can join.

3. Click Join now. The next screen is similar to the one shown when you create a homegroup. It prompts you to choose what you'd like to share with other computers in your homegroup, as shown in Figure 7-13. Most items are preselected, except for Documents.

Figure 7-13. When you join a homegroup, you can select what you want to share with other computers in the homegroup.

4. Select or clear the check boxes to specify what to share and then click `Next`. In the next screen, shown in Figure 7-14, Windows requests the homegroup password. If you don't know the password, follow the instructions on the screen to locate it.

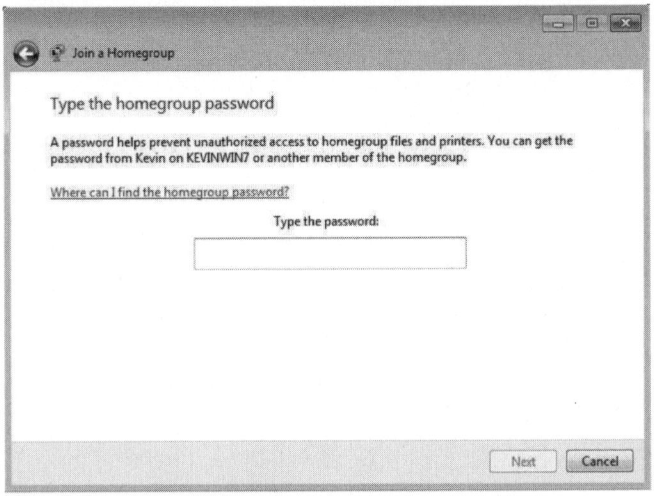

Figure 7-14. Type the homegroup password, or click the link to find it.

5. Type the password that was created by the first computer in the homegroup, as shown in Figure 7-15.

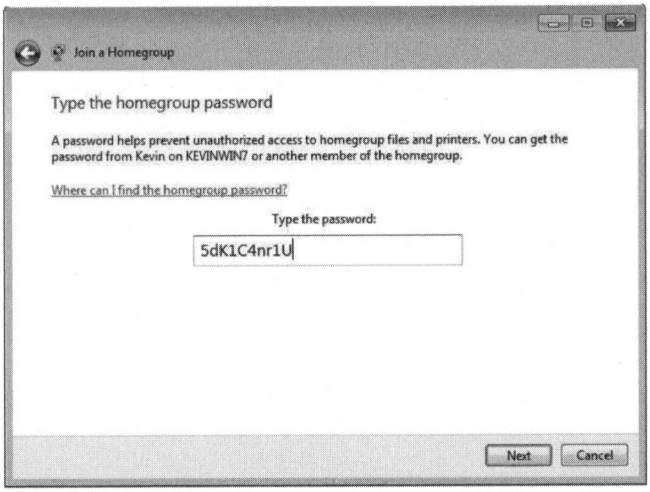

Figure 7-15. To join the homegroup, enter the homegroup password.

211

Windows verifies the password and then confirms that you have joined the homegroup, as shown in Figure 7-16.

6. Click Finish.

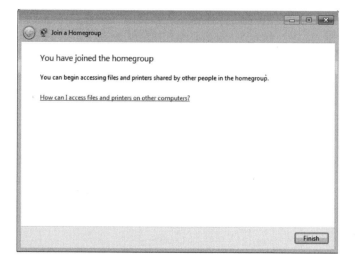

Figure 7-16. You have successfully joined the homegroup.

Changing homegroup settings

When you create a homegroup or add a computer to a homegroup, the settings are applied to the current user. If you have several other users on the computer, each will have to specify what to share by logging in to his or her own user account.

You can change the sharing, password, and other advanced settings through the Change homegroup settings page.

To change the homegroup settings, follow these steps:

1. Click the Start button, and in the Start menu's search box, type homegroup.

2. In the list that appears, click Choose homegroup and sharing options. The Change homegroup settings window appears. Yours will be similar to Figure 7-17, but the options and commands listed vary depending on whether any sharing settings were previously specified, or whether this is the first time you have viewed the homegroup settings.

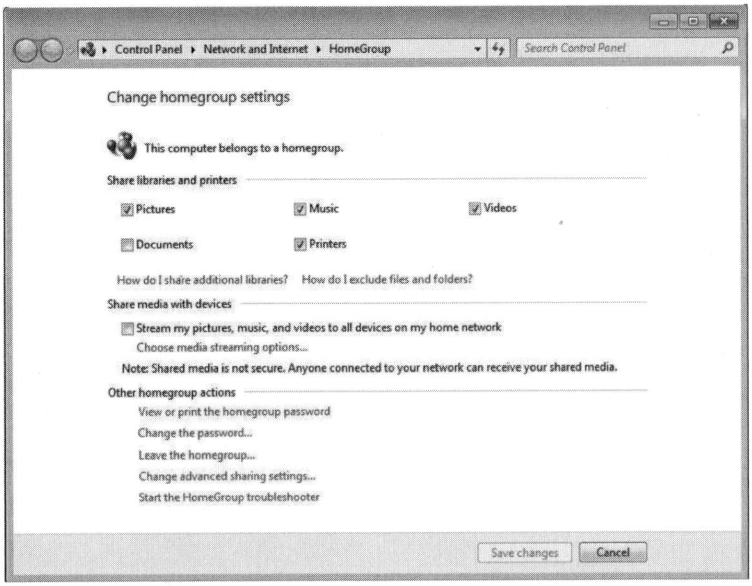

Figure 7-17. The `Change homegroup settings` window provides links to change or view the homegroup passwords and sharing selections.

Leaving the homegroup

The reasons for joining a homegroup are to share files and to share printers. If you have no need to share either, you can leave the homegroup. This does not remove or delete any files; it only removes them from access by the homegroup.

To leave the homegroup, click the `Leave the homegroup` link on the `Change homegroup settings` page.

Excluding files or folders from sharing

Sometimes you may want to exclude specific files or folders from sharing, without blocking an entire library type. For example, you may have a document library that you want to share, except for a few confidential or private documents. Even if you select to share your Documents library, you can still exclude files or folders in that library from sharing.

To exclude or limit specific files or folders from sharing, follow these steps:

1. Navigate to the folders or files you want to exclude.

2. Right-click the file or folder, and on the `Share with` menu, click one of the following:

    - **Nobody**: If you don't want to share this file or folder with anybody
    - **Homegroup (Read):)**: If you want people to be able to read but not change the file
    - **Homegroup (Read/Write):)**: If you want people to be able to read or change the file
    - **Specific people**: If you want to select from a list of specific people to share it with

You cannot exclude files or folders within the Public folders, for example `C:\Users\Public`.

LinkED

The preceding section described how to share files through a homegroup, and the following section describes how to share printers through a homegroup. But what if you have computers in your home network that are not running Windows 7? If computers in your home network are running Windows XP or Windows Vista, you can use their version of file and printer sharing. Or if your other computers are running Windows Vista (and none are running Windows XP), you might also consider upgrading the Windows Vista computers to Windows 7. According to Microsoft, most computers that can run Windows Vista should also be able to run Windows 7 just as well if not better.

For most people, though, upgrading computers to or replacing them with Windows 7 is not necessary. "Installing a printer that is not attached to a homegroup computer" and "Sharing files with computers or devices that are not part of a homegroup" describe how to do this without upgrading or replacing computers, or buying any extra equipment.

Sharing printers on a home network

There are several reasons to connect and share printers on a home network. You can print to a network printer from any computer on the network, place your printer anyplace you have wired or wireless access in your house, and reduce printer ink and paper costs by using fewer printers.

As you've seen previously in this chapter, there are several ways to connect a computer to a network, wired and wirelessly. It's the same with printers, except there a few more options. The following list describes the more typical ways of connecting a printer to a network:

- **A connection to a network computer:** Attach a printer to a computer on the network, install the printer on that computer, and then share the printer through your HomeGroup settings. You can do this with any printer that attaches to your computer with a cable.
- **A connection directly to your router:** If you have a printer that is wired-network ready, you can connect an Ethernet cable from the router to the printer. The only limit on placement of the printer is how long you want to run the cable from the router to the printer.
- **A wireless connection to your network:** If you have a printer that is wireless-network ready, you can place the printer anyplace within range of your wireless network.
- **Through a network-attached storage (NAS) device on your network:** A NAS is an external hard drive that attaches directly to your network, usually via an Ethernet cable. Some NAS devices have one or more USB ports, which you can plug your printer into directly.

Choosing which printers to attach to your network

Have you ever wanted to print a photo, only to realize that the photo printer is attached to another computer, not the one you are using? Or most of the time you need only plain black-and-white printing, but the color printer is more convenient (and more costly) because it is attached to the main family computer everybody uses? If you want to use the right printer for the job, either you have to copy the files to the computer that has the printer you want, and print from there, or you have to physically move the printer from the other computer to the computer you are now using. These are great reasons to put your printers on a network.

Printers are cheap. Sometimes computer retailers practically give them away when you buy a computer. Printer ink is expensive, especially color. So having the right printer available can save you money, especially if most of the time you need only black-and-white printing.

The following sections describe the most common types of printers used at home.

Color printers

Color printers usually have separate cartridges for the three primary colors and a separate cartridge for black ink. Most of these printers today use *inkjet* technology, but some now use laser cartridges, which previously were available for only black-and-white printing. Usually you replace the color cartridges as a set, and the black cartridge separately. Color printers are versatile, because they can print in colors or black-and-white, and can be used for everything from a plain document to a high-quality glossy photo, comparable to what you would get if you took your photos into the drug store for printing.

All-in-one printers

All-in-one printers are usually color printers with a scanner and fax built in. These are handy because most allow you to use them as a straight copier, the scanner allows you to digitize photos or documents from a hard copy, and you can use the scanner to send a page as a fax.

Though you can share an all-in-one printer on your home network, with some models you cannot share the scanner or fax features. To use those features, you must use them from the computer that is attached to the all-in-one.

Photo printers

What makes photo printers different from regular color printers is that they are designed to print a little finer detail, and often have optional printer cartridges designed especially for photos. They also usually include camera card slots so that you can plug your camera's memory card directly into the printer, and select which photos to print without ever connecting to a computer. Some offer a small screen to help you locate, crop, and edit the photos before printing. Many regular color printers now offer memory card slots. The paper input tray can accommodate paper from standard size 8 1/2×11 inches down to 4×6-inch photographs.

Personal photo printers

These printers are much smaller, sometimes about 2/3 the size of a shoe box or tissue box. Their main purpose is to print photos from digital cameras, and they are usually limited to printing 4×6-inch photographs. Because these printers are so small, they are very portable. Some offer rechargeable battery options. With this portability, and the capability to download and print directly from the camera or memory card, you can use these much like people used Polaroid cameras to print out pictures on the spur of the moment at parties and get-togethers.

Black-and-white (monochrome) laser printers

These printers use a single black-ink laser cartridge, and the technology is similar to that used in copying machines. Monochrome laser printers will save you huge amounts in printing costs. They print faster than the inkjet color printers, and the ink does not smear on the paper as it does for the first few minutes after inkjet printing. A single cartridge for a laser printer costs more than color printer cartridges, but it lasts two to three times longer.

Recommendations

There is no perfect printer or one-size-fits-all solution for you or your home network, but the following tips, along with the preceding descriptions of the printer types, should help you choose. Don't rush right out and buy a printer or printers based on these recommendations.

- Use a black-and-white printer whenever possible. On every computer, make this your default printer. Otherwise, when people print something, they may not take the extra step to select the black-and-white printer if a color printer is your default printer. Black-and-white laser printers may cost more up front, but if you do any amount of printing, it will pay for itself in a year or so.
- Use your local drug store or camera store for printing large quantities of photos, if not all photos. Studies have shown that printing photos from your home computer costs about the same or more than the regular price of ordering prints from your local drug store or camera store.
- If you must have a color printer, most all-in-one printers offer nearly all the features and quality of a color photo printer.

- If you receive a "free" printer when you buy your computer, and you already have printers you use and like better, consider using the free printer only until the ink needs replacing. Then compare the ink replacement costs of your old and new printers and decide which one makes more sense to keep.
- If you do decide to buy a new printer, consider one that offers wired/wireless network connections.

Installing a shared printer

The simplest way to share a printer on a network is to share a printer already attached to one of the computers on the network. Even if you are starting from scratch, meaning you have a printer but have not installed it on any computer, the process is pretty straightforward to install it and share it on a network. You may have already completed some of these steps.

These steps are divided into two sections: attaching the printer to a computer in your homegroup, and then installing the printer on other homegroup computers.

Attaching a printer to a computer in your homegroup

To attach, install, and share a printer on a homegroup computer, follow these steps:

1. Connect the printer to your computer with a USB cable and then turn on the printer.

   Windows may automatically install the printer on your computer the first time you connect it to your computer with a USB cable. Windows comes with printer drivers for most brands of printers, but sometimes cannot find a printer driver that matches your model because the printer is old or very new.

   If Windows cannot find a printer driver, it will offer to search for drivers on another location such as the Web or another folder on your computer. Insert the printer installation disc that came with your printer, and either run the printer installation program (the installation screen usually pops up after you insert the disc) or click the `Browse` button in the `Add printer` wizard, and navigate to the CD or DVD drive that contains your printer installation disc.

   If you cannot find your printer installation disc, or Windows displays a message that the printer drivers are not compatible with Windows 7, go to the printer manufacturer's website. Look for their support pages, and look for something like `downloads` or `printer drivers`. Most printers should be able to use the same printer drivers for Windows 7 as were used for Windows Vista. Download the printer installation program to your computer. When the download completes, run the installation program.

2. After the printer is installed, click the `Start` button, and in the `Start` menu's search box, type `share printers`.

3. In the list that appears, click `Share Printers`. The `Change homegroup settings` window appears.

4. Make sure the `Printers` check box is selected. If it is already selected, you don't need to do anything more in this window, so click `Cancel`. If it is not selected, select it and then click `Save Changes`.

Installing the printer on other homegroup computers

To install a shared printer on another homegroup computer, follow these steps:

1. On the homegroup computer, click the `Start` button, and in the `Start` menu's search box, type `share printers`.

2. In the list that appears, click `Share Printers`. The `Change homegroup settings` window appears. Windows detects that there is a shared printer available in the homegroup, as shown in Figure 7-18.

Figure 7-18. Windows will detect when a shared printer has been added to the home network, and will offer to install it.

3. Click `Install Printer`. Windows searches for drivers on this homegroup computer, or on the computer that the printer is attached to, and installs the printer. The `Change homegroup settings` window then refreshes, and the Install printer message disappears, as shown in Figure 7-19.

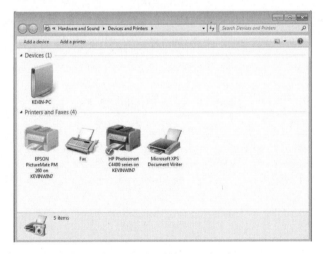

Figure 7-19. The prompt to install the new shared homegroup printer goes away after the printer is installed.

4. (Optional) Check to see whether the printer is now available for this computer. Click the `Start` button and then click `Devices and Printers`. The `Devices and Printers` window shows that the new printer HP Photosmart C4400 attached to the homegroup computer KEVINWIN7 is available, as shown in Figure 7-20. The green check mark means it is the default printer.

Figure 7-20. HP Photosmart C4400, shared by another homegroup computer KEVINWIN7, is the default printer on this computer.

221

AdvancED

Whether you are using homegroup in Windows 7, or File and Printer Sharing in Windows XP or Windows Vista, there is a universal truth about sharing printers or files attached to a computer. If the computer with the shared files or shared printer is turned off or not attached to the network (for example, a laptop that somebody has taken out of the house and out of range of your network), you won't be able to use any printers attached to it, or access files that are shared on it.

So how do you make printers and files available to all home network computers all the time? There are several solutions, which may require additional computer devices or using more energy (electricity):

- ***Keep one network computer on all the time, and attach all shared printers and store all shared files on this computer.*** *This is the simplest solution, which requires no new equipment but does require a computer to be on all the time. Not only does this drive up your electrical bill, but it also gives off heat and may warm up your room more than you normally want. Ideally, you could use an older desktop PC that would otherwise be surplus or obsolete, running Windows XP. You could also use a laptop, but they are not as good a choice because laptops are more susceptible to overheating than desktop PCs and tend to have much smaller hard drives for storage. You won't be able to use the HomeGroup feature with this computer if it is running Windows XP or Windows Vista, but it is not that difficult to set up sharing between Windows 7 computers and Windows XP or Windows Vista. You can minimize the power usage by turning off the monitor when you are not actually sitting at the computer using it.*
- ***Buy a wireless or wired network printer.*** *These can be attached directly to your home network router. They are only a little more expensive than printers that offer USB-only connections. This, however, does not address the problem of providing shared file access all the time.*

- **Buy an external portable hard drive.** *This can provide file access to any computer on your network if you share it from the computer it is attached to. If you want to share files with any single computer anytime, you can move the portable drive around from computer to computer. This does not address the problem of providing shared printer access all the time. There are also external desktop hard drives. They are not as compact as a portable hard drive and may not have as much protection from accidental drops. But they are almost as easy to move around from computer to computer as needed. Desktop hard drives are larger because they use a larger disk inside, a 3.5-inch drive, vs. 2.5-inch drives in portable hard drives. This larger size allows desktop hard drives to offer significantly larger storage capacity. Currently, 320GB capacity is a popular size for portable hard drives, though larger sizes are available. Desktop hard drives are commonly available in even higher capacities including 500GB, 750GB, 1TB (1000GB), and 1.5GB.*
- **Buy a network-attached storage device (NAS).** *It can provide access to shared files and printers. These are fairly new to home computer users, but have long been in use in corporate networks. For home users, a NAS device is a special type of external hard drive that attaches directly to your network. Many of the examples in this chapter show a device listed as //Storage. That is a NAS device, which happens to also have three printers attached directly to it. The NAS device can also be useful if you want to stream music or videos to other devices on your home network, such as a media player to display videos on a TV, or certain types of stereo receivers, so that you can share music throughout your house. NAS devices are more expensive than an external hard drive, but may well be worth it because they provide around-the-clock access to files and printers, and their large capacity provides plenty of space to regularly back up the files on all of your computers.*
- **Buy a home server.** *Don't be scared by the idea of setting up a server. It is not much more complicated to set up than setting up a regular computer. A home server works similarly to the first alternative, of having one computer on all the time. A home server doesn't run Windows 7, but may run a special version of Windows, Windows Home Server, or another operating system*

designed to run as a home server. Though it is running an operating system, controlled by a mouse and keyboard, you cannot use a home server as a desktop PC to run programs or surf the Web. A home server offers all the features of a NAS device, but in addition offers more flexibility to add storage (extra hard drives) as needed.

Installing a printer that is not attached to a homegroup computer

There are several common scenarios where you may want to share printers on your home network but cannot do it through the homegroup. Fortunately, Windows 7 provides other ways to install shared printers on your network. The process is similar to the one previously described for homegroup printers: install the printer, share it, and then install it on the individual computers in the home network. You can use this process to share printers that are attached to the home network but not through homegroup computers:

- Wired or wireless printers attached directly to the home network through a router
- Printers attached to a NAS that is attached to the home network through a router
- Printers attached to non-Windows 7 computers on the home network running Windows XP or Windows Vista

The steps in this process are provided in two sets. In the first set, you will install the printer so it is available to computers on the home network. In the second set of steps, you will install the printer on the other computers in your home network.

Installing and sharing a wired or wireless printer

For your initial setup, you will need an Ethernet cable, even if you plan to use the printer wirelessly. If you will be using this printer wirelessly, and your network is configured for wireless authentication and encryption, you will also need the wireless encryption key or password. The manufacturer's instructions may vary, but generally follow these steps:

1. Insert the printer's installation disc in a computer on your network.

2. Turn on your printer.

3. Follow the onscreen instructions from the printer manufacturer's installation disc.

4. Attach the printer to the router directly with an Ethernet cable when prompted by the installation program. If you are installing the printer as a wireless device, the installation program will tell you when you can remove the Ethernet cable and use the printer wirelessly.

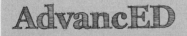

Wireless printers require a large amount of data to pass back and forth between the router and the printer. Wireless printers are just as susceptible as wireless routers and computers to interference and blockage by walls and devices. After you've completed a wireless setup, print a test page to make sure that your printer location has a strong signal. If you don't have strong signal between your router and printer, printing may take a long time or not work at all. Move either the printer or the router and try printing the same test page again to see if it works better. If you try multiple locations and still have difficulty, you may need to use an Ethernet cable all the time to connect to your network. Most, if not all, wireless printers also have an Ethernet jack, so if wireless doesn't work for you, you will need to locate the printer within reach of your Ethernet cable.

Installing and sharing a printer attached to a NAS device

Check the documentation for your NAS device to verify that the device supports attaching printers and has a USB port for connecting printers. The exact steps for adding a printer to a NAS device vary, but generally follow this process:

1. Attach the printer directly to the NAS device via a USB cable.

2. Turn on the printer.

3. Open the configuration program for the NAS device. You will need to log in as an administrator on the NAS device.

4. Click the command for managing printers. Check your NAS documentation for the exact command to do this.

5. The printer may be displayed in a list of printers attached to the NAS device. Select the printer and select the command to attach the printer. The NAS device will not have the printer drivers even if the printer was previously used and installed on the computer you are running the NAS configuration program from.

6. When prompted, insert the printer installation disc. The NAS configuration program should find the needed drivers on the disc. If you have problems installing a printer on your NAS device, consult the NAS device documentation.

ExplainED

To access printers or shared folders on the NAS device, you may have to install the NAS interface on each computer. When opening the NAS interface on any of the computers, you may need to provide a login name and password for the NAS device if you previously configured it for password-controlled access.

Installing and sharing a printer attached to a Windows Vista or XP computer

You may need administrator-level privileges to install and share a printer on a Windows Vista or XP computer. Follow these steps:

1. Turn on the computer.

2. Attach the printer directly to the computer via a USB cable.

3. Turn on the printer.

   Windows may automatically install the printer on your computer the first time you connect it to your computer with a USB cable. Windows comes with printer drivers for most brands of printers, but sometimes cannot find a printer driver that matches your model because the printer is old or very new.

   If Windows cannot find a printer driver, it will offer to search for drivers on another location such as the Web or another folder on your computer. Insert the printer installation disc that came with your printer, and run the printer installation program (the installation screen usually pops up after you insert the disc) or click the Browse button in the Add printer wizard, and navigate to the CD or DVD drive that contains your printer installation disc.

4. If installation is required, complete the Add printer wizard or the printer manufacturer's installation program.

5. In Control Panel, open Printers.

6. Right-click the printer you just installed, and click `Sharing`. The `Printer properties` window is displayed.

7. On the `Sharing` tab, follow the instructions to enable sharing for this printer.

Adding a shared printer to a Windows 7 computer from a non-Windows 7 computer or device

After you've installed the printer on your router (wired or wireless), NAS, or Windows XP or Windows Vista computer, and configured it for network sharing, you can add the printer to your Windows 7 computers on your home network. If you want to install and share another printer, you must repeat the preceding procedures for each printer. After a printer is installed and shared on the home network, you can add it to other computers on the network.

To add a shared printer from a non-Windows 7 computer or device to a Windows 7 computer, follow these steps:

1. Click the `Start` button, and in the `Start` menu's search box, type `Printers`.

2. In the list that appears, click `Add Printer`. The `Add Printer` wizard is displayed, as shown in Figure 7-21.

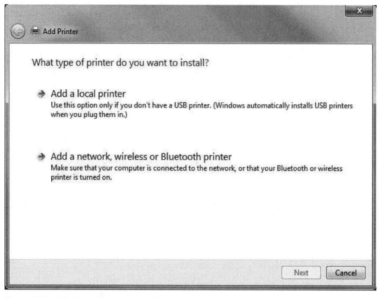

Figure 7-21. To install a printer that is shared on your network, click `Add a network, wireless or Bluetooth printer`.

3. Click `Add a network, wireless or Bluetooth printer`.

Windows quickly finds any printers attached to your homegroup. Eventually, it should list all printers on your home network, including those that are attached to non-homegroup computers or devices, as shown in Figure 7-22. In this example, the first three printers were attached to Windows 7 computers named KEVINWIN7 and KEVIN-PC. The next three printers listed were attached directly to a NAS device, named STORAGE. The last printer was attached to a Windows Vista computer named Kevin-PC64HP. Though no wired or wireless printers were installed on the network used in this example, if they were attached and shared on the network, they would appear in this list also.

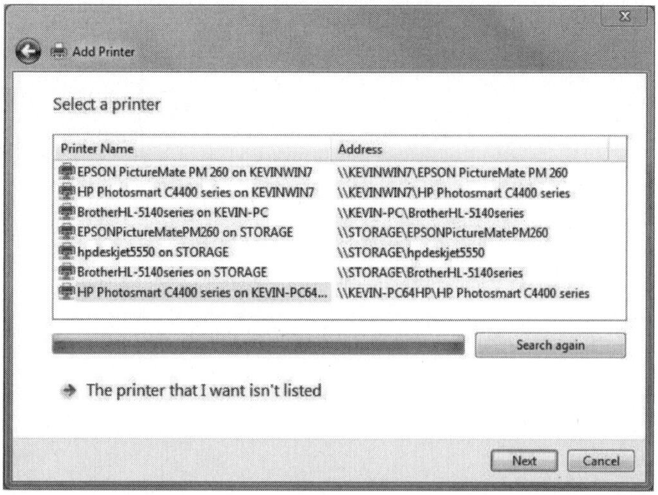

Figure 7-22. Windows may not at first find printers attached to non-Windows 7 computers or devices. Eventually, Windows should find all printers on the home network.

4. Click the printer you want to add and then click `Next`.

    —or—

    If you don't see the printer you want, click `The printer that I want isn't listed`. Then choose one of the options for locating the printer via browsing, typing the computer name, or typing the IP address. If you still cannot find the printer you want, the computer that the printer is attached to might be off, or the printer might not be enabled for printer sharing.

5. After you select or locate the printer, Windows will attempt to connect with it, as shown in Figure 7-23.

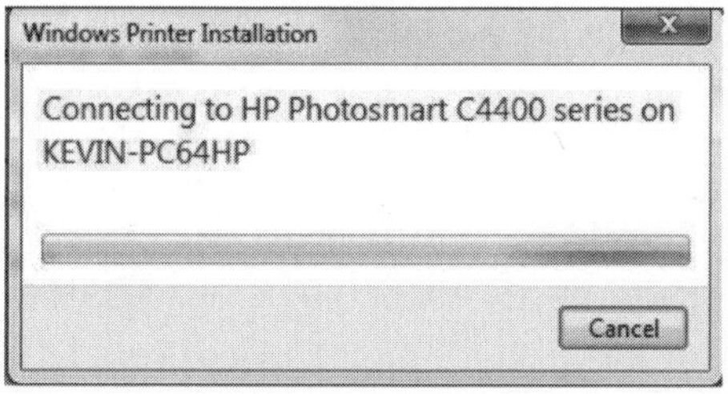

Figure 7-23. Windows attempts to connect to the printer you selected.

When Windows finds and installs the printer, it will confirm that the installation was successful, as shown in Figure 7-24.

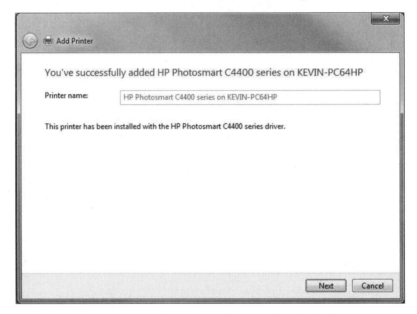

Figure 7-24. The printer is installed and ready to use from the local computer. Note that the printer named in this message is referring to the location of the printer on the network, KEVIN-PC64HP, not the local computer you just made the printer available to.

Repeat the steps in this section for each computer you want to add the shared printer to.

Sharing files with computers or devices that are not part of a homegroup

If all of your computers on your home network are running Windows 7, you can manage file sharing with a homegroup. If you have a mixture of Windows 7, Windows Vista, and Windows XP computers on your home network, you can still share files, but the steps are slightly different for each version of Windows.

Because you cannot use a homegroup, in order for the computers to recognize and share files with each other, they need to belong to the same workgroup. The default name that Windows assigns to workgroups is MSHOME, so most if not all of your computers may already belong to that workgroup. If some computers belong to different workgroups, you can change the workgroup name on each computer until they all have the same workgroup name.

Viewing and changing the workgroup name on Windows XP

To view and change the workgroup name on a Windows XP computer, follow these steps:

1. Click the `Start` button, right-click `My Computer`, and then click `Properties`. The `System Properties` page is displayed, as shown in Figure 7-25.

Figure 7-25. The `System Properties` page in Windows XP

2. On the `Computer Name Changes` page, type the workgroup name you want to use for all computers on your home network and then click `OK`, as shown in Figure 7-26. Click `OK` again to close the `System Properties` dialog box.

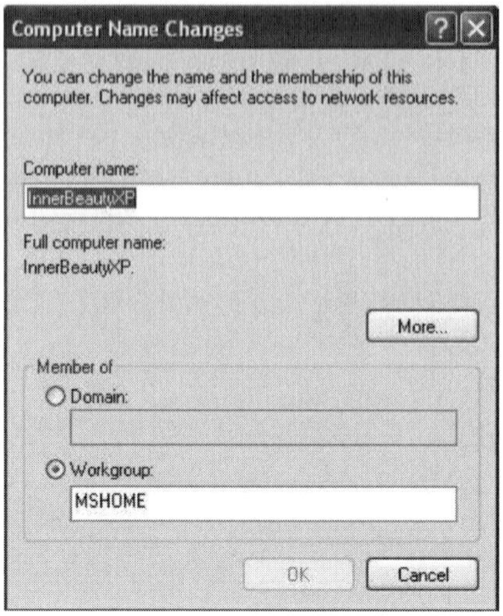

Figure 7-26. Change the workgroup name to the name you want to use for all computers on your home network.

Viewing and changing the workgroup name on Windows Vista or Windows 7

To view and change the workgroup name on a Windows Vista or Windows 7 computer, follow these steps:

1. Click the `Start` button, right-click `Computer`, and then click `Properties`. The `System` page is displayed, as shown in Figure 7-27.

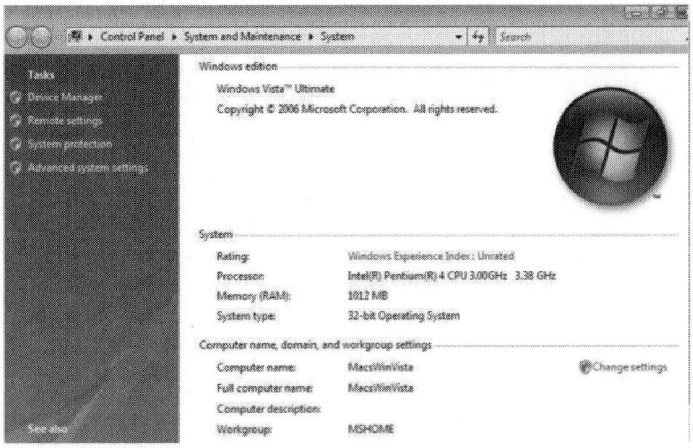

Figure 7-27. The Windows Vista `System` page is identical to the Windows 7 `System` page.

2. If the workgroup name is correct, close this window. If it is not correct, under `Computer name, domain, and workgroup settings,` click `Change settings.`

3. Click `Continue` if prompted for permission by `User Account Control.` The `System Properties` page `Computer Name` tab is displayed, as shown in Figure 7-28.

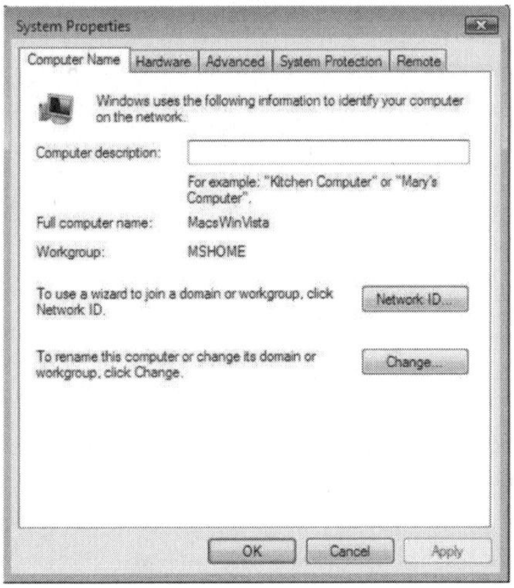

Figure 7-28. Windows Vista `System Properties Computer Name` tab`System Properties Computer Name` tab. Windows 7 displays an identical page.

4. Click `Change`. The `Computer Name/Domain Changes` window appears, as shown in Figure 7-29.

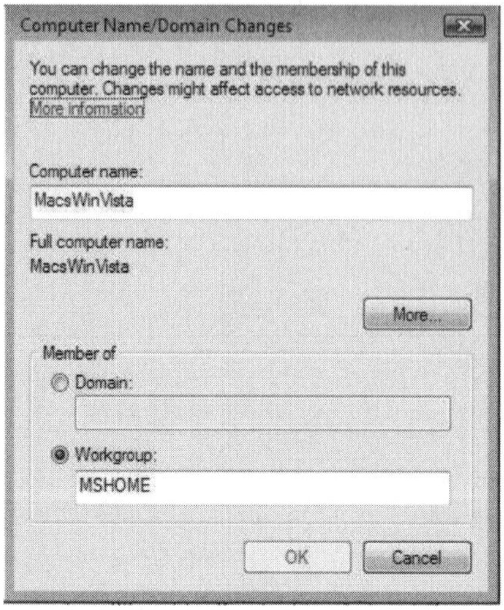

Figure 7-29. The `Computer Name/Domain Changes` window provides text boxes for renaming the computer or workgroup.

5. On the `Computer Name/Domain Changes` page, type the workgroup name you want to use for all computers on your home network, and then click `OK` twice.

After you have changed all computers to the same workgroup, and restarted them so that the name takes effect, all computers should be able to detect each other on the network. When all computers on your home network belong to the same workgroup, they can share folders and printers.

Viewing and accessing shared folders on your network

Each version of Windows has a slightly different way of displaying the shared folders and computers on your home network. You can check to see what's shared, so if there is something that you want to share that's hidden, or something that's shared that you want private, you can go back to the computer that contains the folders and change the sharing settings.

Accessing shared folders from Windows XP

To view from a Windows XP computer what computers are available and what they are sharing on your network, follow these steps:

1. Click the Start button and then click My Network Places. My Network Places displays the folders that are shared, and on what computer, similar to Figure 7-30.

Figure 7-30. Windows XP lists shared folders on computers and network storage devices on your home network.

2. Perform any of the following tasks to see what is available:

   - Double-click a folder icon to open it, and access files in the folders that are shared.

- View what is in your workgroup, by computer or device. In the `Network Tasks` list in the left column, click `View workgroup computers`. Figure 7-31 displays the computers and storage devices in the MSHOME workgroup. There are fewer icons displayed here than in the previous figure of shared folders, because some computers or storage devices have more than one shared folder.

Figure 7-31. A list of computers and storage devices in the MSHOME workgroup

- Open a computer or device in the list and view the shared folders and printers, as shown in Figure 7-32.

236

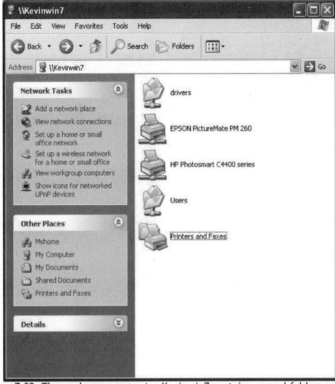

Figure 7-32. The workgroup computer Kevinwin7 contains several folders and printers that are shared.

Accessing shared folders from Windows Vista

To view from a Windows Vista computer what computers are available, and what they are sharing on the home network, follow these steps:

1. Click the Start button and then click Network. The Network window displays the computers and devices that are shared on the home network, similar to Figure 7-33. Windows Vista also displays other devices besides computers and storage devices. In this example, the Network list includes a wireless router, WGR614V9.

237

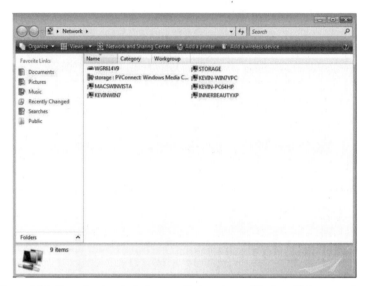

Figure 7-33. Shared network devices as displayed on a Windows Vista computer

2. Double-click a computer or device to view what folders and printers are shared. Windows Vista displays the contents, similar to Figure 7-34.

Figure 7-34. Shared folders and printers available on the computer KEVINWIN7

AdvancED

One way to make it easy to access your network is to add the Network *command to the* Start *menu. Right-click the* Start *button and then click* Properties. *On the* Start Menu *tab, click the* Customize *button. In the* Customize Start Menu *dialog box, scroll through the list until you find the* Network *check box, and then select it.*

Accessing shared folders from Windows 7

To view from a Windows 7 computer what computers are available, and what they are sharing on the home network, follow these steps:

1. Click the Start button, and in the Start menu's search box, type Network. In the list that appears, click Network.

   The Network window displays the computers and devices that are shared on the home network, similar to Figure 7-35. Windows 7 provides grouping and more detail of the devices on the network than Windows Vista.

Figure 7-35. Windows 7 groups network devices by type in the Network window.

2. Double-click a computer to view what is shared. Windows 7 displays the shared contents, similar to Figure 7-36.

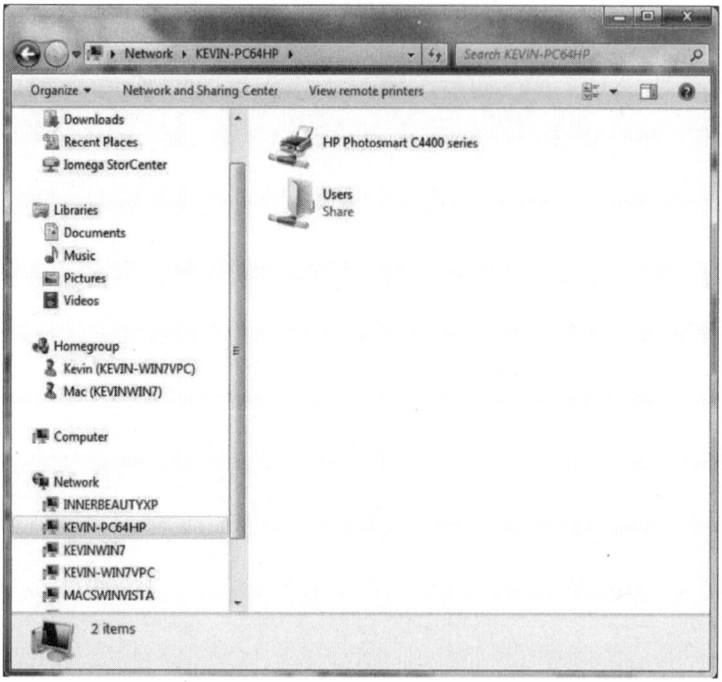

Figure 7-36. Folders and printers shared on the computer KEVIN-PC64HP, as seen from a Windows 7 computer

Sharing a folder if it does not appear available from another computer

After you've added all of your computers to the same workgroup, you may still need to mark folders in order for them to be shared with other computers in the workgroup. There are three ways to share files in Windows 7:

- Create or join a homegroup, as described previously in this chapter. This method is available only for Windows 7 computers.
- Add folders to a public or shared folder. You can do this with Windows XP, Windows Vista, and Windows 7 computers. You can share a folder locally with other users on the same computer, or you can share the folder with other users on this computer and users on the network.
- Specify who can view or change a folder. You can do this with Windows Vista and Windows 7 computers.

The easiest way to broadly share files and folders with other users on your computer or any computer on the home network is to place them in special folders called Shared Documents (Windows XP) or Public Documents (Windows Vista and Windows 7).

LinkED

Chapter 3 covers the Windows 7 Public Documents folder, as well as its siblings Public Downloads, Public Music, Public Pictures, Public Recorded TV, and Public Videos. They can all be found in C:\Users\Public.

In Windows XP, the shared folder is named Shared Documents in the folder list of `My Computer`, and is usually located at C:\Documents and Settings\All Users\Documents.

There are more options for sharing than just adding the Shared Documents folder, such as sharing the folder on the network and giving it a share name. The following procedure provides additional sharing options.

Sharing a folder on Windows XP

To share a folder on Windows XP, follow these steps:

1. Navigate to the folder in `Windows Explorer`.

2. Right-click the folder and then click `Sharing and Security`. The properties for the folder are displayed, similar to Figure 7-37.

241

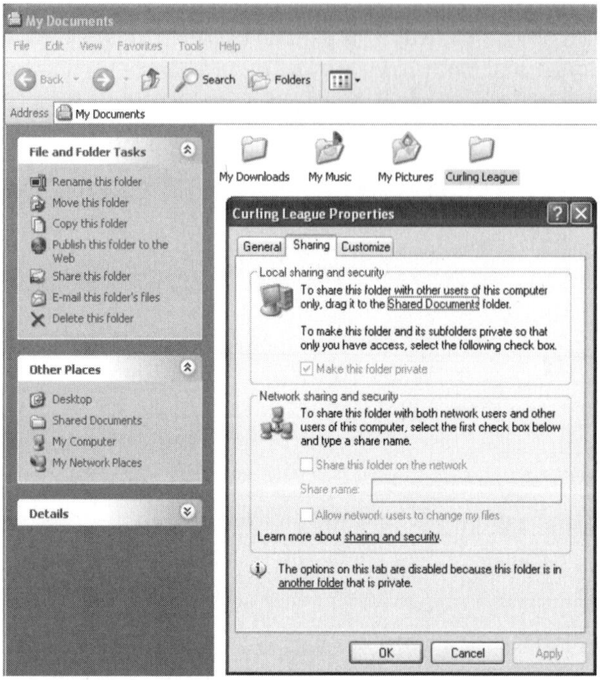

Figure 7-37. The sharing settings of a folder in `My Documents`

If some options are grayed out, that means they are not available. Follow the instructions and links in the dialog box to enable sharing as needed.

Sharing a folder on Windows Vista

To share a folder on Windows Vista, follow these steps:

1. Navigate to the folder in `Windows Explorer`.

2. Right-click the folder and then click `Share`. The `File Sharing` dialog box appears.

3. Click the down arrow to the left of the `Add` button, and then click who you want to give sharing access to. Figure 7-38 shows the list of users who can be given access on this computer. As the user logged in to the computer at this time, you automatically have full access.

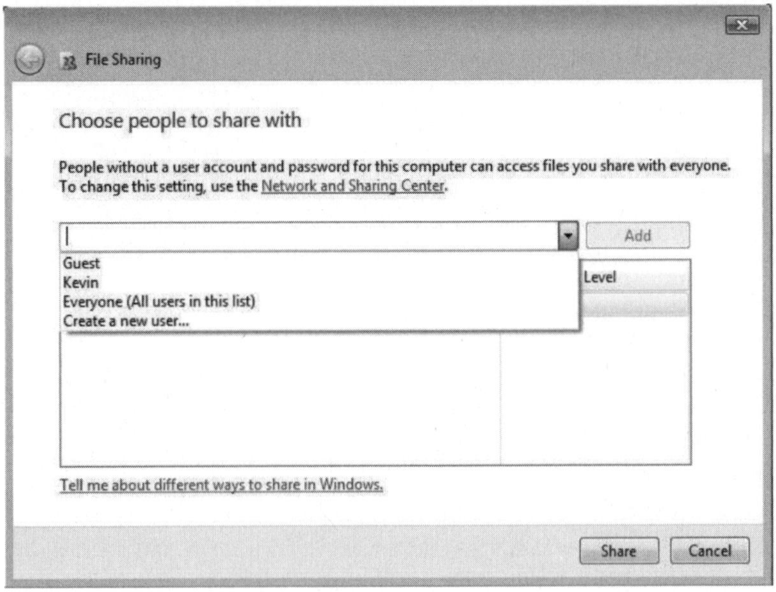

Figure 7-38. You can share a folder with any, all, or no users on this computer.

4. Click `Add`. When the name appears in the list, you can change the permission level. By default, when you add a user, the permission level is Reader. Continue adding users if needed.

5. After adding your last user, click `Share`.

Sharing a folder on Windows 7

To share a folder on Windows 7, follow these steps:

1. Navigate to the folder in `Windows Explorer`.

2. Right-click the folder and then click `Share with`. A submenu appears, as shown in Figure 7-39.

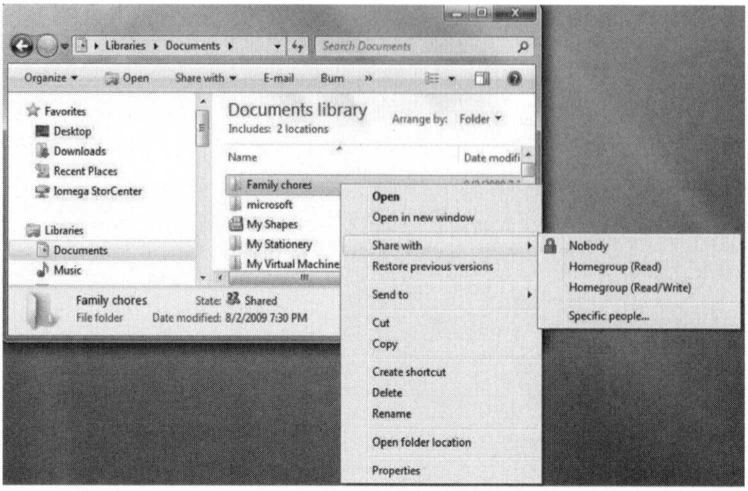

Figure 7-39. Windows 7 provides several options for sharing a folder.

3. Click one of the following:

- **Nobody:** To keep the folder completely private. Only you will be able to access it, when you are logged on to this computer. If you select this option, Windows applies it and you are finished.

- **Homegroup (Read):):** To allow any user in the homegroup to read but not add, change, or delete files in the folder. If you select this option, Windows applies it and you are finished.

- **Homegroup (Read/Write):):** To allow any user in the homegroup to read, add, change, or delete files in the folder. If you select this option, Windows applies it and you are finished.

- **Specific people:** To select users and their permission level from the list of users on this computer. If you select this option, the `File Sharing` dialog box appears, just like the one in Windows Vista. Click the down arrow to the left of the `Add` button, and then click who you want to give sharing access to.

Enhancing network security

Networks connect computers to each other and to the outside world (the Internet). This exposes your computer and network to all sorts of threats from outside, and even from other users within the network. This section highlights some security issues and solutions specific to home networks.

LinkED

Chapter 6 provides a much more comprehensive look at security issues and how to set up Windows 7 to provide as much protection as possible.

A home network is only as safe as its weakest link, whether that link be a particular user or a particular machine. The following list of ten good ways to make your network safer is by no means all that you should do to protect your network, but are good practices that are worth the time and effort.

- **Use a wireless encryption key for your wireless router.** When you install a wireless router, follow the instructions to create a wireless encryption key. Though there are several types of encryption methods offered with similar-sounding names, avoid using WEP, which is older and not very secure. Use WPA2. If you don't encrypt your wireless router, anybody can tap into your wireless network if they can get within range. Some of the newer wireless routers have a very large range. For example, when I turn on a laptop at home with wireless networking turned on, my computer detects anywhere from one to four other wireless networks from neighboring houses. If I can see their wireless networks, they can see mine. If you live in a higher-density neighborhood, such as apartments or dormitories, you will see many more nearby networks, and more people will detect yours.

- **When using public wireless hotspots, assume the worst and use the highest security settings.** When you first connect to a wireless hotspot, Windows may prompt you to verify whether you feel safe connecting to this new unknown connection. Even if you do trust the Wi-Fi service provider, use the Public profile recommended by Windows. Whether it be a free service at your library or a subscription service at your local coffee shop, assume that somebody could intercept your data as you surf the Internet or use your e-mail. Do not perform any kind of banking, financial, or shopping tasks from a public hotspot.

- **Restrict what types of programs users on your network can download and install.** Free doesn't always mean free. A free screensaver program may have a virus or spyware embedded in it. Popular file-sharing services for swapping videos or music files may require unsafe access through your Windows firewall, and some of these services may violate copyright laws. Downloading lots of videos may soon take up a lot of your hard disk or storage space.

- **Make sure all computers on the network are up-to-date with the latest Windows updates, antivirus, and antispyware software.** Turn on automatic updating for any of these types of programs. One unprotected computer on your network can easily infect other protected computers on your network because within a network, computers trust each other more than they do computers outside the network. For more information, see Chapter 9.

- **Make sure all users have their own accounts, and that all accounts on all computers require a password.** If your laptop or desktop PC gets lost or stolen, it does no good to have passwords for most of the user accounts if one has no password. Hackers could access your password-protected accounts by logging on with the account that has no password. For more information about creating user accounts, see Chapter 2, and for keeping your computer safe, see Chapter 9.

- **Make sure you have a password reset disk for every computer on your network.** If everybody or most users have administrator-level permissions on a computer, they may be able to change the passwords of other users on the computer. With a password reset disk, you can recover control over your computer.

- **Do not give anybody any passwords for any account on your computers.** Set up a guest account for limited access to web browsing or e-mail. Typically, when you log in with your user account, you also have other programs that have your personal user accounts such as e-mail, instant messaging, websites, shopping sites, and so forth. Some of these accounts, or Windows, may offer to remember to save your name and password so that you don't have to enter it the next time you visit the site or check the e-mail account. If you give somebody access to your user account, you also give them access to any account with a saved password. If you have a short-term visitor, you can set up a limited guest account. If they are going to be visiting longer term, you can set up a regular user account on the computer, and then remove the account when they leave. For more information, see Chapter 2.

- **Back up every computer and storage device with another computer or storage device.** Windows 7 provides backup and recovery software that will help you protect the data on your computer. The Windows operating system and applications can be reinstalled from the original disks. But unless you back up your pictures, files, documents, music, videos, and so forth, you won't have any way to recover them if your computer crashes, is stolen, or is irreparably damaged. Saving all of your important files on an external drive or storage device is not enough. If the only place you store important files for long-term storage and safekeeping is a single storage device, you need to back up that storage device too. Most backup programs send the backups to a separate location from the original place the data came from. Many external hard drives and storage devices (such as network-attached storage) come with or have built-in backup and recovery programs. Use them. For more information about backup and recovery, see Chapter 6.

- **Do not share everything with every user on the home network.** People accidently delete or move files all the time. One of the reasons for having separate user accounts is so that you can control access to your files. If a member of your family has just about filled up the hard drive with downloaded videos, you don't want them to start deleting your stuff to make room for their downloads. Use Public folders for files that you want to share with other users, or be selective such as sharing your music, pictures, and video folders, but not your other documents.

- **Encourage every user on your home network to use the same user account name and password on every computer they use in the network.** This is partly practicality and partly security. Sometimes when accessing files, printers, or devices on another computer in your network, you may be prompted for an authorized user account and password. If you use the same username John on every computer and the same password with it, you won't have to worry about which password was used with which John account on each computer. For more information, see Chapter 2.

Summary

Here's a review of what you've learned in this chapter:

- How to connect your computers to the Internet
- How to connect your computers to a network
- How to create and join a homegroup
- How to share printers and files with other Windows 7 computers in a homegroup
- How to share printers and files with Windows 7, Windows XP, and Windows Vista computers all on the same home network
- How to protect your network from common security problems and issues

Chapter 8

Using Windows 7 Programs

An operating system like Windows 7 is only as good as the things you can do with it. That's why software programs that come with the operating system—or those that you install yourself—are what you'll use on a daily basis to perform tasks such as opening and creating documents, browsing the Web, using e-mail, viewing photos, playing audio and video, and more.

There are lots of programs with lots of features in Windows 7, and covering them all is beyond the scope of this book, but in this chapter, we'll explore the basics of some of Windows 7's major programs. We'll also cover some of the handier minor programs, as well as group of programs that doesn't come with the operating system but that Microsoft offers to Windows 7 users as a free download.

Then you'll learn how to add and remove new programs and how to specify which programs are used for specific activities such as web browsing or opening a digital photo.

Using Internet Explorer

Browsing the Web is probably one of the most frequently performed tasks, so Internet Explorer 8, Windows 7's built-in web browser, seems like a good place to start. The most convenient way to run Internet Explorer is to click its taskbar button (Figure 8-1).

Figure 8-1. You can conveniently run Internet Explorer via its taskbar button.

Viewing a website

The large box at the top of Internet Explorer is called the **address bar** (Figure 8-2). To visit a site, type the site's address into the address bar, and press Enter.

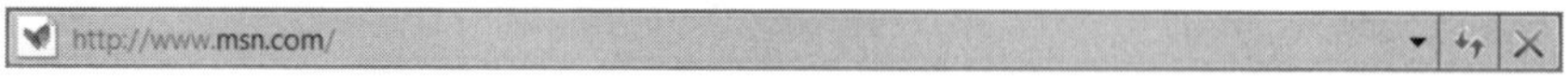

Figure 8-2. Type into the address bar to visit a website.

Because Internet Explorer remembers your browsing activity, as you begin typing in a site address, it will automatically display a list of site suggestions as well as addresses for sites you've already visited that contain the same word (or portion of a word) you've typed (Figure 8-3). To use one of the suggestions, select it with the down arrow key, and press Enter (or click it with the mouse).

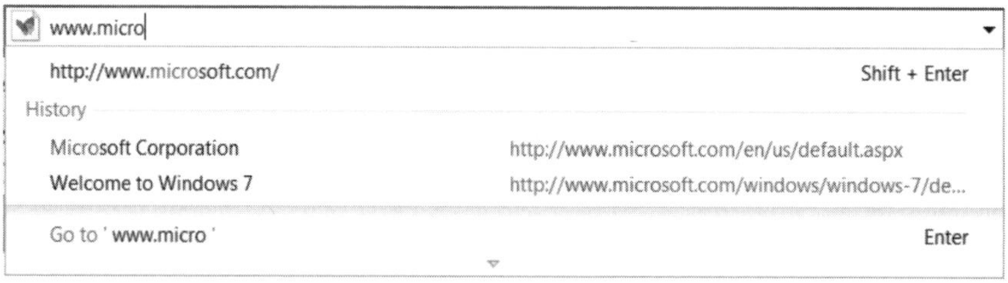

Figure 8-3. Internet Explorer tries to anticipate what site you want and makes suggestions based on sites you've already visited (which means suggestions you see will vary from those shown here).

Viewing multiple websites

Internet Explorer 8 uses a tabbed interface that makes it possible to have multiple web pages open at the same time. To open a new tab, click the New Tab button, which is the small square located to the right of the tab for the currently open page (Figure 8-4), and then type in the address for a new site. To switch between open tabs, just click the tabs.

Figure 8-4. Click the small square to the right of the tab to open a new tab.

Whenever you have multiple tabs open, you'll see a Quick Tabs button (with four squares on it) appear to the left of the tabs (Figure 8-5).

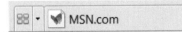

Figure 8-5. When you have multiple tabs open, the `Quick Tabs` button appears to the left of the tabs.

Click the `Quick Tabs` button, not the down arrow, and you'll be able to see thumbnail views of all your open tabs, as shown in Figure 8-6. To switch the view to a specific tab, just click its thumbnail.

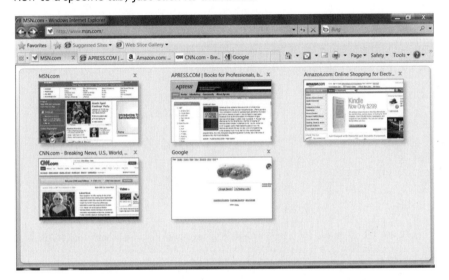

Figure 8-6. The `Quick Tabs` button lets you view all your open tabs at the same time.

If you click the down arrow, you will see a list of the open tabs, where each tab is identified by the title of the web page it is displaying.

Another way to see thumbnails of all open tabs is to place the mouse pointer over Internet Explorer's taskbar button. For more information on taskbar previews, see Chapter 1.

Saving favorite sites

To avoid having to repeatedly type in the address of a frequently visited website, you can add it to your list of Favorites so it's never more than a click or two away. To save a site as a Favorite, follow these steps:

1. Make sure the site is visible (in other words, that it's the currently selected tab if you have several open).

2. Click the `Favorites` button under the address bar (the one with the gold star) to open the `Favorites` window (Figure 8-7).

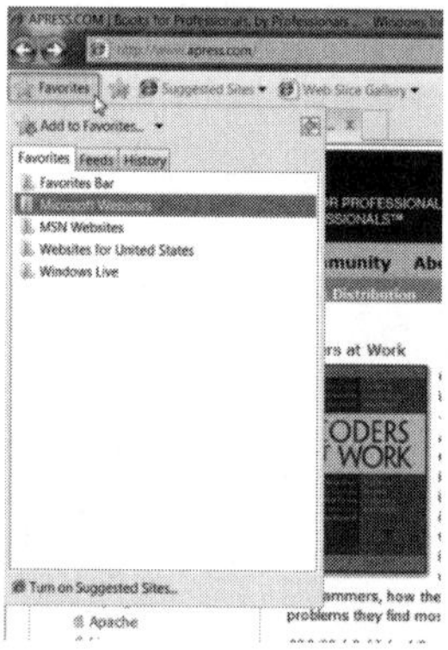

Figure 8-7. Click the `Favorites` button to save or access frequently visited sites.

3. Finally, click the `Add to Favorites` button, change the default name of the favorite if desired (often you'll want to shorten it), and click `Add` (Figure 8-8).

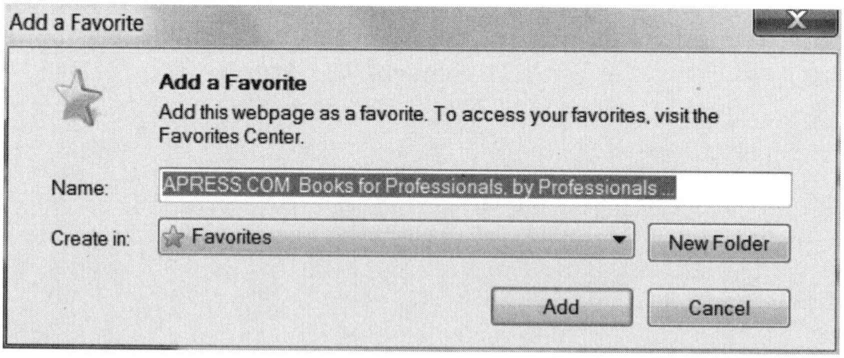

Figure 8-8. You can pare down the name of a favorite before saving it.

Your new favorite will be listed and easily accessible each time you click the Favorites button.

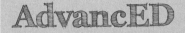

The Favorites window will automatically close after you click a site, but you can keep it open at all times by clicking the green arrow in the upper-right corner of the window. Also, when you type all or part of the name of a favorite site into the address bar, potential matches will be displayed along with the browsing history, as shown in Figure 8-3.

Configuring a home page

When you start Internet Explorer, it automatically loads a default, or **home**, page. Depending on how you got Windows 7 (that is, whether you installed it yourself or it came with your computer), your home page may be Microsoft's MSN website or different site chosen by your system manufacturer. Clicking the Home button (Figure 8-9) will return Internet Explorer (or the currently selected tab, if multiple tabs are open) to the home page.

Figure 8-9. The Home button (which looks like a house) returns Internet Explorer to its default home page.

To set your own home page, follow these steps:

1. Open the page you want to use, and then click the down arrow to the right of the Home button.

2. Select Add or Change Home Page.

3. Click Use this webpage as your only home page to replace your current home page. If you want to add a second (or third or fourth, and so on) home page, click Add this webpage to your home page tabs instead. This will add the new home page to any you already have. Then click Yes to save the change (Figure 8-10).

Add or Change Home Page

Would you like to use the following as your home page?

http://www.apress.com/

- Use this webpage as your only home page
- Add this webpage to your home page tabs
- Use the current tab set as your home page

Yes   No

Figure 8-10. You can replace your current home page or add to one you already have.

AdvancED

If you want Internet Explorer to automatically start up with a customized group of tabs, open all the tabs you want, and then select `Use the current tab set` *as your home page.*

Searching

You'll probably often find yourself searching for various types of information on the Internet. In the upper-right corner of Internet Explorer, you'll find a search box where you can type in a word or phrase and see a list of results (Figure 8-11).

Figure 8-11. Type a word or phrase into the search box to find information on the Internet.

Internet Explorer's default search provider is Microsoft's Bing, which is quite a good search engine. However, if prefer to use another search provider or just want to have multiple search options, you can configure additional providers.

To add a new search provider, follow these steps:

1. Click the arrow to the right of the search box, and select `Find More Providers` (Figure 8-12).

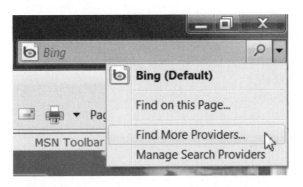

Figure 8-12. Click `Find More Providers` to add search options.

2. This will open Internet Explorer to a page of search providers. When you find one you want to use, click its `Add to Internet Explorer` button (Figure 8-13).

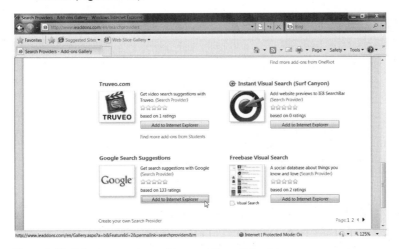

Figure 8-13. Select a search provider, and then click `Add to Internet Explorer`.

3. If you want the new search provider to be your default search option, click `Make this my default search provider`, and then click `Add`. If you only want it to be available as an option, just click `Add` (Figure 8-14).

Add Search Provider ✕

Do you want to add this search provider?

Name: "Google"

From: **www.ieaddons.com**

☐ Make this my default search provider
☑ Use search suggestions from this provider

[Add] [Cancel]

Search provider names can be misleading. Only add search providers from websites you trust.

Figure 8-14. Click `Add` (and optionally, `Make this my default search provider`) to add/replace a search provider.

4. If you set up the new search provider as the default, you'll immediately see its name and logo displayed in the search box, and all future searches will automatically be done via that provider. If you chose not to make the new search provider the default, you can click in the search box (Figure 8-15) or on the arrow to display the logos of all your configured search providers. Just click the one you want to use before entering your search term.

Figure 8-15. Click the search box and then a logo to select a non-default search provider.

AdvancED

When you highlight text on a web page, a blue-and-white arrow icon will appear nearby. This is Internet Explorer 8's accelerators feature, which lets you do things with the highlighted text without having to copy and paste it into another location first. Clicking the icon will display a menu of accelerators, which include conducting a search on the highlighted text, translating it into another language, or, in the case of a street address, showing a map of the location. You can download additional accelerators by visiting http://ieaddons.com/en/accelerators/.

Using Windows Media Player

Windows Media Player is a program to organize and play digital media such as audio and video files. The quickest way to run Windows Media Player is to click its taskbar button (Figure 8-16).

Figure 8-16. You can run Windows Media Player directly from the taskbar.

When you run Windows Media Player, the program starts in the Player Library, as shown in Figure 8-17. From the left pane, you can select the library you want to access (such as Music, Videos, or Pictures) and see the contents of the selected Library displayed in the right pane.

ExplainED

In addition to files stored on your computer, Windows Media Player can also play audio CDs and DVD movies. When you insert one, you'll see it appear in the left pane.

To play an item, highlight it, and then use the playback and volume controls at the bottom of the window (or double-click an item to begin playing it immediately).

257

Figure 8-17. Windows Media Player's Player Library mode lets you browse and play its content.

While Windows Media Player is playing music, click the button in the lower-right corner (the one that's three squares and an arrow) to enter Now Playing mode, a smaller and simplified view optimized for the type of media you're playing. For example, while playing music, Now Playing mode displays only basic playback controls and cover art (if any) for the song (Figure 8-18).

To return to Player Library from Now Playing mode, click the corresponding three boxes and an arrow button.

Figure 8-18. Windows Media Player's simplified Now Playing mode while playing music.

Windows Media Player automatically goes into Now Playing mode when playing video.

Creating a playlist

A **playlist** is a list of items (such as a group of your favorite songs) you can create and save for convenient access.

To create a playlist, follow these steps:

1. Make sure Windows Media Player is in Player Library view, and then click the `Play` tab in the upper-right corner, which will open a new right pane.

    To add an item to the playlist, drag it over to the new pane (Figure 8-19). Your playlist will automatically begin playing as soon as you add the first item; if you don't want to hear anything while building the list, click the `Stop` (square) button in the playback controls.

Figure 8-19. Build a playlist by clicking the `Play` tab and dragging items over to the right pane.

A playlist can consist of any combination of music, video, or pictures.

2. As you add items, the total number of items and total playing time will be shown at the bottom of the list. When you've finished building your playlist, click the `Save list` button, and then type over the `Untitled playlist` label. After your playlist is saved, you'll see it listed in the left pane under the `Playlists` category.

AdvancED

While in the Player Library, Windows Media Player can burn items to CD/DVDs and sync them to certain portable media devices.

Using WordPad

WordPad (Figure 8-20) is Windows 7's built-in word processor program—essentially a "light" version of Microsoft's full-featured Word program. You can find it by searching for *wordpad* from the `Start` menu's search box.

WordPad is easy to use, with a simple interface that provides a basic set of features without overwhelming you with too many options. Although WordPad has some major limitations—it lacks a spell checker and can have only one document open at a time—it can open files created in other word processors, including Microsoft Word 2003 (.doc extension) and the OpenOffice.org word processor (.odt). WordPad can also create and save files in .doc, .odt, and several other formats.

AdvancED

You can also use WordPad to open and save files in Microsoft Word 2007 format (.docx extension), though they may have some missing or incorrectly formatted content. WordPad will display a reminder message when you open or try to save a Word 2007 file.

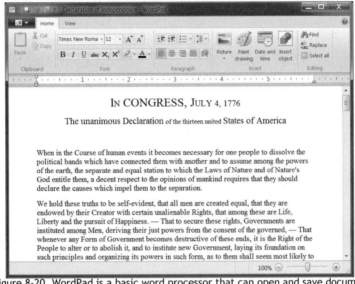

Figure 8-20. WordPad is a basic word processor that can open and save documents created with other word processing programs.

Using Windows Photo Viewer

Although you won't find Windows Photo Viewer in any of Windows 7's menus (nor will it appear in results if you search for it), this is the default program for viewing many kinds of picture files, including JPEG (.jpg) photos created by most of today's digital cameras.

LinkED

For more information about default programs in Windows 7, see "Configuring default programs" later in this chapter.

Whenever you click to open a photo in Windows 7—say from the Pictures Library—it will likely open in Windows Photo Viewer, shown in Figure 8-21. By using the menu options at the top of the program, you can print, e-mail, or burn a photo to a disc, while the controls at the bottom let you zoom, rotate, and delete a photo, as well as display a slide show of all the photos in the folder. (Just place the mouse pointer over a button to see what it does.)

Figure 8-21. Windows Photo Viewer is the default program for opening photos.

Using Windows Fax and Scan

With Windows Fax and Scan, you can use your computer to send and receive faxes, essentially allowing it take the place of a dedicated fax machine. Windows Fax and Scan also lets you to scan printed material such as documents and photos—being able to convert printed material into digital form can help you cut down on paper storage, and it's a good way to preserve old photos taken before the advent of digital cameras.

To run Windows Fax and Scan (Figure 8-22), search for *windows fax* from the `Start` menu, and then run Windows Fax and Scan.

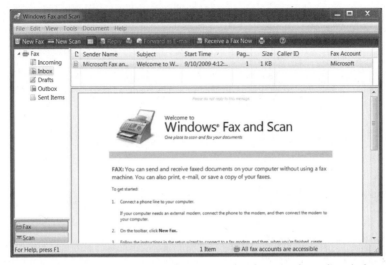

Figure 8-22. Windows Fax and Scan lets you send and receive faxes directly from your computer, as well as scan printed documents into digital form.

To send and receive faxes, your system must be equipped with a fax-capable modem that's connected to your home phone line. (Although rarely used for Internet access anymore, most systems still include a built-in modem.) To scan documents, you'll need either an all-in-one printer with scanning capabilities or a stand-alone scanner.

AdvancED

To send and receive faxes from your computer (or a standard fax machine, for that matter), your home phone service should be delivered by a conventional telephone circuit commonly known as a "land line." If your home phone service is provided via your broadband Internet connection—often referred to as a digital phone or Voice over Internet Protocol (VoIP)—it may not be compatible with fax.

263

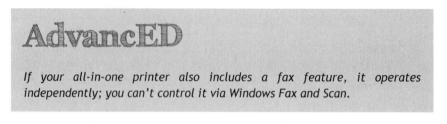

AdvancED

If your all-in-one printer also includes a fax feature, it operates independently; you can't control it via Windows Fax and Scan.

Configuring Windows Fax and Scan

Before you can send or receive faxes in Windows 7, you must configure some initial settings, which you can do by clicking New Fax.

1. The first time you click New Fax, a Fax Setup Wizard will appear (Figure 8-23). Choose Connect to a fax modem.

2. Give your modem a name (or leave the default of Fax Modem in place).

3. Choose how you want Windows 7 to handle incoming calls. You can choose Answer automatically to have the phone picked up after five rings or Notify me to display a message about incoming calls so you can decide whether to pick up.

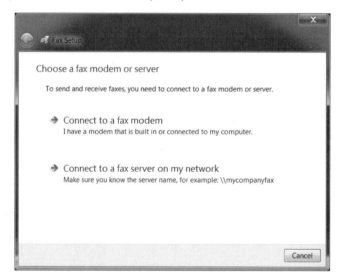

Figure 8-23. Use the Fax Setup Wizard to configure initial settings such as whether you want the computer to pick up incoming calls.

ExplainED

If your computer is connected to the same phone line as an answering machine or you have voice mail service provided by your phone company, you should choose the Notify me *option. Otherwise, your answering machine/voice mail may prevent incoming faxes from reaching your computer, or your computer may prevent messages from reaching your answering machine or voice mail system.*

Sending and receiving faxes

Once you've configured your fax settings, clicking the New Fax button will open a window where you can specify a recipient, select a cover page, and choose a document to send (Figure 8-24).

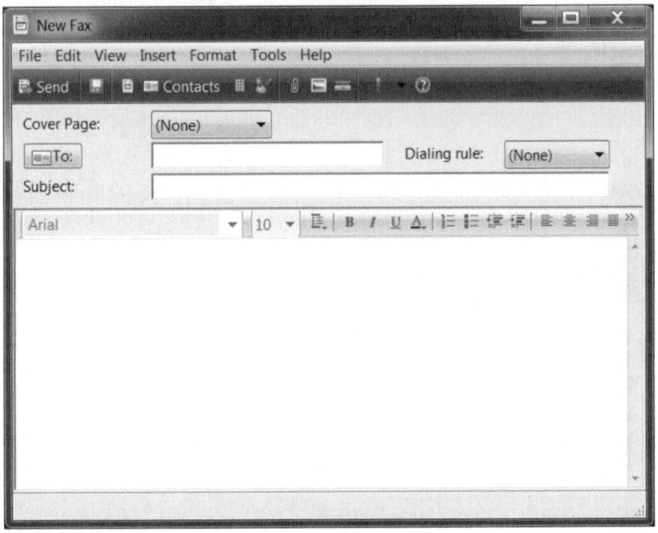

Figure 8-24. Once you've configured fax settings, the New Fax button will open a window for sending a fax.

The first time you send a fax, the program will prompt you for information such as your area code and give you the opportunity to customize a cover page with your own name and fax number.

Windows Fax and Scan will automatically receive faxes if you've selected the `Answer automatically` option described earlier. If not, Windows will display a notification message and automatically start Windows Fax and Scan when it detects an incoming call. Click the `Receive a Fax Now` button while the phone is ringing to accept the fax.

Scanning a document

To scan a document or photo, follow these steps:

1. Click the `New Scan` button. Windows Fax and Scan will take a moment to communicate with your scanner and then display the window shown in Figure 8-25.

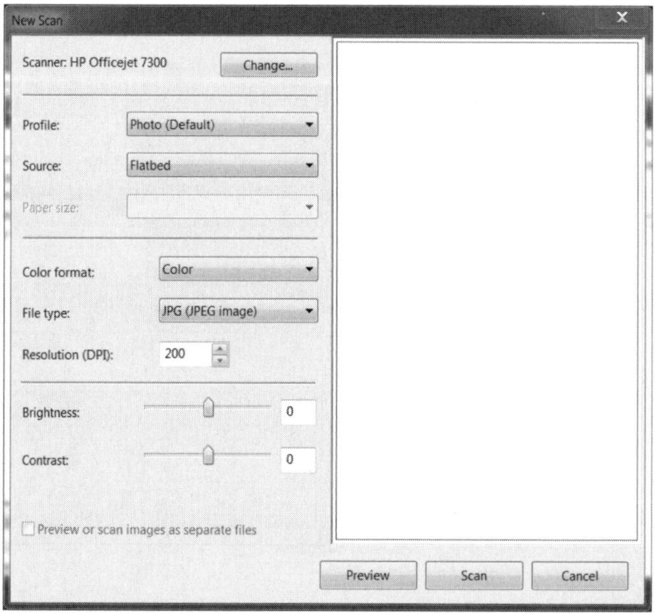

Figure 8-25. The `New Scan` window lets you select scan options and preview your scan in advance.

2. In the `New Scan` window, you can specify settings such as the kind of scan you want to perform (photo or document), the file type you want to save it as, and what resolution you want to use. (Higher resolution means better quality scans, but they take slightly longer to perform and result in larger files.)

AdvancED

The scan options available will depend on the capabilities of your scanner and the type of document you're scanning. For example, if your scanner includes a document feeder, you will be able to select this option under Source, *which in turn will activate the* Paper Size *option.*

3. After you've chosen your scan options (and verified your document or photo is in the scanner), click the Preview button. Within a few seconds, an image of what the scan will look like will appear in the large pane at the right of the New Scan window, as shown in Figure 8-26. You can preview your scan as many times as you want, so feel free to experiment with different settings.

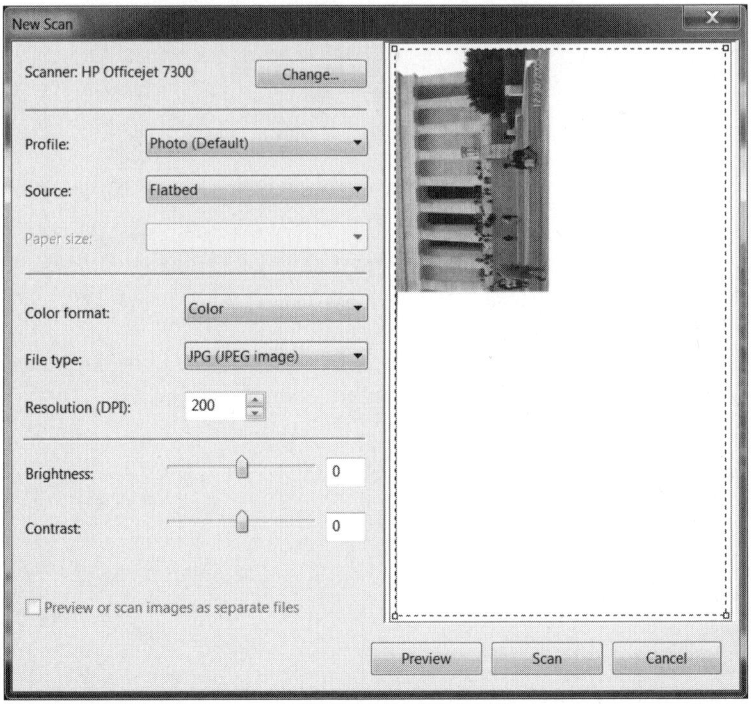

Figure 8-26. You should preview your scan before saving it as a file.

4. If the surface of the scanner is much larger than the item you're scanning, your scan preview will contain a lot of white space (as is the

case with Figure 8-26). To prevent this white space from included in your saved scan, use the mouse to drag one of the four small boxes in the corners of the preview pane so that the dotted line surrounds only the scanned item and not the entire pane.

5. Once you're satisfied with the preview, click the `Scan` button. After your scan is saved (all scans are stored in the Documents folder under Scanned Documents), Windows Fax and Scan will reappear, and you'll see your new scan highlighted in the list with a preview window underneath (Figure 8-27).

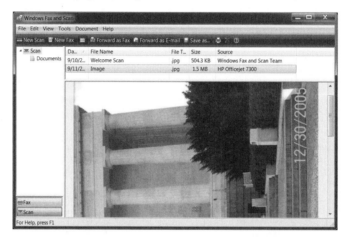

Figure 8-27. After your scan, is complete, you can rename or forward it.

6. To rename the scan from the default of `Image`, right-click anywhere the list entry or the preview image, and choose `Rename`.

7. To save it in another file format, use the `Save as` button, or to send your scan to someone else, use the `Forward as Fax` or `Forward as E-mail` button.

AdvancED

If you don't change a scan's default name, any subsequent scans will be automatically named using incremental numbers, like Image (1), Image (2), and so on.

Using Calculator

When you need to do some quick math, Windows 7's Calculator is always within easy reach and probably offers all the features of the physical calculator buried in your desk drawer.

To open Calculator, just type `Calc` in the `Start` menu's search box. Calculator starts out with a standard no-frills keypad, but by clicking the `View` menu, you can switch the calculator into one of several specialized modes, including a scientific mode handy for high school or college math.

The following are two particularly noteworthy Calculator features new to the Windows 7 version; they are both accessible from the View menu:

- Unit conversion lets you quickly convert Fahrenheit to Celsius, miles to kilometers, quarts to liters, and so on.
- Worksheets can calculate mortgage/car lease payments and fuel economy (MPG) figures (Figure 8-28).

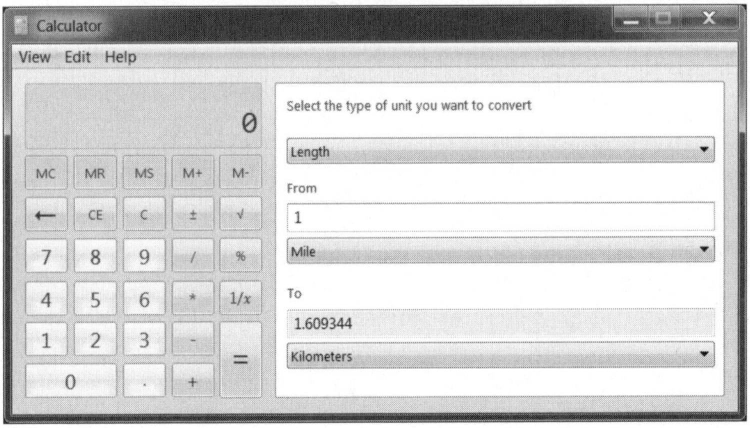

Figure 8-28 Windows 7's built-in calculator can handle simple and complex calculations, as well as unit conversions.

Using Sticky Notes

If you're the type who jots down info or reminders onto scraps of paper, Sticky Notes may be for you. To run it, type `Sticky` in the `Start` menu's search box. Then you can type directly onto a note on the Windows desktop (Figure 8-29) and right-click a note to change its color. Your notes are saved when you close the Sticky Notes program.

Figure 8-29. The Sticky Notes program is good for jotting down quick information or reminders.

ExplainED

If the notes are obscured by open windows, you can hover the mouse over the program's taskbar button and then over the preview window to make them visible. You can also search for information saved in Sticky Notes from the Start *menu.*

LinkED

For more information on previewing windows via the taskbar, see Chapter 1.

Exploring the Windows Media Center

Like Windows Media Player, Windows Media Center (which comes with all Windows 7 versions except Starter) can be used to browse and view digital media stored on your computer (such as audio, video, and pictures) or to play back content stored on a disc, such as audio CDs or DVD movies.

Unlike Windows Media Player, however, Windows Media Center features a special interface (Figure 8-30) that's similar to the kind found on your TV set-top box and is designed for use with a remote control (though you can also use a mouse).

When a system is equipped with the proper hardware, such as a TV tuner card, you can use Windows Media Center to view and record live television programming.

To run Windows Media Center, search for and run Windows Media Center from the `Start` menu. Depending on your hardware, you may see warning messages the first time you run Windows Media Center, and you will need to go through a setup wizard before you see the screen shown in Figure 8-30.

Figure 8-30. Windows Media Center uses a set-top-box-style interface best accessed via a remote control.

AdvancED

Some Windows 7 systems include the hardware—TV tuner and remote control—necessary to take full advantage of Windows Media Center. These are commonly referred to as Media Center PCs.

LinkED

For a detailed online tour of Windows Media Center's features, visit www.microsoft.com/windows/products/winfamily/mediacenter/demos/windowsmediacenterdemo/default.html.

Using gadgets

Gadgets are miniature programs that run directly on the Windows 7 desktop and that allow you to obtain information and perform tasks without having to take the time to visit a website or run a conventional piece of software. For example, you might use a gadget to monitor the local weather, sports scores, or news headlines. You can also use gadgets to perform tasks such as monitoring the status of your computer

To use gadgets, right-click any open area on the desktop, and then choose `Gadgets`. (Figure 8-31).

Figure 8-31. To use Windows 7 gadgets, right-click a free area of the desktop, and choose `Gadgets`.

This will open the Desktop Gadget Gallery (Figure 8-32). If you want more information about what the gadgets do, click `Show details`. As you can see, there aren't many gadgets included with Windows 7, but you can browse and download many more (for free) by clicking the `Get more gadgets online` link in the lower-right corner of the gallery.

Figure 8-32. Windows 7 ships with a handful of gadgets out of the box, and you can go online to find more.

To make a gadget appear on your desktop, double-click it, and then use the mouse to drag each gadget into the exact position you want. When you put the mouse pointer over a gadget, a small toolbar will appear letting you enlarge or close the gadget. You can also right-click a gadget to configure various gadget options (Figure 8-33), including opacity, which makes gadgets transparent so you can see what's beneath them.

Figure 8-33. Here you see five desktop gadgets—Calendar, Clock, CPU Meter, Currency, and Weather—and the options available when right-clicking one.

LinkED

The `Show desktop` *feature described in Chapter 1 can come in handy when your gadgets out of view because of open windows. Placing the mouse pointer over the* `Show desktop` *button at the extreme right edge of the taskbar will make all your gadgets visible.*

Finding games to play

For those times you'd rather play than be productive, Windows 7 includes a group of ten games including checkers, chess, backgammon, and various card games (including several you can play against people from around the world via the Internet). To access the Windows 7 games, click the `Start` button, and then choose `Games` from the right side of the `Start` menu to open Games Explorer (Figure 8-34).

The first time you visit the games folder, Windows 7 will ask you whether you want to use the recommended update and folder settings, which will automatically download game updates, artwork, and other information as well as save information about recently played games.

Figure 8-34. You can find all of Windows 7's built-in games in the Games Explorer folder.

LinkED

Remember that by turning on Parental Controls, you can block access to games for certain accounts. For more on Parental Controls, see Chapter 2.

LinkED

If you click the More Games from Microsoft *link, you'll be taken to Microsoft's game website where you find other games to sample or purchase.*

Exploring Windows Live Essentials

Windows Live Essentials is a group of programs from Microsoft—free and available for download—that provides added capabilities not offered by the programs included with Windows 7.

Windows Live Essentials consists of the following programs:

- **Messenger:** Messenger is an instant-messaging program you can use to communicate, play games, and exchange files with others.
- **Mail:** Mail is an e-mail program that works with accounts from popular web-based mail providers such as Google, Microsoft, and Yahoo! or an e-mail account provided by an Internet service provider (ISP), such as Comcast, Time Warner, Verizon, and so on. Mail can manage multiple accounts and includes a built-in calendar.
- **Writer:** Not to be confused with WordPad, Writer is a tool used to compose, format, and post blog entries. (A **blog** is a kind of online journal.)
- **Photo Gallery:** Photo Gallery offers a way to transfer photos to the computer from a digital camera, organize and edit them, and then share them with others by posting snapshots to an online album.
- **Movie Maker:** Movie Maker is a video-editing tool you can use to trim home movies and apply things such as titles, background music, or transitions and effects.

- **Family Safety**: A complement to the parental control features included with Windows 7, Family Safety allows you monitor a child's online activity (not just their use of the computer) and block access to certain websites or Internet services.
- **Toolbar**: This is an Internet Explorer toolbar that provides convenient access to Microsoft's Bing search engine as well as various Windows Live services.

Getting Windows Live Essentials

To download Windows Live Essentials, follow these steps:

1. Search for `Windows Live Essentials` from the `Start` menu's search box.

2. Select `Go online to get Windows Live Essentials.` This will open Internet Explorer to the Windows Live Essentials download page (Figure 8-35).

LinkED

You can also reach the Windows Live Essentials download page by typing `download.live.com` *directly into Internet Explorer.*

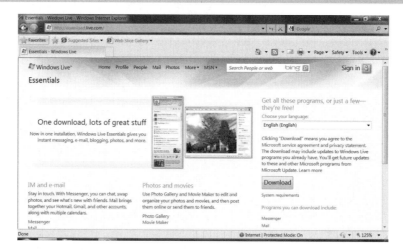

Figure 8-35 The Windows Live Essentials download page.

3. Click the Download button on the http://download.live.com web page, and then choose Run to launch the installation wizard. (Before installing the software, the wizard will let you deselect any individual Windows Live Essentials components you don't want.)

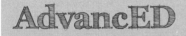

Several of the Windows Live Essentials programs require a Windows Live ID to use certain features. After installing the software, the wizard will give you the opportunity to sign up for one.

Configuring default programs

In Windows 7, a default program is one that's automatically used in conjunction with a particular task (such as accessing a web page) or to open a specific type of file. For example, when you first install Windows 7, the default program to visit a website is Internet Explorer, and the default program to open a .jpg image file is Windows Photo Viewer.

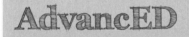

*The default program for a particular kind of file is considered to be **associated** with that file type.*

Over time, however, the default program for a task or file can change. This usually results from installing a new program that does the same thing or opens the same kinds of files as a program that comes with Windows 7 or another program you already have. For example, you may install a new web browser such as Mozilla Firefox or Google Chrome or another program that can view photos like Windows Photo Viewer or play audio and video like Windows Media Player.

When you install a new program, you usually have the chance to specify which file types it will open or configure it to automatically open all the file types it supports (often the default option). But sometimes programs don't give you the choice—or at least don't make your options clear during the installation process—and you may wind up with a situation where the default program for a task or file is no longer the one you want.

Windows 7 lets you view and modify default programs and file associations so that if a default program changes unexpectedly—or even if you change one knowingly and then change your mind later—you can still decide which programs are used to perform tasks and open files.

Choosing default programs

To make a program a default so that it's automatically used for all tasks and file types it supports, follow these steps:

1. Click the `Start` button, and then click `Default Programs` on the right side of the `Start` menu to display the window shown in Figure 8-36.

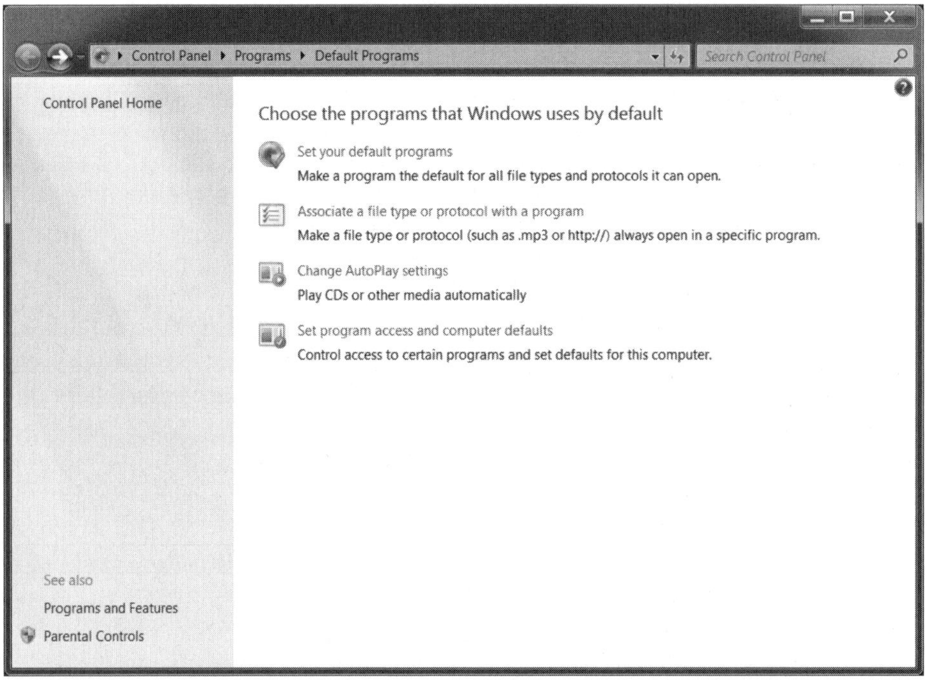

Figure 8-36. Windows 7 lets you control which programs are used to perform certain tasks or open specific files types.

2. Now click `Set your default programs`, and a new window will appear listing major programs installed on your system (Figure 8-37).

3. Highlight the program you want, and then click `Set this program as defaultSet this program as default`. (After setting a program as default, the message under the program description will change from `This program has x out of x defaults` to `This program has all its defaults`).

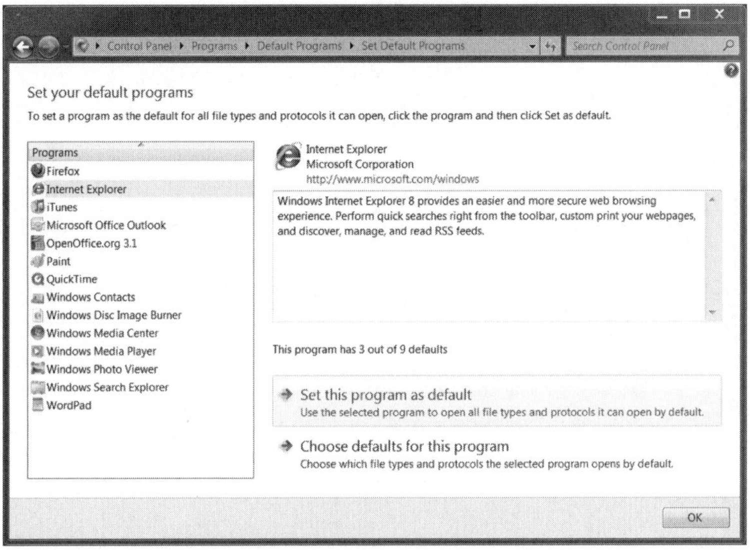

Figure 8-37. Select a program, and click `Set this program as default` to ensure it's automatically used for all supported tasks or file types.

ExplainED

Making Internet Explorer a default program as we've done in Figure 8-37 means it will automatically be used to open web pages even though there may be another web browser installed on the system.

Configuring file associations

If you don't want to make a program the default for all file types and would rather configure it to open one or more specific file types, after selecting the program in the `Set your default programs` window, click `Choose defaults for this program`. From the `Set Program Associations` window, you'll be able to view a list of all the file types the program is capable of opening (Figure 8-38). Make sure there's a check mark next to the file types you want the program to open, and then click `Save`.

Figure 8-38. You can view and individually configure the file types associated with a particular program.

AdvancED

To view or modify a comprehensive list of all the file associations on your system, instead of using the `Set your default programs` option, use the one labeled `Associate a file type or protocol with a program`.

Opening a file with a non-default program

Although double-clicking a file will automatically open it with the default program for that file type, you always have the option to choose which program you want to use to open a file.

To open a file using a program other than the default for its file type, right-click the file and select `Open with`. You'll see a menu of programs you can choose from (including the default program) that are capable of opening the file (Figure 8-39).

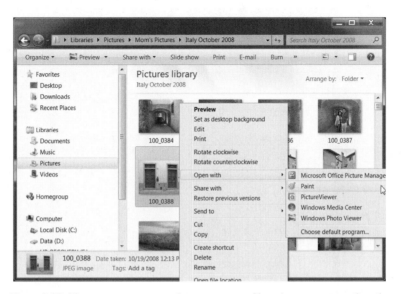

Figure 8-39. The `Open with` menu lets you open a file using a program other than the default.

AdvancED

Choosing a program from the `Open with` *menu will open the file in the selected program on time only without altering file type's default program. However, if you select the* `Open with` *menu's* `Choose default program` *option, you'll see all the* `Open with` *programs listed under a* `Recommended Programs` *heading. Double-clicking one of the recommended programs will make it the new default for the file type.*

Changing AutoPlay settings

AutoPlay is a Windows 7 feature that automatically runs a specific program or performs a certain task (or asks you what to do) based on the content found when you insert or connect media such as a DVD or other storage device. Figure

8-40 shows what AutoPlay might look like when inserting a music CD. (The options you see will differ depending on what software is installed on your computer.)

Figure 8-40. If you haven't chosen a default action/program, AutoPlay will ask you what to do when you insert or connect various kinds of media.

Just as you can tell Windows 7 which program to use when you open a certain kind of file, you can also tell AutoPlay what to do when you pop in something like a DVD movie, an audio CD, or a flash memory drive filled with photos or home videos.

To change AutoPlay settings, click `Change AutoPlay settings` from the `Default Programs` window to display the window shown in Figure 8-41.

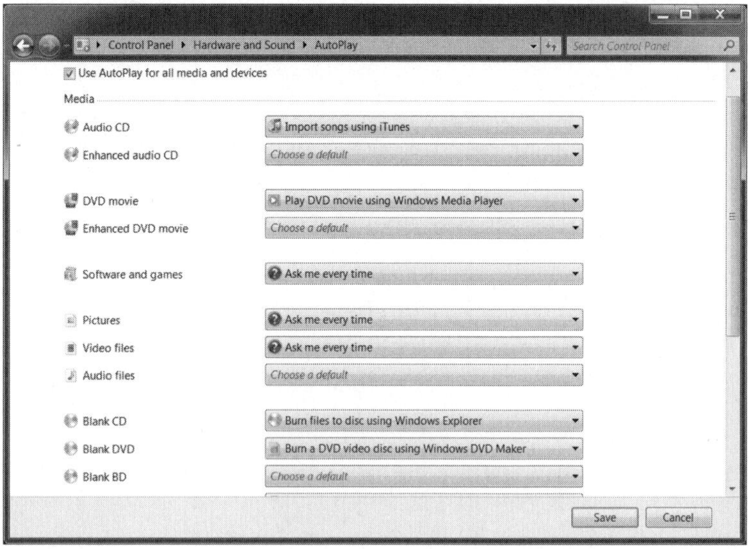

Figure 8-41. AutoPlay lets you decide what happens when you use different kinds of media or storage devices.

Now find the type of media or storage device you want to configure, and use the adjacent drop-down menu to choose an action. For example, you can set AutoPlay to automatically play a DVD movie using Windows Media Player or use another movie player program you have.

The actions available for each media or device type will depend on what programs you've installed and what their capabilities are. For example, if you have a third-party disc-burning utility installed, you'll see it as an option in the menus for `Blank CD` and `Blank DVD`.

Installing programs

When you install new software onto your computer, the software usually comes from one of two forms—a store-bought disc or a file that was downloaded from a website (though these days, it's more likely than not to be the latter).

When you click a link to download a program from the Web, you'll typically see a message giving you the option to either run or save the installer file (Figure 8-42).

File Download - Security Warning

Do you want to run or save this file?

> Name: WeatherBugSetup.msi
>
> Type: Windows Installer Package, 5.42MB
>
> From: **wdownload.weatherbug.com**

[Run]   [Save]   [Cancel]

While files from the Internet can be useful, this file type can potentially harm your computer. If you do not trust the source, do not run or save this software. What's the risk?

Figure 8-42. When downloading a program from the Internet, you usually have the choice to run the file or save it first.

Choosing the `Run` option will automatically run the file as soon as it's finished downloading, while the `Save` option will save a copy to your Downloads folder where you must run it manually (by double-clicking it). Note you must have access to an administrator account to install software.

ExplainED

You can find your Downloads folder in your account folder, which you can access by clicking your account name in the upper right of the `Start` *menu.*

A program's install process will be the same whether you run the file directly or save it to your Downloads folder before running it. (Most let you select an install location, choose program options, and so on.) The benefit of the latter method is that saving a copy of the file makes it more convenient to install the software on multiple computers or reinstall the software. (In either case, you won't need to visit the website again to re-download the file.)

LinkED

To have Windows 7 automatically run the installation wizard when you insert a software disc, visit the AutoPlay settings described earlier in this chapter, and make sure `Software and Games` *is set to* `Install or run program from your media.`

To make them easier to find, recently installed programs will appear highlighted in the `Start` menu, as shown in Figure 8-43.

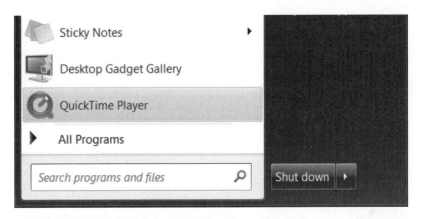

Figure 8-43. The highlighting of QuickTime Player in the `Start` menu indicates it's a recently installed program.

Uninstalling programs

If you install a program and later decide that you don't need it, it's a good idea to uninstall it from your computer. This will ensure you don't have unneeded programs running in the background (consuming system resources) as well as free up storage space by removing the program from the hard disk.

To uninstall a program in Windows 7, follow these steps:

1. Click the `Start` button, and then search for `programs and features and run it` to display the window shown in Figure 8-44.

285

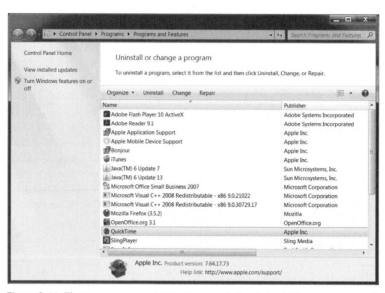

Figure 8-44. The `Programs and Features` window lists all the programs you've installed. (The list you see will differ somewhat from the one shown here.)

2.   Next, highlight the program you want to remove.

3.   Click the `Uninstall` button that appears at the top of the list of programs.

4.   A confirmation window will appear asking whether you're sure you want to uninstall the program; click `Yes`, and the program will be removed.

ExplainED

In some cases after confirming you want to uninstall a program, you may see another window—this one from User Account Control—confirming you want to remove the program or asking for an administrator password. You may also sometimes be prompted to restart the system to complete the uninstall process.

ExplainED

Some programs will offer a Change *option, which can be used to remove specific program components or features without uninstalling the entire program or to add features that were not selected when the program was first installed.*

LinkED

If an installed program is not working properly, choosing the Repair *option, which checks the program and reinstalls any damaged or missing files. This can often fix the problem. If there's no* Repair *button shown when you highlight a particular program, click the* Change *button instead. This will launch the program's installation wizard, which will usually offer the option to repair the program. For more information on using the uninstaller to fix problems with programs, see Chapter 5.*

Turning off Windows 7 programs

Windows 7 gives you the flexibility to turn off specific operating system features along with several of its major built-in programs like Internet Explorer, Windows Media Center, or games. This can be handy if you don't need these programs—usually because you prefer to use a third-party program for a particular purpose, such as browsing the Web with Mozilla Firefox instead of Internet Explorer 8.

You don't have to turn off programs or features just because you're not using them, but doing so will remove them from menus (and search results) so they're no longer available to any system user.

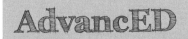

AdvancED

Turning off Windows 7 programs requires administrator account access.

To turn off Windows 7 programs, follow these steps:

1. Type `Windows features` into the `Start` menu search box, and choose `Turn Windows Features` on or off to display the window shown in Figure 8-45. (Note: We've lengthened the window and expanded several of the items to provide a better view of some of the options available.)

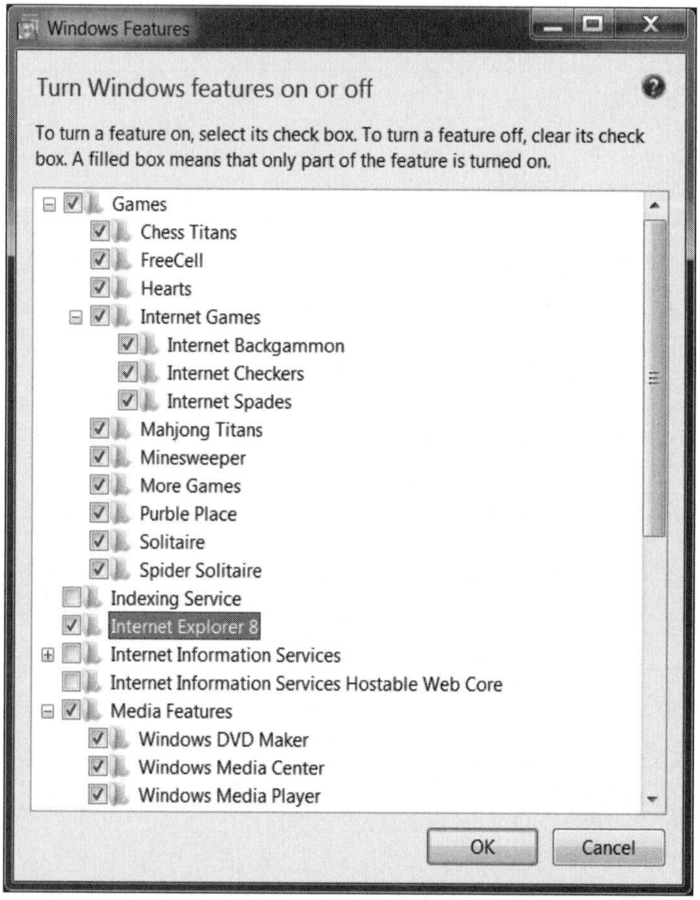

Figure 8-45. Windows 7 lets you turn off many built-in programs and features.

2. To turn off an item, click to remove the check mark next to it in the list. When selecting certain items, you may see a warning indicating that turning off the item may affect other features or programs or may require deactivating another program or feature that's dependent on the one you're turning off. If so, you'll be asked to confirm that you want to continue, and see a `Go Online to learn more` link to click for more information on the ramifications of turning the item off.

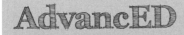

Turned off items are not deleted from the hard drive, so you can add them back at any time without having to provide your Windows 7 installation disc.

3. After selecting items to turn off, click `OK`. Windows 7 will make the changes and in some cases prompt you to restart the system in order for the changes to take effect.

Just as you can use the process described here to turn off features and programs, you can also use it to activate features or programs you (or your system manufacturer) chose not to include when installing Windows 7. Many of the features listed are technical in nature, however, so if an item is turned off by default, be sure you know what it does and that you need it before turning it on.

Summary

- Here's a review of what you've learned in this chapter:
- How to use the following programs:
  - Internet Explorer
  - Windows Media Player/Windows Media Center
  - WordPad
  - Windows Photo Viewer
  - Windows Fax and Scan
  - Calculator
  - Sticky Notes
  - Games
  - Windows gadgets

- How to download Windows Live Essentials
- How to add and remove programs
- How to configure default programs to open supported file types automatically
- How to associate programs with particular file types
- How to open a file in a non-default program
- How to configure AutoPlay to automatically run a program and perform a task when you connect or insert storage media
- How to turn off Windows 7 features

Chapter 9

Safeguarding Your Computer

This probably isn't the first chapter you wanted to read. You didn't buy a computer so that you could fiddle with security settings. You want to get to work or play with the fun stuff. But hackers aren't resting. They're already hard at work—attacking your computer. Don't worry, you can have fun and keep your computer safe at the same time.

There is no bullet-proof protection that can guarantee no harm comes to your computer or your data. But there's a lot you can do with Windows 7 and with how you use your computer and programs to minimize the risks. In this chapter, we'll cover how to use Windows 7 to protect your computer now and what you should do to keep it safe tomorrow:

- Setting up your computer for protection from logon to logoff
- Checking the security status of your computer
- Adjusting Automatic Update and Windows Firewall settings
- Obtaining and using virus protection and antispyware
- Surfing the Internet and exchanging e-mail safely

Setting up your computer for protection from logon to logoff

Windows 7 provides features and programs to protect you and your data from the moment you log on to your computer to the time you shut down the computer.

You need security protection the moment you turn on your computer. One of the first threats to your computer is unauthorized people with physical access to your computer. You don't want them to be able to log on to your computer and get to its contents. There are ongoing threats to your computer such as physical damage, loss, theft, and of course viruses. You can take some of the sting out of these threats by preparing for the worst with a disaster recovery plan that includes thorough and consistent backups. So, before covering the Windows 7 security features, we'll cover two other Windows 7 features that you should use hand in hand with Windows security: user accounts and Windows Backup. When you use these features together, you can't quite "set it and forget it." But most of these features require only a few one-time setup steps, such as setting up a schedule to perform a given task daily or weekly.

Every person using your computer should have a user account, and every user account should have a password

When you start your computer, even if you are the only person who uses the computer, you need to set up Windows to require that you log on with a name and password. If more than one person uses the computer, each person must have a username and password. A user account ensures that each person authorized to use your computer has their own settings, libraries, and preferences. In addition, requiring a user account and password restricts who has access to any information on your computer.

ExplainED

User accounts also provide a way of specifying what level of changes the user can make to the computer. The highest level of permissions is administrator. An administrator can add or remove programs, change Windows settings, and set the permission levels of users. Most users should be assigned standard accounts to prevent them from making changes that could affect other users on your computer.

LinkED

You'll find all the information you need to add user accounts and passwords in Chapter 2.

Adjust User Account Control to an appropriate level

User Account Control (UAC) controls how you are notified when you or programs you are using try to make changes to your computer that might put your computer at risk. The purpose of UAC is to warn you when viruses and other malware try to make changes to your computer. When Windows detects a request to make changes to your computer that could be dangerous, UAC can alert you and require that an administrator approve those changes. If you are not an administrator or if you are logged on as a standard user, you will be prompted to provide an administrator username and password.

The default setting for User Account Control is suitable for most people, and you should not need to change it. Some people find these notifications annoying or disruptive and change the UAC settings so that they receive fewer notifications and interruptions. Or, they are using programs that they know are safe, but UAC does not recommend them as safe.

In the `User Account Control Settings` dialog box, you can view the different levels of notification available and the consequences of each level.

To change your User Account Control settings, follow these steps:

1. Click the `Start` button, and in the search box type `User Account Control`. In the list that appears, click `Change User Account Control settings.`

    The `User Account Control Settings` dialog box appears, as shown in Figure 9-1.

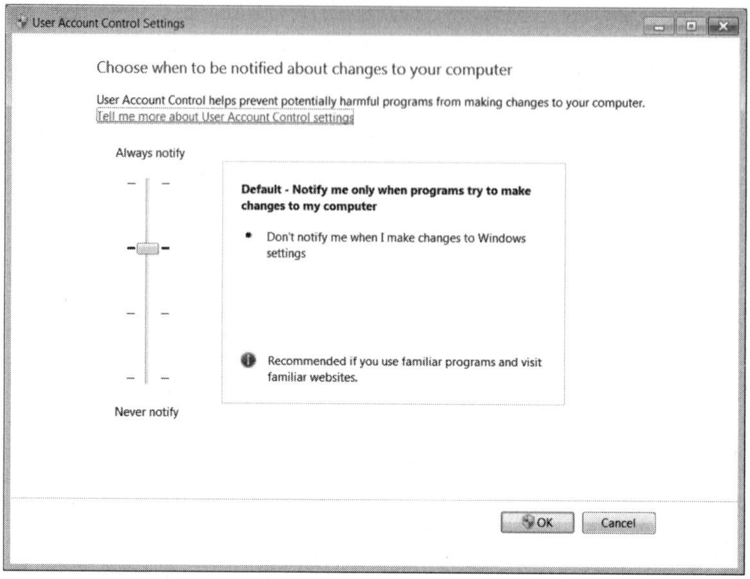

Figure 9-1. For most users, the default setting provides strong protection without being disruptive.

2. Move the slider up or down to view a description of each setting. If you want to learn more about UAC, click the `Tell me more about User Account Control settings` link. This opens a separate help window but does not close the `User Account Control Settings` dialog box.

3. When you are done with the `User Account Control Settings` dialog box, click `OK` if you have selected a different level. Otherwise, if you do not want to make any changes, click `Cancel`.

Creating and using a disaster recovery plan

A **disaster recovery plan** just means that you've already taken steps before disaster strikes to protect your data and programs so that you can restore them to your computer after the disaster. Disaster can strike your computer in many ways:

- **Your computer is lost or stolen**: Your car is broken into, you lose your laptop at the airport, or your home is burglarized.
- **Your computer is damaged by electricity, heat, cold, or water**: A power surge or spike can damage the chips, board, or hard drive in your computer; your computer is left in a car on a very hot day or on a very cold day; or your house is flooded or a water pipe bursts.
- **Your computer's hard drive fails, and you cannot access any of the data on it**: It is not a question of if, but when, your hard drive will fail.
- **Your computer is attacked by a virus, worm, or Trojan horse**: Even with good antivirus protection, some of these still get through to people's computers. Sometimes the only way to fix your computer is wipe everything clean and reinstall Windows and all of your programs.

We hope you don't experience any of these catastrophes, but being prepared can reduce the pain and damage.

ExplainED

To prepare for disaster recovery before you need it, as discussed in Chapter 6, you can take the following measures:

- *Create a system repair disc.*
- *Put your original Windows installation discs (and your product key) in a safe place. If you bought a computer with Windows 7 already installed, your computer may have either a Windows recovery disc or a hidden partition on the hard drive that you can reinstall Windows from. Check the documentation that came with your computer.*
- *Keep the installation discs for any programs you installed in a safe place.*
- *Schedule a weekly backup of your entire computer (system image) using Windows Backup. Back up the data to an external hard drive or storage, not the hard drive on your computer.*

- *If you store most of your information on an external drive already, back up that external drive to another drive or storage.*
- *Perform daily backups of important files, such as documents you are actively working on. For small backups (not the entire computer), you can use data CDs, DVDs, or USB flash drives (sometimes called **memory sticks**, **USB thumb drives**, **USB fingers**, or **pen drives**). A data CD can hold up to 600MB of data, a standard data DVD can hold 4.7GB (8.4GB dual layer), and USB flash drives are available in a wide range of capacities such as 1GB, 2GB, 4GB, 8GB, 16GB, 32GB, and 64GB.*

- *Whenever possible, keep your backups in a different physical location than the computer the data came from. Another alternative to backing up your computer or files to a hard drive or disks is to use an online backup service like Carbonite Online Backup (www.carbonite.com), IDrive Online Backup (www.idrive.com), or Mozy Online Backup (www.mozy.com), to name a few.*

AdvancED

For most people, Windows Backup provides all you need for complete protection of your computer and data. However, many other backup and recovery programs are available that provide enhanced features such as more advanced schedule options. You can buy another backup program separately. If you buy an external hard drive or storage for backing up your computer, it may come bundled with its own built-in backup software.

It is not as important what backup and recovery program you use as it is that you actually use it.

Security features that protect your computer

Setting up user accounts and setting up a backup plan are vital to the overall health and security of your computer. But once you are logged onto your computer, you need protection against threats from outside your computer. The Internet is the host of all sorts of threats, such as viruses, spyware, hackers, phishing, and spam. Fortunately, Windows and other programs can protect you against all of these.

The following tools and features are the basis for your protection:

- **Action Center** provides the status of your current security settings and notifies you if there is a security issue that needs attention. Third-party Internet security suite programs often provide their own security center page that lists the overall security status of your computer and any issues that need attention.
- **Windows Firewall** blocks unauthorized access to your computer by other computers on the Internet. Windows 7 comes with the Windows Firewall built in and already on the first time you start your computer. You need and can use only one firewall on your computer. Many third-party Internet security suites provide their own firewall program as well.
- **Windows Update** downloads and installs the latest Windows patches and security fixes.
- **Virus protection** scans your computer, downloaded files, and e-mail attachments for viruses and dangerous file types and blocks or removes them. Microsoft does not provide virus protection software; you must obtain it from a third party. You can use only one virus protection program on your computer. If you want to use a different program, you must uninstall your old one first.
- **Spyware protection** detects and removes programs that may be collecting personal information and programs that hijack your Internet search and home pages. Windows 7 includes Windows Defender, but Internet security suites often include their own spyware protection. You can install and use more than one spyware protection program on your computer.
- **E-mail filtering of dangerous attachments, junk mail, phishing, and spam** is not a feature of Windows itself but is usually provided by your e-mail program or provider. Some Internet security suites also include filtering or scanning of e-mail messages and attachments when you try to view or open them on your computer.

- **Browser security settings** in Internet Explorer, Mozilla Firefox, and most other browsers provide their own security settings and features. These features include managing cookies, blocking pop-ups, and blocking dangerous code on web pages.

AdvancED

Windows 7 includes its own firewall, Windows Firewall, and its own spyware protection program, Windows Defender. It does not provide virus protection software, so you must obtain a third-party virus protection software program. Some companies offer a virus protection program by itself or as part of an Internet security suite. Security suites usually include their own firewall that replaces Windows Firewall, spyware protection, and their own security center page that tells you at a glance what the status is of your system. See "Getting virus protection software" later in this chapter for more information, including how to get this software for free or low cost.

Checking the security status of your computer

You can check your security status in several ways. You can wait until Windows detects something wrong and displays a notification, or you can check it yourself any time.

If you wait, when you start your computer, you may see a notification pop-up similar to the one displayed in Figure 9-2.

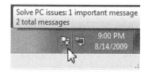

Figure 9-2. The red and white *x* on the notification flag tells you there is an important message in the Action Center.

The message in Figure 9-2 is a general message that doesn't tell you specifically that there is a security issue. Or you might see a more specific message like Figure 9-3 or Figure 9-4.

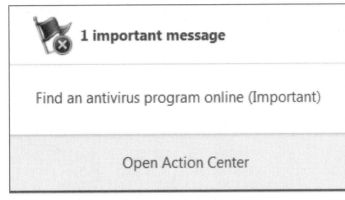

Figure 9-3. A notification appears if you do not have an antivirus program installed.

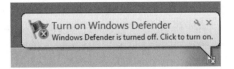

Figure 9-4. A notification may appear if a security feature is turned off.

Whether or not you see one of these notifications, you should check to see what the status is of your security settings.

To check your security status, follow these steps:

1. Right-click the notification icon in the taskbar, and then click Open Action Center.

2. Alternatively, click the Start button, and in the search box type Security status. In the list that appears, click Check security status.

3. The Action Center appears. It may indicate that there are security issues that need addressing, as shown in Figure 9-5. Or, if everything is OK, it may list the current status of your security features, as shown in Figure 9-6. Figure 9-6 also illustrates how Windows will report the status of security features even if they are not provided by Microsoft or Windows. McAfee Security is an optional program you can buy.

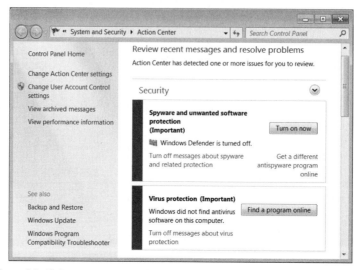

Figure 9-5. If there are any security issues that need attention, they will be listed in the Action Center.

Figure 9-6. All the necessary security features are set to the proper safety levels and settings. Third-party security programs may be included in the security status.

ExplainED

If you have installed third-party protection software, such as an Internet security suite that contains its own spyware protection or firewall, those will be listed. In Figure 9-6, a McAfee security suite has been installed and is providing the virus and spyware protection. McAfee Security is one of many products that you can buy for protection. McAfee Security is not provided by Windows or Microsoft.

Fixing security issues

The two most likely security issues you may see when you start your new computer are that you need to obtain or turn on virus protection and that you have no spyware protection because Windows Defender is turned off. During setup of your computer, you are asked to turn on Windows Update. If you did not turn it on then, it will also show up as a security issue. Your firewall should always be on. It is really rare for a person to turn off the firewall by accident or on purpose. If you are installing a program that requests that you turn off or open the firewall, Windows may warn you and discourage you from doing it. If the software is from a legitimate company, visit its website, and check its support pages to see whether the company provides more information about issues you may encounter with Windows blocking firewall changes. You may also want to check Microsoft's support site to see whether it has any information about this issue. Go to www.support.microsoft.com, and search for articles about this particular product. If you are not sure that the program or its request to open the firewall is safe, do not do it.

If your security status shows several issues, which one do you fix first, and which ones can you put off until later? The short answer is fix all of them as soon as you can. Virus protection is the only issue that may require that you purchase additional software that is not already available on your computer.

Adjusting Windows Update

Microsoft is constantly improving Windows to make your computer more secure and to fix bugs. You don't have to wait for a service pack or the next version of Windows to get these improvements. Microsoft makes them available on an ongoing basis through Windows Update. With Windows Update you can set up your computer to automatically download and install new updates whenever they are available. Or you can choose to download the updates automatically, and Windows will wait for you to install them.

Important and optional updates

Windows Update classifies the updates as Important or Optional:

- **Important** updates are usually to fix security problems or to fix other issues in Windows that could disrupt programs, cause loss of data, or prevent programs from working correctly. If an update is classified, you should install it. Oftentimes, viruses and other harmful programs get on computers because the user did not install an update that would have prevented it.

- **Optional** updates can be things such as noncritical updates to Windows or Microsoft programs you use on your computer, updated drivers for devices attached to your computer, and language packs that help Windows display the characters and symbols of a specific language on your computer, to name a few examples. If an update is optional, you might skip it if it pertains to a program, feature, or device that you don't really use and you don't want to tie your computer up with running the download and installation. For example, you may be notified that 35 new language packs are available for Windows. If you do not browse websites or receive mail or documents in languages other than the one you currently use on your computer, you may not want or need to install other language packs.

Setting Windows Update to automatically install updates

Most of the time, Windows can install the updates in the background and not disrupt you while you are using your computer. But the inconvenience, if any, cannot compare to having a computer disabled by a virus or security vulnerability.

To set Windows Update to automatically install updates, follow these steps:

1. Click the `Start` button, and in the search box type `Windows Update`. In the list that appears, click `Windows Update`.

2. In the left column of the `Windows Update` window, click `Change settings`.

   The `Change settings` window appears, as shown in Figure 9-7.

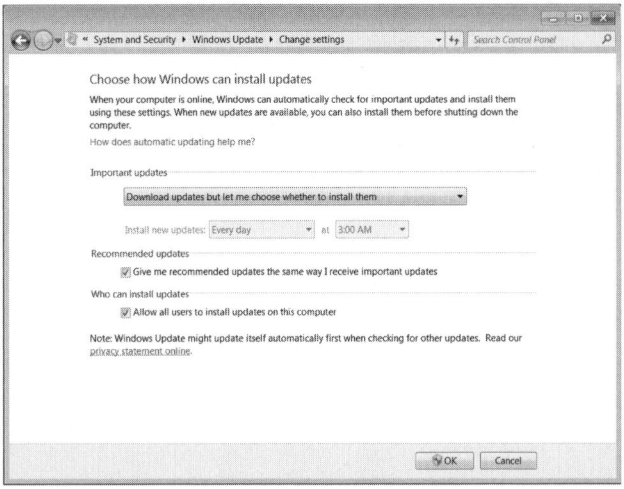

Figure 9-7. The `Change settings` window allows you to change how to handle downloading and installing updates.

3. Click the drop-down list under `Important updates`, and then select `Install updates automatically (recommended)`, as shown in Figure 9-8.

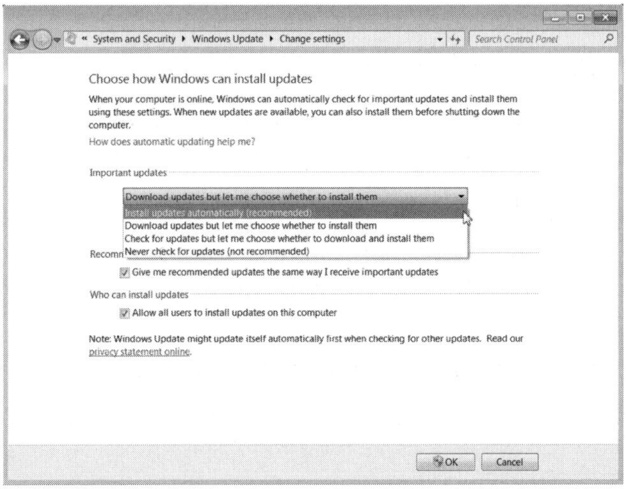

Figure 9-8. With `Install updates automatically`, you don't have to remember to check for updates, download them, and install them. Windows can do that for you.

4. If desired, set how often you want Windows to install updates and at what time, as shown in Figure 9-9.

Figure 9-9. When you choose `Install updates automatically (recommended)`, you can specify how often and at what time to install new updates. Note the green shield with a check mark, indicating that this is an approved safe setting.

If your computer is not on at the scheduled time, Windows will install the updates the next time your computer is on.

ExplainED

How often have you read about a virus or Trojan that is expected to hit computers tomorrow? How do they know this, and why didn't they stop it? Often Microsoft or the virus protection software already fixed it, and the fix was included in a Windows update (or the virus protection software company's updates). But the computer attackers know that a percentage of the computer users do not install updates. That's what the attackers are counting on.

Checking for new updates available for download or installation

If you do not have automatic updates turned on, you should check at least once a week to see whether any new updates are available. As a reminder, you can set up a Windows notification to tell you when new updates are available.

To turn on Windows Update notifications in the notification area, follow these steps:

1. Right-click in the notification area at the bottom right of the desktop, and click `Customize notification icons`, as shown in Figure 9-10.

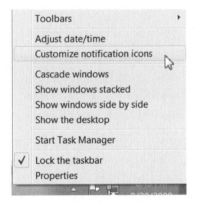

Figure 9-10. You can customize a notification to let you know when new Windows updates are available.

2. In the `Notification Area Icons` window, scroll down to `Windows Update`, and click the down arrow to view the options available, as shown in Figure 9-11.

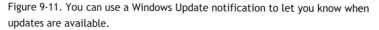

Figure 9-11. You can use a Windows Update notification to let you know when updates are available.

3. Choose how you want Windows Update notifications displayed.

If you choose `Only show notifications`, the Windows Update icon will be displayed in the notification area only when there are new updates available. A `New updates are available` notification will pop up when there are updates available, similar to Figure 9-12.

Figure 9-12. The Windows Update icon is the icon to the left of the flag icon.

If you select `Show icon and notifications`, the Window Update icon will always be displayed in the notification area, like the first icon shown to the right of the up arrow in Figure 9-13. When an update is available, a `New updates are available` notification will pop up, as shown in Figure 9-12.

Figure 9-13. With `Show icon and notifications`, the Window Update icon is the same as what is shown in `Only show notifications`, but the icon doesn't go away when the notification is gone.

4. Click `OK`.

To install updates that have already been downloaded, follow these steps:

1. If you don't know if there are updates available because you have turned off Windows Update notifications, click the `Start` button, and in the search box type `Windows Update`. In the list that appears, click `Windows Update`.

   Alternatively, if you do have notifications on, click the Windows Update icon in the notification area.

   The `Windows Update` window appears, as shown in Figure 9-14.

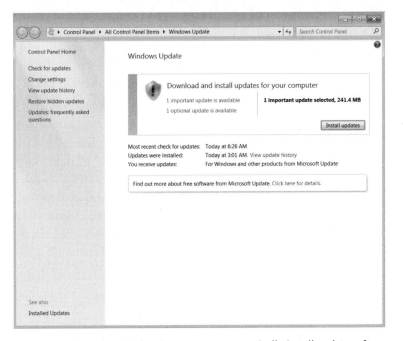

Figure 9-14. If Windows Update is not set to automatically install updates after downloading, you will need to select and install them yourself. Image-0031.tif

2. Click `Install Updates`.

    Alternatively, click the `important update` or `optional update` link to view and select the individual items in the update.

    Sometimes when you select to install the updates, Windows may need to download additional files for the update. Depending on the type of update, you may be prompted to restart your computer. Or, Windows may need to install the files after you choose to shut down your computer. In that case, after you've logged off, the screen may read `Installing update x of x`. Do not turn off your computer yet.

Adjusting Windows Firewall settings

A **firewall** is a barrier that restricts the flow of information in and out of your computer across the Internet or a network. Think of it as a castle wall, meant to keep the enemy from coming in or taking things out.

You should always have Windows Firewall on, unless you are using another firewall from an Internet security suite.

Windows Firewall works by identifying what types of programs and traffic to allow in and out of your computer. If a program attempts an **unsolicited request**—a request that you didn't make or authorize a program to make—Windows Firewall blocks the connection. It then allows you the opportunity to unblock the program. If you unblock it, Windows Firewall creates an exception and won't ask you the next time that particular program requests information from your computer.

You can change whether Windows Firewall is on or off, change what programs are allowed to communicate through the firewall, and open specific ports in the firewall required by a program. If you use several different networks, such as at home and on a public network, you can also customize the firewall settings for each type of connection.

ExplainED

The default settings in Windows Firewall, or the firewalls provided by third-party security suites, will work quite well without you having to make any adjustments. Even though you can turn the firewall on or off and change other settings to allow programs access to your computer, most of the time you should not need to do anything with the firewall. Do not turn off the firewall or change the settings unless instructed to do so by a person or program you trust.

To check the status of the firewall on your computer, follow these steps:

1. Click the `Start` button, and in the search box type `Windows Firewall`. In the list that appears, click `Windows Firewall`.

   The Windows Firewall settings are displayed. There are three types of states for the firewall, as shown in Figures 9-15 to 9-17.

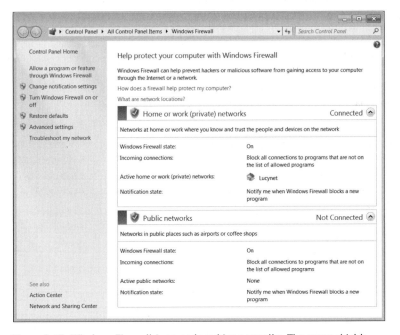

Figure 9-15. Windows Firewall is on and working normally. The green shields indicate that the status of the firewall is good.

309

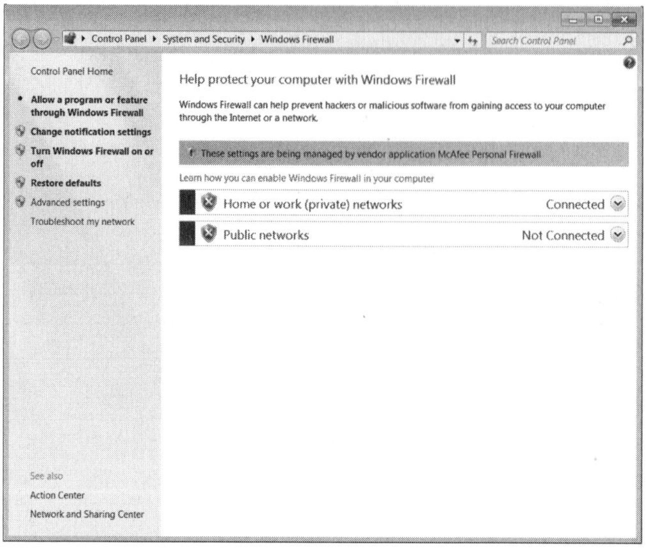

Figure 9-16. Windows Firewall is off, but your computer is using another firewall. The red shields don't mean there is a problem; in this example, it means Windows detects that a firewall from a third party is in use.

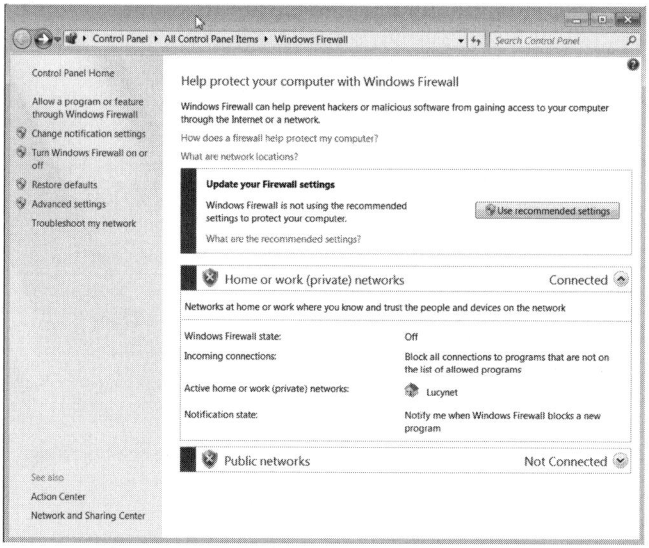

Figure 9-17. Windows Firewall is off, and there is no other firewall on. This is dangerous and should be avoided.

310

Note that if you are using a third-party firewall program, you will need to go through that program to change firewall settings.

To turn Windows Firewall on or off, follow these steps:

1. In the `Windows Firewall` **window, click** `Turn Windows Firewall on or off`. **The** `Customize Settings` **window is displayed, as** shown in Figure 9-18.

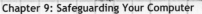

Figure 9-18. Windows Firewall recommended settings are `Turn on Windows Firewall`.

AdvancED

By default, Windows Firewall is on for all network connections. If you use more than one network, Windows Firewall provides separate settings for each type of network. For example, if you use your laptop on a work network, your local coffee shop, or your home network, each of these network locations requires different Windows Firewall settings. Depending on what types of networks Windows detects, your Windows Firewall settings may display separate settings for home networks, work networks, public networks, or domain networks. The settings for a domain network are controlled by a domain network administrator and cannot be changed by the individual from his or her own machine.

Adding or removing programs from the Windows Firewall allowed programs and features list

Windows keeps a list of software programs and Windows features that are allowed through the firewall. There are three common ways programs and features get added to the firewall allowed list:

- **Windows automatically adds it**: When you turn on or enable Windows features such as File and Printer Sharing, HomeGroup, and Remote Desktop, Windows adds them to the allowed list. Since these are part of Windows, they are known to be safe and trustworthy.
- **Windows asks whether you want to unblock a program that is currently blocked by Windows Firewall**: When you install a program that is not part of the operating system, Windows may display a security message notifying you that Windows Firewall is blocking the program or parts of the program and ask whether you want to unblock the program. Some common programs that require access through the firewall include instant message programs such as Windows Live Messenger, Yahoo Messenger, or AOL Messenger; media players such as Windows Media Player; backup programs; and antivirus programs.

- You manually add them to the allowed list: Sometimes Windows automatically blocks a program and does not offer to add it to the allowed list. You can also remove programs from this list and select different settings for a program depending on what type of network you are on. You should add programs to this list on an as-needed basis. When you view the list, you will see many programs listed that are not selected as allowed. Every program allowed through the firewall presents a potential risk, so be careful about adding programs to the allowed list.

To add or remove programs from the allowed programs and features list, follow these steps:

1. Click the `Start` button, and in the search box type `Allow a program`. In the list that appears, click `Allow a program through Windows Firewall`.

   The `Allowed Programs` window is displayed, as shown in Figure 9-19.

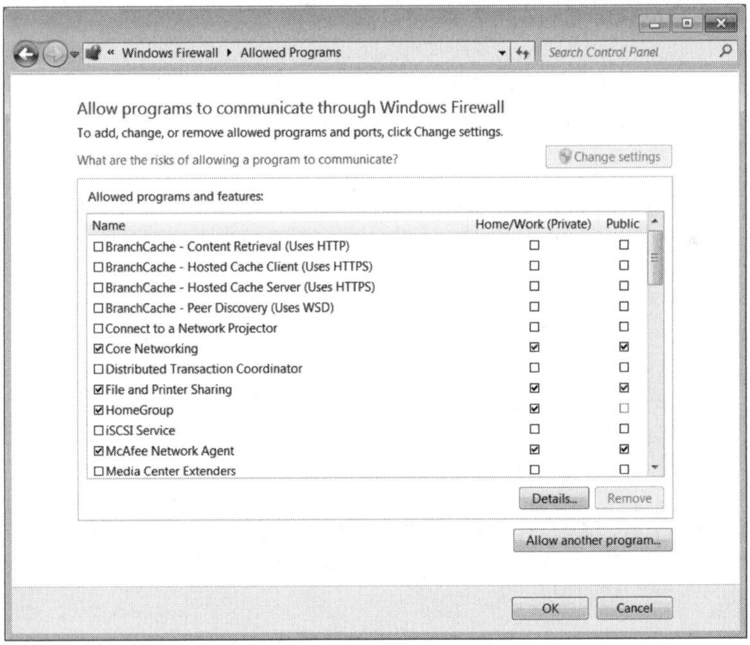

Figure 9-19. The `Allowed Programs` window window displays programs and features and whether they are allowed through the firewall.

If the list items are grayed and you cannot select or clear a check box, that may mean you are using a third-party firewall or your settings are controlled by a network administrator.

2. If the `Change settings` button is not grayed, click the button to see whether that gives you access to the list items. If the `Change settings` button is grayed, then you must use the third-party firewall or security suite program to change these settings or contact your network administrator if you are on a company network. See the documentation or online help provided by the third-party software for instructions.

3. Locate the program or feature you want to change.

    If the program you want to change is not on the list, click `Allow another program`. In the `Add a Program` dialog box, select the program from the list or locate it with the Browse button, and then click `Add`.

4. In the `Allowed Programs` window, select the check box next to an item to allow it through the firewall, or clear the check box if you don't want to allow the item.

5. When you are done with your changes, click `OK`.

Protecting against spyware

OK, scary stuff first. In its most malicious form, **spyware** (sometimes called **adware**) can record the websites you visit and your keystrokes—such as what you type in your login name and password boxes—and send that information to thieves or criminals on the Internet. For example, when you log on to your online banking account, spyware can record your username and password and send that information to somebody else on the Internet. A thief can then log on to your banking account and wreak havoc.

LinkED

*There's another tactic for getting your online bank account information via a faked website called **phishing**. You can find out more about phishing and how to avoid it later in this chapter; see "Surfing the Internet and exchanging e-mail safely."*

Spyware in most cases usually isn't as dangerous as viruses but can be quite annoying. Once on your computer, spyware can do things without your permission:

- Change your home page in your browser
- Add toolbars to your browser
- Change your preferred search service
- Display pop-up advertisement windows
- Slow down your computer

Those are the things you see. In the background, spyware may be gathering personal information by tracking the websites you visit or, worse yet, recording keystrokes.

How does spyware protection work?

A spyware protection program works similarly to a virus protection program. It offers a multipronged approach to detecting, intercepting, quarantining, and deleting spyware:

- It scans your computer for known spyware programs.
- It detects and notifies you of suspicious activities or downloads that might be spyware actions.
- It quarantines suspicious programs so that you can decide whether to remove them or allow them to perform on your computer
- It automatically updates the antispyware signature files on your computer, which are used to detect and deal with new spyware programs as they appear on the Internet

Window 7 includes its own antispyware software, Windows Defender. Many antivirus programs and security suites also include antispyware. You can run more than one antispyware program, unlike virus protection or firewalls. You only need one, but if you use more than one, they usually do not interfere with each other.

Fortunately, Windows Defender and other antispyware programs are designed fix this.

Using Windows Defender for spyware protection

Windows 7 comes with its own antispyware program. The first time you run Windows Defender, you'll want to do a full scan of your computer. After that, you can set up a schedule to automatically scan your computer daily, weekly, or however often you want.

If you use another antispyware program, the commands, buttons, and menus will be different, but the general process is the same:

1. Turn on the spyware protection program or feature.

2. Set up a schedule for daily or weekly scans, usually a quick scan.

3. Adjust how the program should deal with any issues it finds.

4. Run a full scan the first time, and then let the schedule you set up automatically run scans on a regular basis.

Using Windows Defender for spyware protection is optional but is highly recommended if your antivirus program does not already provide spyware protection.

Turning on Windows Defender

To turn on Windows Defender, follow these steps:

1. Click the `Start` button, and in the search box type `Windows Defender`. In the list that appears, click `Windows Defender`.

   If you have not turned on Windows Defender, you will be prompted to turn it on, as shown in Figure 9-20. If you see this message, click the `click here to turn it on` link.

Figure 9-20. Windows Defender is usually in a turned-off state when Windows 7 is installed.

   If Windows Defender was already on or you just turned it on, the `Windows Defender` window is displayed, as shown in Figure 9-21.

Figure 9-21. The `Windows Defender` window provides the current status of your scans, as well as toolbar buttons to run, schedule, view, or configure scans.

2. In the toolbar, click `Tools`, and when the `Tools and Settings` window appears, click `Options`.

The `Options` window appears, as shown in Figure 9-22.

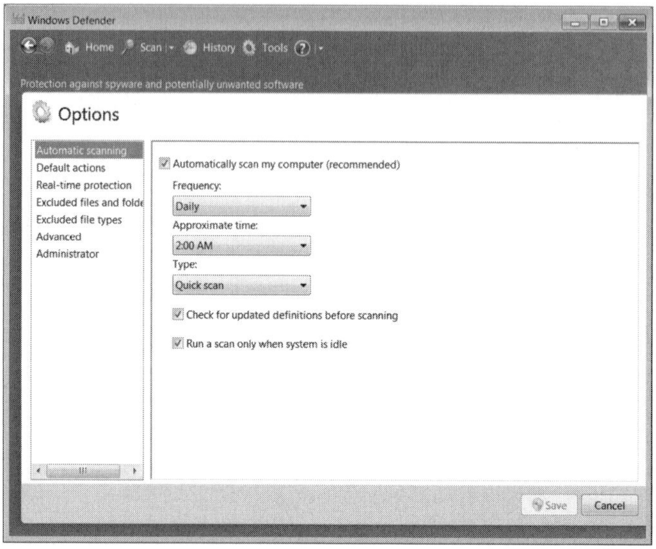

Figure 9-22. The `Options` window allows you to set a schedule for automatically scanning your computer.

3. Make sure `Automatically scan my computer (recommended)` is selected, and then choose your options to schedule the scan:

4. Click the down arrow for `Frequency`, and then choose `Daily`, or a day of the week if you want to run it weekly. If you connect to the Internet daily, schedule a daily scan for the best protection.

Click the down arrow for `Approximate time`, and then choose a time when your computer is normally on. The scan cannot run when your computer is off.

Click the down arrow for `Type`, and then choose `Quick scan` if you will be running the scan frequently, such as daily, or `Full scan` if you will be running the scan less frequently, such as weekly.

5. Select `Check for updated definitions before scanning`. This is how you keep Windows Defender automatically updated. Windows Defender will check the Web for new definitions before running the scan. Microsoft and other antispyware programs are

constantly discovering new threats, and these updates allow the program to detect and deal with these new threats.

6. Select `Run a scan only when system is idle`. The scan can slow down your computer, so this setting minimizes the effect on your computer by running it only when the computer is on but you are not actively using it.

7. Click the other options in the left column to see other settings you can configure.

   You may not need to change or set any other options for now; for most people, the default settings are OK. If you want Windows Defender to notify you of issues but not take any actions without your approval, you can change that in `Default actions`.

8. Click `Save` when you are done changing options.

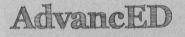

The first time you turn on and use Windows Defender, it is a good idea to run a full scan. A full scan takes several hours, so be sure when you start the scan that you can leave your computer on for as long as Windows Defender needs to complete it. That may mean leaving your computer on overnight when nobody is using it. If you leave your computer on but unattended, you can lock the computer by pressing Windows+L. Also, if you're leaving your computer in an idle state while the scan is running, make sure that in the `Control Panel` item `Power Options`, the settings for `Put the computer to sleep` are set to as long as possible or `Never`. You can access these settings by typing `change when the computer sleeps` in the `Start` menu's search box.

Scanning your computer for spyware

To scan your computer for spyware, follow these steps:

1. In Windows Defender, click `Home`.
2. Click the arrow next to `Scan`, and select `Full Scan`, as shown in Figure 9-23.

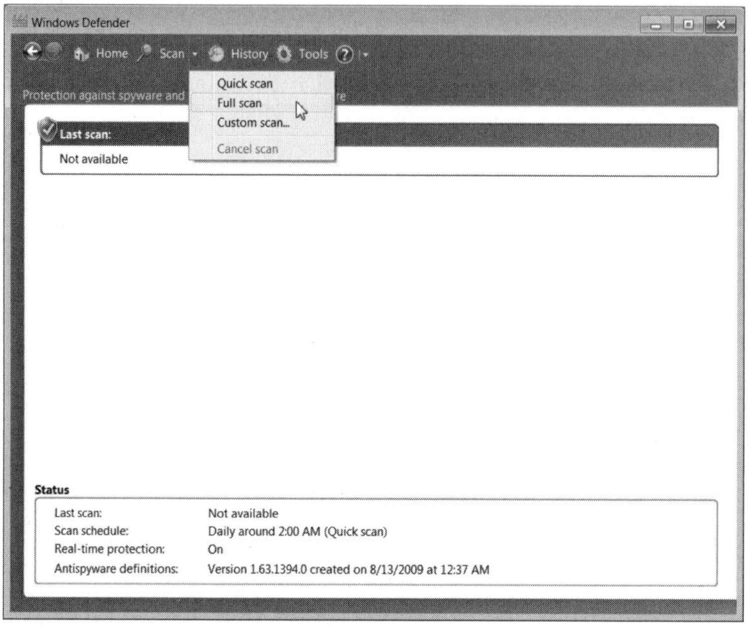

Figure 9-23. If you've never run a scan with Windows Defender or have not run one for quite awhile, run a `Full scan`.

3. When the scan is complete, a summary is displayed similar to Figure 9-24.

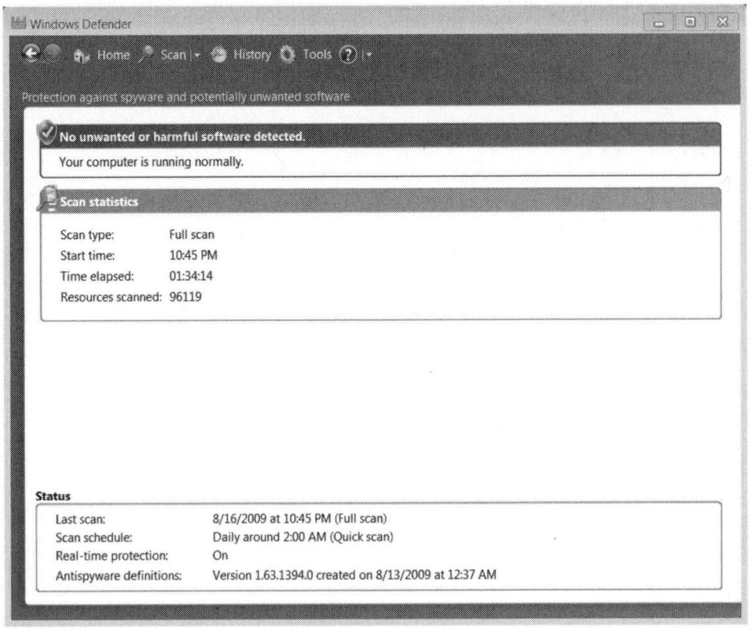

Figure 9-24. The larger the hard drive, the longer it will take the scan to complete. A full scan takes much longer than a quick scan.

When Windows Defender detects spyware, it uses an alert level system to let you know how severe the problem is and what you should do about it. If get an alert from the scan and are not sure what the levels mean, click the help icon (the round blue and white question mark button) to the right of `Tools` on the toolbar. If you do not want to see these alerts in the future, you can click the `Tools` button, click `Options`, and then click `Default actions`.

Choosing an antivirus program

The cost of this software is very small compared to cost of the time you can lose fixing your computer or redoing lost work. If your computer did not come with a virus protection program, you can buy the software either in a retail box with an installation disc or as a software download from a website. Or, you may be able to get it free or at a low cost from your Internet provider.

Once you've installed it, you will receive free updates to the software for a set subscription period, usually a year. This subscription is a very important part of your protection. Just as Microsoft releases patches and updates on a regular basis through Windows Update, your virus protection program checks for regular updates from the virus protection program service. Like Windows Update, most virus protection programs allow you to schedule these updates so that they download and install automatically in the background, without any action required on your part.

Getting security software for free or cheap

Many companies offer antivirus software separately or in security suites that include a firewall, antivirus software, and antispyware. You can purchase and download this software directly over the Web, through Microsoft's referral site, or in a retail box from a store.

However, you may be able to get this software for free or inexpensively. Make no mistake about this—you do need this software, and it is well worth it even if you have to pay for it.

ExplainED

Free or cheap still means a legal, licensed copy of the software. Borrowing, copying, or loaning software without a license for each installed copy is illegal.

Tips for getting security software

Here are some tips for obtaining security software:

- Look for free versions already on your computer. Check your computer for free or trial versions provided by your computer manufacturer. Check the `Programs` menu, your desktop icons, or any extra program disks that came with your computer for antivirus, virus protection, or security suite programs. You may be eligible for a free 30-day to one-year subscription.
- Get free software from your Internet service provider. Check with your Internet service provider or your broadband provider—many offer free security software with their service, which you can install on all your computers in your household.
- Get free software through your work. Some companies buy a site license, which allows employees to install a copy of the software on their computer at home. If you use a computer at home for your work, your company may pay for the cost of security software even if they don't have a site license.

- Purchase a family pack. Every computer in your home should have security software. Many security software companies offer a discount when you buy several copies at the same time. These "family packs" usually include three to five licenses so that you can install it on all of your computers. Most antivirus programs or security suites are available for multiple versions of Windows so that you can install it on your Windows 7 computer, as well as older versions of Windows such as Windows Vista or Windows XP.
- Don't overbuy. You need only one firewall and one antivirus program on each computer. If you run more than one of each of these, they will not work together, and you'll have to uninstall or disable one. Microsoft already provides a good firewall, automatic updates, and antispyware program free with Windows. You really only need to purchase and install an antivirus program—if there aren't any free ones available on your computer, from your Internet service provider, or from your employer.

Getting antivirus software through Action Center

If you do not have antivirus protection, Windows Action Center can help you locate third-party security suites, antivirus, and spyware protection. Action Center provides links to pages where you can purchase, download, and install this software without leaving your desk.

Before you install any virus protection or security suite program, make sure you will be able to leave your computer on for several hours after installation. Typically, these programs prompt you to run a full virus scan when installation is complete. Some programs even run a scan before installation to make sure there aren't viruses already on your computer that could block or interfere with your virus protection software installation. A full virus scan can take several hours, but it is really important that you run this as soon as possible. After the first full virus scan, you usually have an option to schedule quick scans daily or weekly. Even with frequent quick scans, it is a good idea to run a full scan once in awhile. Many people find it convenient to run the full scan overnight while they are asleep.

1. Right-click the notification icon in the taskbar, and then click `Open Action Center`.

    If you do not have a virus protection program installed, Action Center provides a link to obtain a program online, as shown in Figure 9-25.

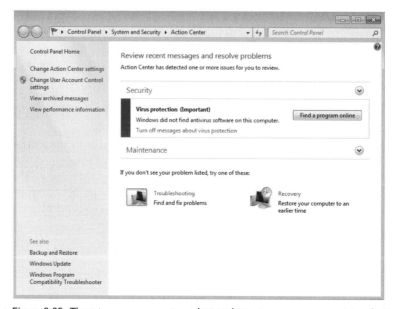

Figure 9-25. The `Virus protection` alert and `Find a program online` button are displayed when there is no antivirus program installed.

2. Click `Find a program online`.

Windows will connect to the Internet and access a Microsoft web page similar to Figure 9-21. The programs listed will be compatible with Windows 7.

Note that web pages change frequently, and the list of companies may change at any time.

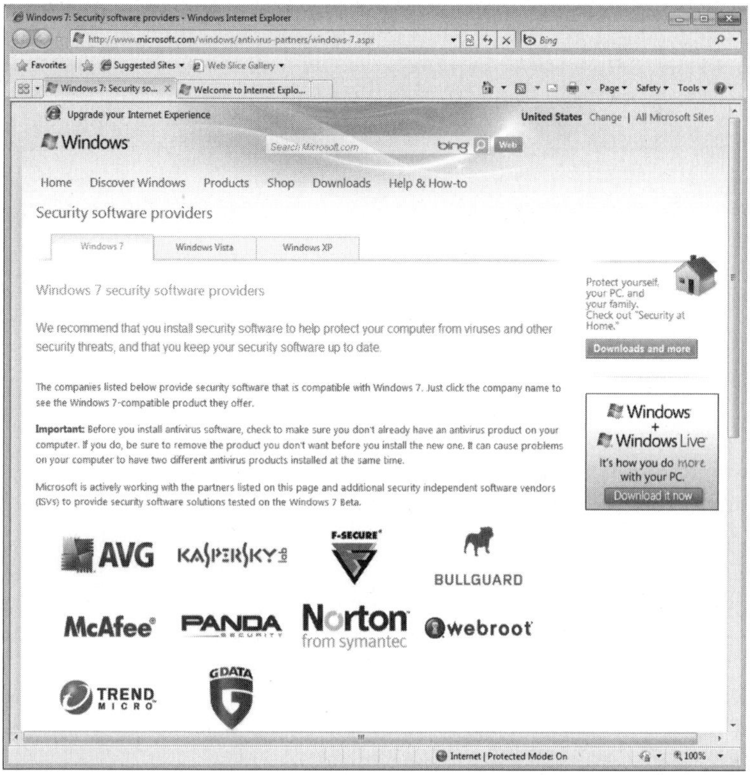

Figure 9-26. Security software providers that are compatible with Windows 7. Microsoft may change the list of programs displayed here from time to time.

3. Click the company logos to go to the websites and view the offerings. Most offer a free 30-day trial so that you can install the program and try it before you buy it.

4. When you find one that you like, follow the instructions on your screen to purchase, download, and install the software.

    During installation, you may need to allow the program to shut down other programs that might interfere with the installation. If you already have another virus protection or security suite installed on your computer, you may be prompted to uninstall it. After you download and install the antivirus or security suite program, you will be prompted to run a full virus scan.

Using the Security Center from a third-party Internet security suites

You don't have to use Microsoft's Action Center or security programs. Your computer may have come with other security programs or an alternate security center. The important thing is to make sure that you have these basic security features installed and scheduled to run automatically:

- Firewall
- Virus protection
- Spyware protection
- Windows Updates from Microsoft
- Security software updates from the security program or security suite vendor

The Windows Action Center and third-party security centers or overview pages display the security status of all your security features at a glance and the expiration date for your subscription. In general, green is good and means you don't need to do anything. Red is not good; it means something is off, something needs updating, or a scan hasn't been run recently. The following examples in Figures 9-27 to 9-30 illustrate the different ways these programs may present the status and tools. The choice of examples is not an endorsement of any product, just a random sampling of the many programs available. The software vendors are always improving their programs, so the current versions may differ from these examples.

326

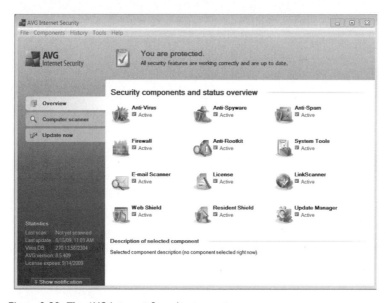

Figure 9-27. A recent McAfee Security Center page. In this example, the security suite is provided by the broadband Internet service provider Comcast.

Figure 9-28. The AVG Internet Security `Overview` page

Figure 9-29. The Norton Internet Security summary page

Figure 9-30. Trend Micro Internet Security

Running and maintaining virus protection

The previous examples of security centers show that each vendor has its own tools, set of features, and status information. The setup and use of virus protection varies, so it is not possible to use an example of one program to demonstrate how all of them work or should work.

The overall process you should follow is similar for most virus protection programs. Consult the documentation or online help for your program for specific steps:

1. Run a full scan soon after you install the security software. No matter which software vendor you use, the first full scan usually takes several hours.

2. Schedule regular virus scans for at least once a week or several days a week. You can use quick scans most of the time and then once in a while run a full scan.

3. Set up automatic updates of the virus signature or detection files. The default setting (meaning it will do this without you having to specify the setting) for most programs is to automatically check the Internet daily for updates when you turn on your computer.

4. Specify what you want the program to do when it detects a virus or issue. Your options vary depending on the vendor, but usually they include creating a report of problems detected for you to review and then waiting for your approval to fix the problems, automatically fixing all the problems for you, or providing a report afterward of the problems that were detected and fixed.

Surfing the Internet and exchanging e-mail safely

Virus protection and spyware protection help protect your computer by detecting bad things on your computer. A firewall is good at preventing outside programs or code from running on your computer or from accessing it. But viruses and spyware don't just magically appear on your computer. They usually get there through e-mail attachments or downloads from web pages. Fortunately, there are many ways that security suites, browsers, and e-mail programs and servers can protect you.

Defending against e-mail threats

You first line of defense is your mail service provider. The better services filter out junk mail and mail with dangerous attachments before the messages even reach your mail inbox. Some junk mail may get through and be sent to a junk mail or spam folder in your e-mail account folders. You can usually adjust the sensitivity of how mail is sorted to your junk mail folder if too much junk mail is getting through to your inbox or too many legitimate e-mail messages are going straight into your junk mail folder instead of your inbox. If, after adjusting your junk mail settings, you still get too much junk mail, you can want to try switching to another e-mail provider. The e-mail program itself may block certain types of mail attachments, for example, blocking any file with the filename extension .exe. But sometimes the danger is in the links or text of the e-mail message itself.

In the examples of security centers shown in Figures 9-27 to 9-30, you'll see that many have e-mail scanning features. That means that when you open an e-mail message you just received, the security software will scan the text and attachments of the message for dangerous links or commands that might not be readily visible to you when you look at the message. Often pictures in an e-mail message have viruses or dangerous scripts that run when you click or view the picture. So, some e-mail programs automatically hide the pictures but offer you the option to view the pictures in the message.

To protect yourself against e-mail threats

This is not a complete list of everything you can do, but just following a few guidelines can make your e-mail much safer:

- **Use the junk mail filtering features in your e-mail program**: Adjust the settings, and if you are still having problems with junk mail, try another e-mail provider. If the program offers something like a `Mark as junk` command, use it on any junk mail that gets through to your regular inbox. Some e-mail programs "learn" from what you mark as junk mail and use that to improve the filtering.
- **Turn on** e-mail message scanning if it is available in your security software: Or consider getting a security suite that includes it.
- **Do not open a mail message if you don't recognize the sender or the message looks suspicious**: Drag it or move it to your junk mail folder if you can without opening it.

- **Add senders you do want to your safe senders list or mail address book**: This will reduce the chance of legitimate mail from a new e-mail contact going into your junk mail folder.
- **Beware of suspicious e-mails**: Beware of anything that looks like a message from your bank asking you to click a link in the message and log on to your bank account to check or fix something; this is called **phishing**. These e-mails, and the sites they link to, are an attempt to get you to provide your login and password so that somebody can log into your accounts and transfer money out of it. If something looks like it needs immediate attention or you are not sure if the website is legitimate, call your bank on the telephone. Many have 24-hour telephone customer service, including technical support for their website and online bank.

Safe surfing on the Internet

Windows 7 provides much of its Internet security through the settings in Internet Options in Control Panel. These settings control what kinds of programs and features on web pages can run on your computer, what kinds of information can be stored on your computer (cookies), and how programs are downloaded and run from the Internet. The default security settings should be safe for most people without being too restrictive. Occasionally the browser's security settings block an action it deems unsafe, and you may need to temporarily change some settings to allow a program to work.

Internet security suites from third-party vendors provide additional protection. They are not mandatory like the firewall, virus and spyware protection, and Windows Update. But if your security suite offers additional Internet protection, make use of it. If you find that it is blocking too much, you can usually adjust settings to be less restrictive.

Security check list

The following checklist summarizes things you can do to help protect your computer and make it safer to use:

- Make sure all users on the computer have password-protected user accounts, at the appropriate user level of standard or administrator, as described in Chapter 2.
- Make sure the User Account Control is set to an appropriate level.
- Make sure you perform regular backups of your computer, as described in Chapter 6.

- Along with performing your regular backups, be ready for disaster recovery in case your computer is lost, stolen, or irreparably damaged.
- Make sure Windows Firewall is on in Action Center, or install and turn on a third-party firewall.
- Use caution when a program requests permission to access your computer through the firewall. Allow only the programs you trust.
- Make sure Automatic Updates is on in the Action Center, and accept the recommended settings to automatically download and install updates daily.
- Turn on virus protection:
    - Scan your computer immediately for viruses
    - Set the program to automatically download the latest virus signatures
    - Schedule follow-up weekly scans
    - Turn on spyware protection:
    - Scan your computer immediately for spyware.
    - Set the program to automatically download the latest spyware definitions and software updates.
    - Accept default settings to enable protection each time you start your computer.
- Use your junk mail features in your e-mail program and service.
- Use e-mail scanning features if they are available in your security suite.
- Avoid opening suspicious e-mail messages.
- Use the default security settings in Internet Options unless specifically told to change them by a person or program you trust.
- Use any additional Internet security settings offered by your security suite.

Summary

Here's a review of what you've learned in this chapter:

- How to require separate user accounts and passwords for each person using the computer through the User Accounts in Control Panel.
- How to specify how you want to be notified by User Account Control when Windows detects a request for program or Windows settings changes that might be dangerous to your computer.

- How to create a disaster plan: locate your original Windows installation disks or media, and your product key; schedule regular backups of your entire computer as well as important document files; regularly store your backups in a location physically separate from your computer, or on an online backup service.
- How to check your overall security status with Action Center.
- How to view or change your Windows Firewall and Windows Update settings.
- How to get virus protection software, which is not included in Windows 7. Microsoft provides a website where you can compare, download, and try or buy virus protection software from third-party vendors. Schedule the virus protection software to regularly scan your computer for viruses, and allow the virus protection software to automatically download and install updates
- How to set up spyware protection by setting up Windows Defender, included with Windows 7, or other antispyware programs. Just like virus protection software, schedule regular scans of your computer and automatic download and installation of updates.
- How to explore and set up e-mail filtering of spam and junk mail, detection of phishing sites, and detection of dangerous attachments. The protection features vary with each e-mail program.
- How to explore and set up the security settings in your Internet browser programs, such as Microsoft Internet Explorer, Mozilla Firefox, and others.

In the next chapter, we'll show you how to use Windows Easy Transfer to make moving to a new computer easy and simple.

Chapter 10

Moving Files and Settings to Your Windows 7 Computer

Most of us do not like moving. You have to pack things carefully and hope they get to the right place without getting lost or damaged. You may decide to throw some things out before you move because you no longer need them. While things are being moved, you cannot use them. When your belongings arrive at the new place, you have to unpack them and sort them out to the rightful owners. Sometimes you hire professional movers to do the moving, which can take some of the load off of you—for a price. That's sort of how it can be with moving to a new computer. Most of us don't want to do it if we don't have to, and it would be nice if somebody else could do it for us.

Fortunately, Windows 7 provides some professional help to make your move to a new computer less stressful: Windows Easy Transfer. With Windows Easy Transfer, you can copy files and settings from your old computer, even another computer running Windows 7, to your new computer running Windows 7.

In this chapter, you'll go through the common tasks associated with getting a new computer, such as moving files and settings with Windows Easy Transfer or alternate methods, installing programs on your new computer, upgrading a computer to Windows 7 from a previous version of Windows, and using or disposing of your old computer.

Moving to a new computer: the big picture

Whether you are upgrading an existing computer from Windows XP or Windows Vista to Windows 7, or moving to a new computer with Windows 7, you probably had your old computer set up just right. You just outgrew it or were ready for a change. You don't need to start all over from scratch to set up new your computer the way you want it.

The process for moving from your old computer to a new Windows 7 computer falls into the following tasks:

1. Running Windows Easy Transfer

2. Installing programs

3. Connecting printers and other devices

4. Cleaning up the old computer—reusing, erasing, or recycling

AdvancED

Which do you do first: reinstall programs or transfer files and settings? The Windows 7 Windows Help and Support suggests that you install your programs on your new computer and then transfer the files and settings. In several tests of the Windows Easy Transfer, this author found no problems performing the Windows Easy Transfer first, and then installing the programs on the new computer. One advantage of doing it in this order is that after the files and settings transfer, Windows Easy Transfer provides a report of programs that should be installed based on what it detected on your old computer, and the documents and settings it transferred over. This takes some of the guesswork out of trying to figure out what you need to install on the new computer by giving you a detailed checklist.

For example, if you had Microsoft Office installed on your old computer but haven't installed it on your new computer, Windows Easy Transfer will still move your Office settings (default file locations, preferences, author information, and so forth) and Office documents (Word documents, Excel spreadsheets, PowerPoint presentations, templates, macros, and so forth) to the new computer. At the end of the transfer, the Windows Easy Transfer report lists the programs you should install based on the settings and documents it transferred, and would list Microsoft Office.

Understanding Windows Easy Transfer

Windows Easy Transfer first appeared in Windows Vista, and prior to Vista was preceded by the File and Settings Transfer Wizard. The purpose of these programs is to make it easier to move from an older version of Windows to another computer running the new version, without losing your settings, preferences, or files.

The way Windows Easy Transfer works is like this:

1. Run Windows Easy Transfer on your old and new computer. (You may have to download and install Windows Easy Transfer on your old computer if it is running Windows XP. Windows Vista already has Windows Easy Transfer.)

2. Choose a method of transfer—through a network connection, an Easy Transfer cable, or by copying to storage media such as a USB flash drive, external hard drive, or removable discs such as CDs or DVDs.

3. Windows Easy Transfer scans your old computer to determine what can be transferred, and the size of the transfer.

4. Choose what to transfer. Windows Easy Transfer suggests what to transfer, but you can customize the list to include or exclude specific files or folders.

5. Transfer the files and settings directly to your new computer (via Easy Transfer cable, or in real time through a network connection) or to a storage location (network share, external hard drive, USB flash drive, or CD/DVD discs) for transfer later to the new computer.

Windows Easy Transfer copies only the files and settings from your old computer. If you want to delete the files from your old computer, you must do that yourself. Or you can perform a clean installation of Windows 7, which will delete everything—the Windows operating system, and all documents, pictures, music, data—before installing the new version of Windows.

Using Windows Easy Transfer for a Windows upgrade installation on the same computer

There are three typical ways to install Windows 7 on a computer:

- Buy a new computer with Windows 7 already installed by the computer manufacturer.
- Upgrade the operating system on your existing computer from Windows XP or Windows Vista to Windows 7. Keep your existing files, settings, and programs on the computer without reinstalling them.
- Install Windows 7 on your existing computer, completely erasing everything on your computer in the process. This is often called a clean install.

Windows Easy Transfer can be used for any of these. Throughout the instructions for Windows Easy Transfer in this chapter, the information you see onscreen, and the online help in Windows Help and Support, you will see references to the *old* computer and the *new* computer. It's easy to assume that this means the old computer and new computer are two different machines, such as when you buy a new computer with Windows 7 already installed and you are moving from an older machine with Windows XP or Windows Vista. But Windows Easy Transfer can also be useful when you are upgrading an existing computer to Windows 7.

AdvancED

Not sure if your existing computer running Windows XP or Windows Vista can be upgraded to Windows 7? Microsoft provides a free tool you can download to your computer to check whether your system is ready to run Windows 7. Web addresses change frequently, so to find this tool, go to the Microsoft website at www.microsoft.com and search for Windows 7 Upgrade Advisor.

If you are upgrading an existing computer to Windows 7, in most cases you can do that without losing any of your files or settings, and you won't need to reinstall very many, if any, programs. But in some cases, you may want to do what is called a **clean install**. In a clean install, Windows erases everything on the computer (cleans) before installing Windows 7; the entire operating system and all of your files, settings, and programs are removed. Some of the common reasons for performing a clean install are as follows:

- Your computer is running poorly under the old version of Windows, and some of the causes may still be there after the upgrade of Windows.
- You have a lot of junk on your computer—files and programs you no longer need or use.
- You don't have much room on your old/new computer's hard drive. A clean install means you won't have any of the old Windows files on your computer.
- You are replacing the hard drive before you upgrade to Windows 7.

If you perform a clean install, Windows Easy Transfer allows you to copy your files and settings to another location that won't be affected by the clean install, such as an external hard drive, a network share, a USB drive, or DVD/CD discs. After performing the clean install, you can then run Windows Easy Transfer on the new computer, and transfer the files and settings from wherever you stored them.

Preparing to move to the new computer

When you move your files and settings to a new computer, you can and should take some steps to ensure that your move goes smoothly and that everything arrives clean and intact.

One of the nice things about moving to a new computer with a new version of Windows is that you have an opportunity to start clean and fresh. You don't have to move *everything* from your old computer. Over time, a computer accumulates a lot of extra files, clutter, and obsolete files. Maybe you have two years of homework files from each of your kids. Your `Programs` menu or desktop lists many more program icons than you regularly use. Your Printers folder lists several printers that you no longer own. Some of these do not take up very much physical disk space, but they clutter things up and can slow down your computer. If you have 50 program items on your `Start` menu `Programs` list, it will take longer for the `Programs` menu to appear, and therefore it will take longer for you to find anything.

Preparing the data on your old computer for transfer

The following tasks are not required but are highly recommended. Performing these steps is sort of like having a garage sale before you move. Not all tasks are applicable to all versions of Windows, and the ones you do choose to complete do not need to be performed in any particular order:

- In Windows XP, right-click an empty area on your desktop, click `Arrange Icons By`, and then click `Run Desktop Cleanup Wizard`. Many of the icons on the desktop are shortcuts, but some could be actual files and folders.
- In any version of Windows, click the `Start` button and click through the submenus: `All Programs` ➤ `Accessories` ➤ `System Tools` ➤ `Disk Cleanup`.
- Have each user on the old computer go through their My Documents folder and delete documents and files they no longer need, or save them to USB flash drives, DVDs, or a hard drive for storage.
- If you have backup software on your old computer, perform a full backup, as well as a backup of your documents. Be sure that you have a copy of the backup software on another computer, and test the recovery, in case you need to recover files from the backup.
- If you don't have a backup program on your old computer, copy the contents of your `C:\Documents and Settings` folder and documents from the Desktop folder to another location outside of your old/original computer. This is not as thorough as running a true backup program, but it will provide something to fall back on if something goes awry in your move to the new computer.

Windows Easy Transfer does not alter or delete files from your old computer. Backing up your files is just a good precaution in preparation for large file and folder moves. These recommendations are not a substitute for running a real backup program but give you an idea of where to find most document files. Some programs store their data files and documents in separate folders outside My Documents folders. Windows Easy Transfer should detect and transfer program data files and settings even if they are not in the My Documents folders. For a more detailed look at Windows 7 backup features, see Chapter 6.

Preparing and verifying a transfer method

When you actually run Windows Easy Transfer, you will be prompted to choose how you will transfer the files and settings. You may already have the hardware or connections for the transfer or you may need to purchase items such as a transfer cable, USB flash drive, external hard drive, or blank DVDs.

You may not have a choice of which method you can use because some methods may not be available to you or practical for your particular situation. The following subsections describe each type of transfer method, advantages, requirements, and limitations.

Easy Transfer Cable

Using an **Easy Transfer cable** is the fastest method for Windows Easy Transfer when connected to USB 2.0 ports on both ends. Microsoft worked with several computer cable manufacturers to develop a USB-based cable to connect two computers directly and use the Windows Easy Transfer in Windows Vista. The Easy Transfer cables sold for Vista will work for Windows 7, so don't worry if you cannot find an Easy Transfer cable labeled for Windows 7.

The Easy Transfer cable looks like a USB cable with two identical USB-A ends that fit in each computer's regular USB ports. However, this cable is more than a USB cable with two identical ends—the middle of the cable has a small chip that enables the two computers to communicate with each other. A plain USB cable with just the USB-A plug on each end will not work.

The Easy Transfer cable package may include an installation disc with a copy of the Window Easy Transfer program for installation on a Windows XP computer. Windows 7 and Windows Vista come with the Windows Easy Transfer program installed. If you have the Easy Transfer cable but don't have a disc with the Windows Easy Transfer program to install on Windows XP, you can download it for free from Microsoft.

The cable may vary in length, but expect it to be about 8 feet. If you need a longer length, you can use a standard USB extension cable. USB speed and data flow decrease with distance, and you need to be able to interact with Windows Easy Transfer on both computers at the same time, so there are practical limits to how many extensions you can string together. The cost of an Easy Transfer cable is more than a regular USB cable of the same length, but not prohibitive.

Network

There are several ways you can use a network for Windows Easy Transfer:

- **Create an Easy Transfer file and copy it to a shared network location.** The old computer and new computer aren't necessarily connected directly to each other; they just need a connection to the same network location. The transfer is in two steps: The old computer creates the Easy Transfer file on the shared computer. Anytime after the file transfer is complete, you can go to the new computer and transfer the file from the network storage location. Neither the old or new computer will be waiting for or communicating directly with each other. Before you create the Easy Transfer file, compare the estimated size given by Windows Easy Transfer, and make sure enough space is available on the network location.
- **Use a network connection to perform the transfer in real time directly from the old computer to the new computer.** This method is similar to the Easy Transfer cable method, but not as fast. If the network connection is wireless, it could be much slower, especially if the signal strength is weak or the network speed is slow. This method will not work at all if the old computer and new computer cannot find each other on the network, which is not uncommon when you have just started integrating your Windows 7 computer with other non-Windows 7 computers on a home network.

LinkED

Chapter 7 describes how you can network computers running different versions of Windows (Windows XP, Windows Vista, and Windows 7) by using Ethernet and wireless connections.

- **Use a crossover Cat5e cable.** This is a variation of the network connection in real time, and very similar to using the Easy Transfer cable. Both computers must have a regular Ethernet (network adapter) jack. You can directly network the old and new computers by using a crossover Cat5e cable. A crossover cable looks like a regular Ethernet cable, except the wire set order on one end is reversed from the wire set order on the other end. Normally, you connect two computers to each other through a router or network switch box. The crossover cable enables two computers to connect directly to each other without the box in between. Essentially, you are creating a small private network.

- In informal testing, using a crossover cable appeared to be comparable in speed to using the Easy Transfer cable. It is not difficult to use, and the crossover Cat5e cable may be available for less than an Easy Transfer cable. The crossover cable works with Windows Easy Transfer, but can also be used to perform a file transfer between computers. Because most network cards can work at either 10 or 100Mbps, you can potentially transfer at 100Mbps.

- The only difficulty in using this method is that you must disconnect both the old and new computer from any other network connections, and then reconnect them to their regular network connections when you are finished. Each time you want to change these network connections, you may need to restart the computers in order for them to correctly detect the current network connections.

External hard disk or USB flash drive

Using an **external disk or flash drive** is similar to using a network location to store a Windows Easy Transfer file. The external hard disk or USB drive is connected to the old computer to receive and store the Windows Easy Transfer file. When the transfer from the old computer is complete, you detach the external device from the old computer and attach it to the new computer. When you run Windows Easy Transfer on the new computer, you specify the external hard disk or USB flash drive as the location of the Easy Transfer file.

If the size of the Easy Transfer file is small enough, it may fit on a large-capacity USB flash drive, or may be broken up to fit several flash drives. It may be a better buy and more practical to get an external hard drive if the estimated file size is more than 8GB. The price of a 16GB flash drive is fairly close to the price of a 250GB external hard drive. If the transfer is larger than the USB flash drive capacity, you can fill the drive, copy it to the new computer, go back to the old computer, get the next set of files, and repeat until you have moved all files from the old computer to the new computer. This may be feasible if you already have one or more flash drives available, but it may be not be practical if you have a large transfer that is many times the size of the flash drive capacity. A 250GB or larger external hard drive may be more practical because you can use it for backup of your documents or important files from several computers, or as a place to store lots of files if you have large music, picture, or video collections.

Ensuring that your computers are not interrupted during transfer

Running Windows Easy Transfer may take several hours. During that time, your old and new computers will need all the attention from the computer's resources—memory, hard drive use, and so forth. Also, Windows Easy Transfer needs to run without interruption. After Windows Easy Transfer starts, both computers will display a message warning not to use the computer during the transfer. Even if you don't intentionally use your computer during that time, routine and automatic computer operations may disrupt the transfer process. To ensure that your computer does not shut down or get interrupted during the transfer, adjust the following settings before you start the transfer. Otherwise, you may come back to your computers only to find that the transfer did not complete, and you will have to start all over again.

Run your computer on AC power, not your batteries

If either of the computers is a laptop, make sure they are all running on AC power from your wall outlet. One to two hours is the most many computers will run on just batteries, and you don't want one of your computers to shut down in the middle of the transfer.

Turn off all sleep, hibernation, standby, and power conservation modes

In Windows XP `Control Panel`, open `Power Options`. On the `Power Schemes` tab, make sure the settings are set to `Never` for `Turn off monitor`, `Turn off hard disk`, and `System Standby` for both `Plugged in` and `Running on batteries`. On the `Hibernate` tab, clear the `Enable hibernation` check box.

In Windows Vista or Windows 7, go to `Control Panel`, open `Power Options`, and then edit or create a Power plan that has all settings for `Turn off the display` and `Put the computer to sleep` set to `Never`.

Some computer manufacturers provide their own separate utility in Control Panel for managing power options. In those cases, you'll need to use their utility instead.

Turn off your screen saver

In Windows XP, in `Control Panel`, open `Display`. On the `Screen Saver` tab, in the `Screen saver` box, select `None`.

In Windows Vista, in `Control Panel`, open `Personalization`. In the `Screen saver` box, select `None`.

In Windows 7, in `Control Panel`, open `Personalization`. Click `Screen Saver`, and in the `Screen saver` box, select `None`.

Turn off scheduled virus scans, spyware scans, and backups

Any kind of antivirus or backup scans will be competing with Windows Easy Transfer for use of the hard drive, memory, and processor resources. Turn off the automatic scans for these programs or reschedule them to run at a much later time, hours after you expect Windows Easy Transfer to finish.

Close down all other programs

Close down all the programs displayed as open in your taskbar. Also close programs that might be running in the background, such as instant messaging or mail programs. Check the notification area of the taskbar and right-click icons to see whether they have a Close or Exit command on the submenu.

Locate installation discs for the programs and devices installed on your old computer

You don't need installation discs before or during Windows Easy Transfer. But the Windows Easy Transfer process will take several hours, which might be a good time to start rounding up installation discs. When the transfer is complete, the transfer report will give you a good idea of what programs you'll need to install on your new computer that were on your old computer.

Transferring files with an Easy Transfer cable

To transfer files with an Easy Transfer cable, follow these steps:

1. If your old computer is running Windows Vista or Windows 7, go to step 2.

   If your old computer is running Windows XP, install the software that came with your Easy Transfer cable. This ensures that your computer has the right hardware drivers installed for the cable. If you are using an Easy Transfer cable for Vista, the installation disc will install the older Vista version of the Windows Easy Transfer software. You will need to update to the Windows 7 version a few steps later in this procedure, but you should still run the cable's installation disc so the drivers are installed.

2. Connect the Easy Transfer cable to the new computer. Windows 7 detects the cable and displays the Windows Easy Transfer screen shown in Figure 10-1.

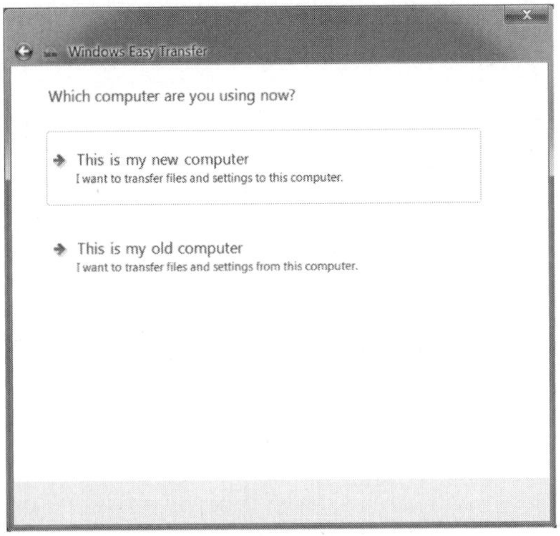

Figure 10-1. When the Easy Transfer cable is connected to a Windows 7 or Windows Vista computer, it triggers the Windows Easy Transfer program. This figure is from Windows 7. The screen in Windows Vista is different.

3. Click `This is my new computer`. The following screen, shown in Figure 10-2, prompts you to install Windows Easy Transfer on the old computer.

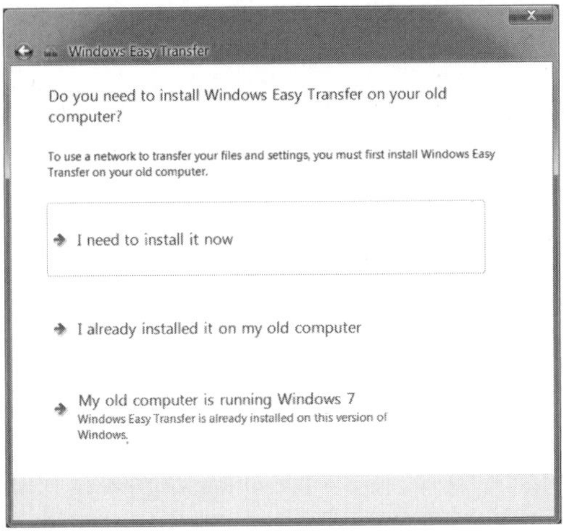

Figure 10-2. If your old computer is Windows Vista or Windows XP, you will need to install the Windows 7 version of Windows Easy Transfer. Though Windows Vista comes with Windows Easy Transfer, you will need to upgrade to the Windows 7 version on the Windows Vista computer.

4. Click I need to install it now. Because the old computer does not have the software installed that will allow it to communicate with the new computer through the Easy Transfer cable, you cannot use the Easy Transfer cable to install Windows Easy Transfer on the other computer. Figure 10-3 displays the choices for installing the Windows Easy Transfer software on the other computer.

Figure 10-3. Windows Easy Transfer software is very small. If you have a USB flash drive, that's the quickest and easiest choice.

5. If you have a USB flash drive, that's the quickest and easiest choice. Attach a USB flash drive to the new computer and then click USB flash drive.

—or—

Attach an external hard drive and then click External hard disk or shared network folder.

6. Click I need to install it now. Windows Easy Transfer prompts you to confirm where you want to copy the Windows Easy Transfer software to. After Windows Easy Transfer is copied to the USB flash drive (or external drive), Windows Easy Transfer prompts you to move the USB to the old computer and install it there, as shown in Figure 10-4.

Figure 10-4. Windows Easy Transfer describes how to install the program on your old computer.

7. Click Next. Insert the USB drive in your old computer. Your old computer should autoplay the Windows Easy Transfer installation software. If the installation program doesn't start, follow the instructions shown in Figure 10-4.

ExplainED

In case you need to rerun Windows Easy Transfer on your old computer, copy the Windows Easy Transfer files to a local folder on your old computer. When you run Windows Easy Transfer on your old computer, it is not an installed program, so it does not appear on your Programs menu, the desktop, or anyplace else. If you need to run it again, you will need to locate it in your local folder and run it from there.

You will be going back and forth between both computers to follow the prompts. The screen shown in Figure 10-5 is displayed on your new computer.

Figure 10-5. Windows Easy Transfer on your new computer prompts you to perform steps on your old computer.

After you install Windows Easy Transfer on your old computer, a `Welcome` screen lists the types of files and settings that are transferred from the old computer running Windows XP (see Figure 10-6).

Figure 10-6. When this `Welcome` screen appears on your old computer, attach the Easy Transfer cable to the old computer.

8. Attach the Easy Transfer cable to the old computer. The cable should now be attached to both computers.

9. Click `Next` on the `Welcome` screen on your old computer. Windows Easy Transfer asks you which computer you are using, as shown in Figure 10-7.

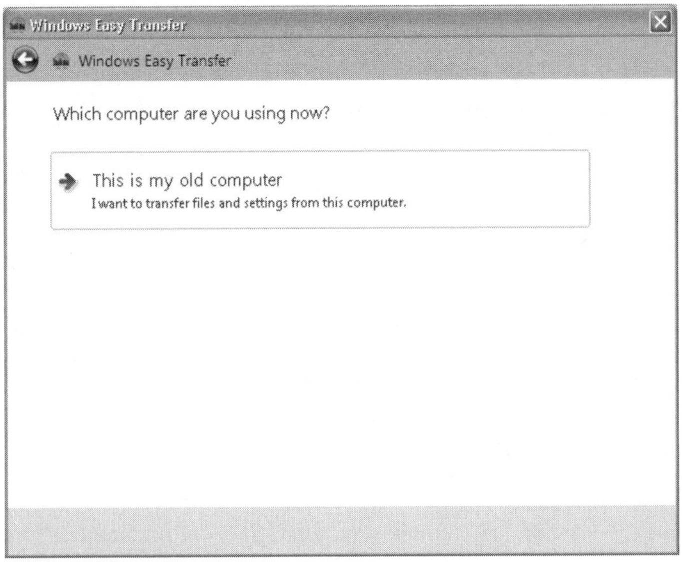

Figure 10-7. Windows Easy Transfer needs confirmation that this is the computer you want to transfer files from.

10. Select `This is my old computer` on the old computer. Both computers will try to connect to each other. When they are connected, Windows Easy Transfer will check for compatibility between the two computers, and then check what can be transferred, as shown in Figure 10-8.

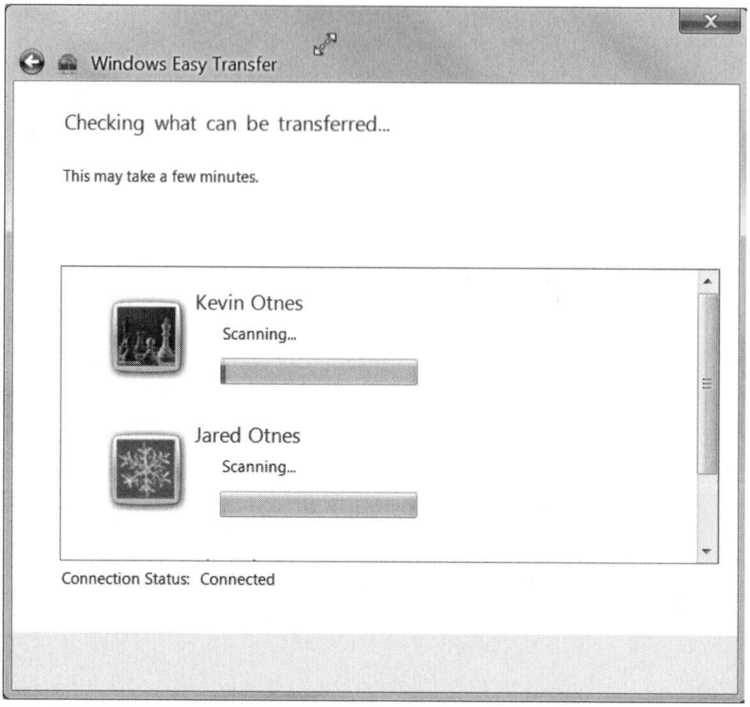

Figure 10-8. Windows Easy Transfer checks the size of the documents and settings files for each user account on your old computer.

After Windows Easy Transfer has reviewed what will be transferred, it displays an estimate of how large the transfer will be for each account, as shown in Figure 10-9.

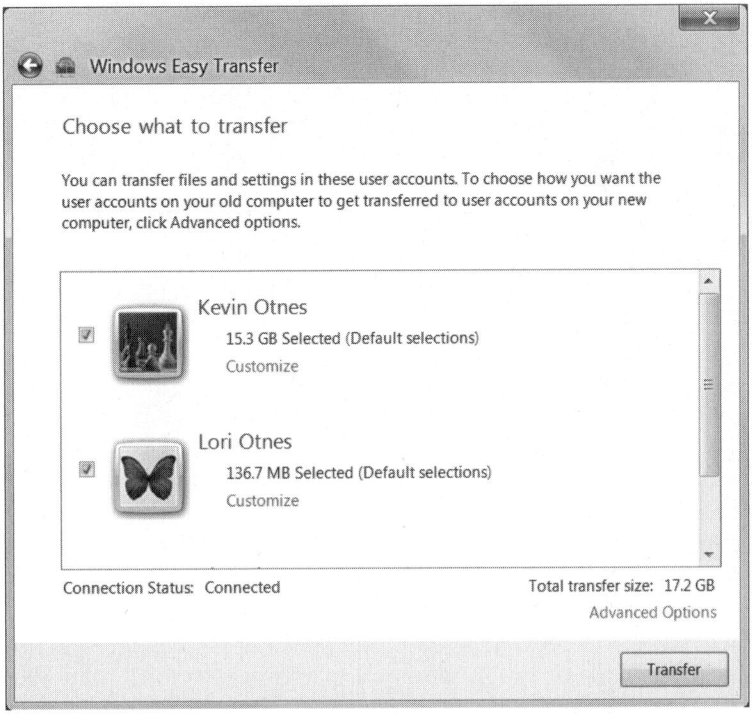

Figure 10-9. Windows Easy Transfer selects the accounts, and the default files and settings for each account.

11. Review the settings on this screen. You can change these settings if needed:

- Remove individual users from the transfer by clearing the check box next to a user's name.
- Customize what files are transferred by clicking the `Customize` link.
- Specify the username to use for each transferred account on the new computer by clicking the `Advanced Options` link.

AdvancED

For most people, the default settings do not need adjustment. Some reasons for changing the defaults are to exclude items from the transfer (for example, one of the document-type folders) or to add a folder of content that is not in one of the default user "My..." folders. Clicking `Customize` *under the user's name displays the default folders and settings that have been selected for transfer, as shown in Figure 10-10.*

Windows Easy Transfer

Choose what to transfer

You can transfer files and settings in these user accounts. To choose how you want the user accounts on your old computer to get transferred to user accounts on your new computer, click Advanced options.

Kevin Otnes
15.3 GB Select
Customize

Lori Otnes
136.7 MB Sele
Customize

Connection Status: Connected

Kevin Otnes

☑ **Desktop** 346.8 MB
☑ **Favorites** 11 KB
☑ **My Documents** 204.5 MB
☑ **My Music** 13.7 GB
☑ **My Pictures** 472.2 MB
☑ **My Videos** 69.4 MB
☑ **Quick Launch** 28 KB
☑ **Program Settings** 4... ⓘ
☑ **Windows Settings** 3.1 MB
Other Items... 889 KB

Advanced

sfer size: 17.2 GB

dvanced Options

Transfer

Figure 10-10. By default, Windows Easy Transfer Windows Easy Transfer selects the default storage folders, desktop, favorites, and other settings.

12. Review the items that have been selected for transfer. To remove an item from the transfer, clear the check box next to it. For example, the large My Music folder may be a duplicate of the user's entire music collection that is already on another computer. The My Music folder will have a significant impact on how long the transfer takes.

13. If you want to select or remove individual folders, on the user's customization list, click the `Advanced` link for an even greater level of detail, as shown in Figure 10-11.

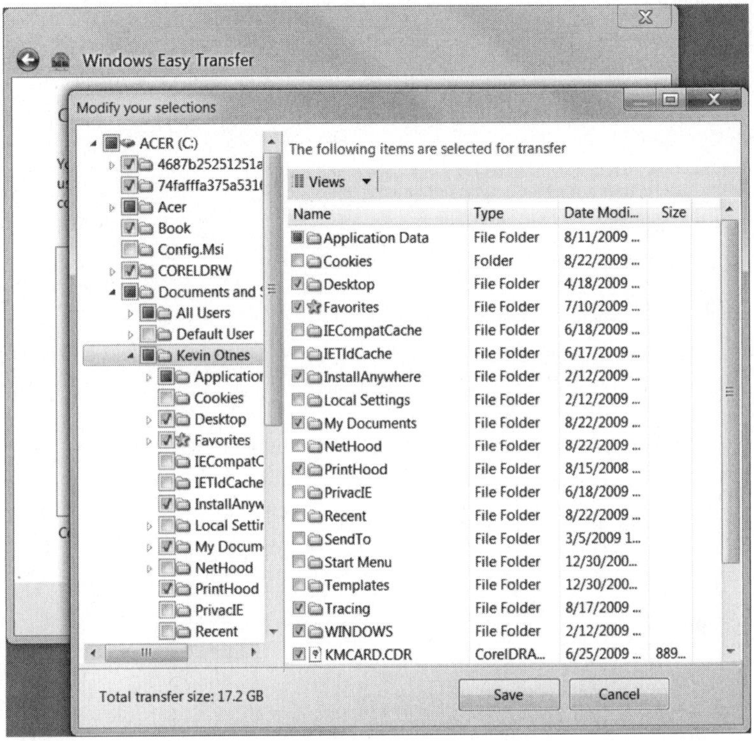

Figure 10-11. The window for selecting folders for transfer is similar to what you might see in a backup program's window.

14. When you are finished viewing or changing settings on this screen, click `Save` or `Cancel`, and then click the `Close` button at the top of the user's customization list that was shown in Figure 10-10.

15. In the `Choose what to transfer` window, click `Advanced Options` at the bottom right of the window. This enables you to select or change the username that will appear for each transferred account on the new computer, as shown in Figure 10-12.

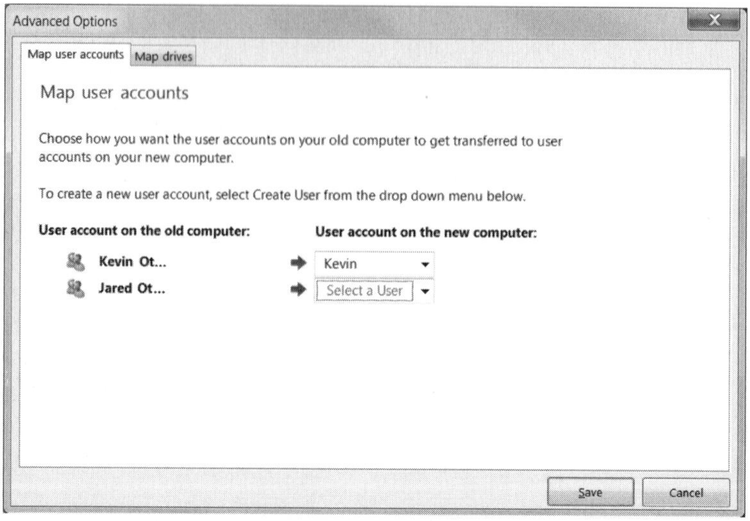

Figure 10-12. Windows Easy Transfer will try to match up the names on the old computer with account names for the new computer.

16. If there is no name specified for an account on the new computer, you can create a new name. When you create a new user, you have the option of creating a password, as shown in Figure 10-13.

Figure 10-13. The `Create New User` dialog box prompts you to create a password for this account. You can leave it blank if you want, and let the user create a password after opening the user account on the new computer.

ExplainED

You can also add new users and set passwords anytime with user accounts. In Chapter 2, you'll learn how to add users, set up passwords, and assign the level of control and privileges for each user. Chapter 9 explains how to use user accounts and passwords as part of a plan to keep your computer safe.

Most people typically have only one drive, C:. Windows Easy Transfer automatically transfers files to the same drive letter on the new computer as the one used on your old computer. The `Map drives` page shown in Figure 10-14 may be useful to advanced users who have multiple drives on their computer; most people will not need to do anything on this page.

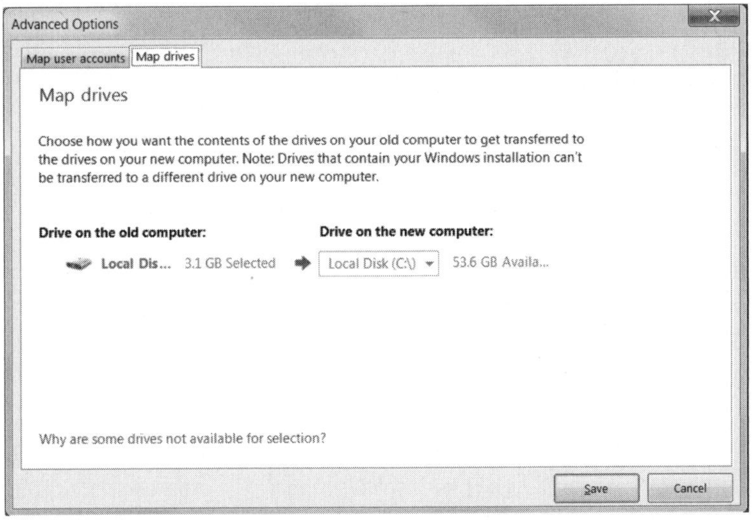

Figure 10-14. The `Map drives` page specifies which drive letter to use for each drive that is transferred. Most people typically have only one drive, C:, and will not need to change anything on this advanced page.

17. When you are ready to perform the transfer, on the `What to transfer` page, click `Transfer`. The transfer can take several hours to complete. During that time, you cannot use the old or new computer, nor can you turn them off, as shown in Figure 10-15.

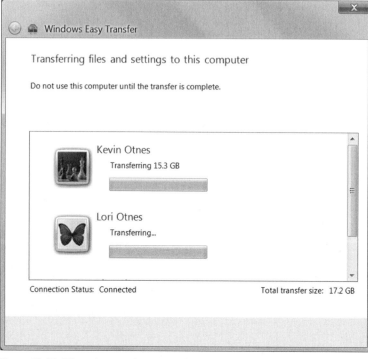

Figure 10-15. When the transfer starts, the new computer displays the size of the transfer, but no indication of how long it may take.

AdvancED

When Windows Easy Transfer starts the transfer, it cannot calculate how long it will take until it has run a few minutes. In this example, it took approximately 10 minutes before Windows Easy Transfer could make an estimate, as shown in Figure 10-16. The estimates are fairly accurate, although when you are watching the progress, it feels like it takes longer. The size of the transfer, the speed of the connection, and the speed of the hard drives on both computers will affect how long it takes. Using either computer during the transfer will slow down the transfer, or even worse, interrupt and stop the transfer.

Figure 10-16. The transfer time does not appear right away. It may take 10 minutes or more for Windows Easy Transfer to make an accurate time estimate based on the transfer so far.

ExplainED

After the transfer begins, you need to leave both computers alone until the transfer is complete. Your screen savers, hibernation, virus scans, backup programs—and anything else that can interrupt the transfer—should all be off. Now is a good time to start rounding up installation discs and product keys for the programs you used on your old computer that you want to install on the new computer. If you will be connecting a printer or other hardware devices to your new computer, locate the installation or driver discs for those too.

If you installed a program on your computer from an Internet download, you may still have the download or setup program on your computer. You will be able to do a more thorough check of what you need when the transfer is complete and you can view the transfer report.

After the transfer is complete, Windows Easy Transfer displays a screen on which you can choose to view a report indicating what was transferred and what programs you should install, as shown in Figure 10-17.

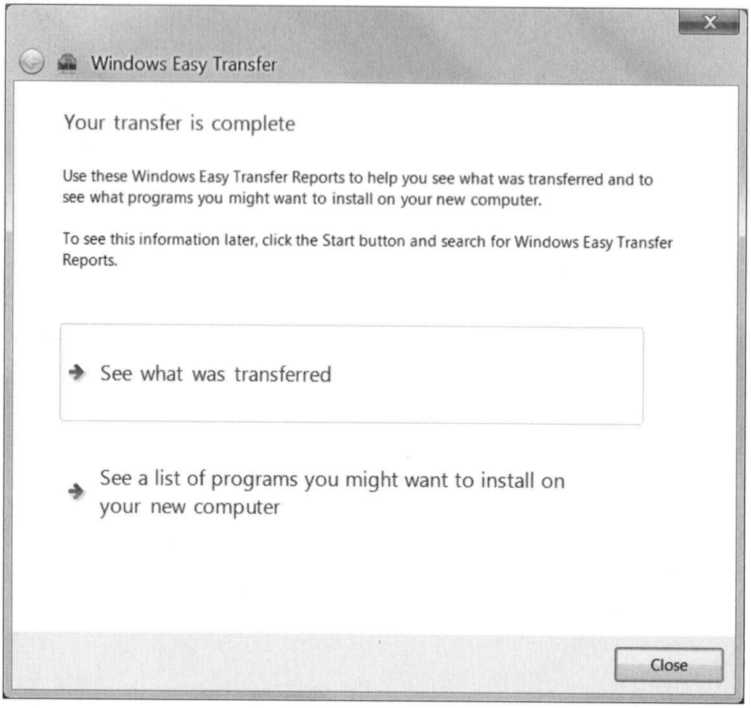

Figure 10-17. Use the transfer reports to determine what programs you may need to install on your new computer.

18. Click `See what was transferred` to make sure there were no problems or errors, and that the things you wanted were transferred, as shown in Figure 10-18.

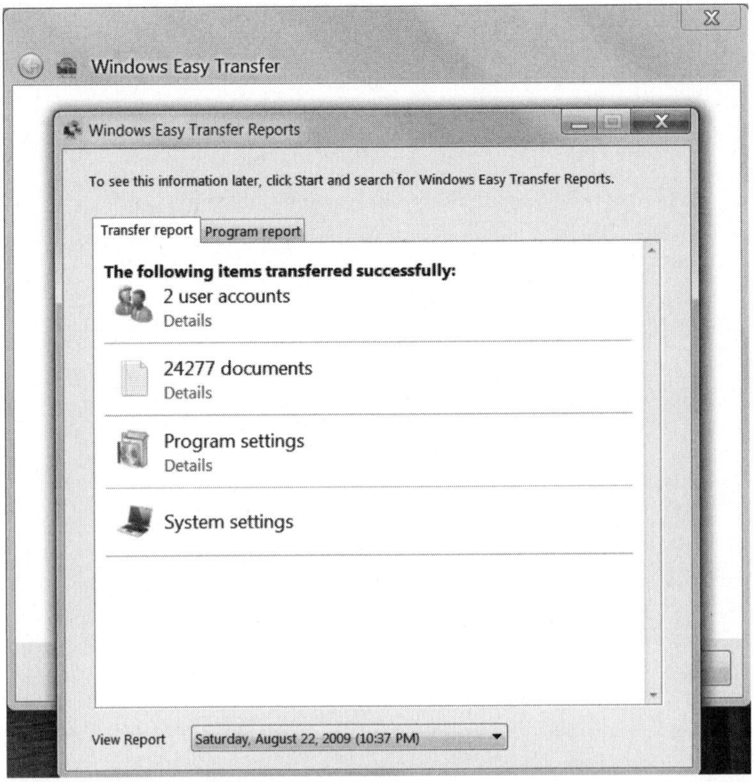

Figure 10-18. The transfer report summarizes what was transferred. You can click the Details links for filename-level detail of what was transferred.

19. Click the Program report tab. This is the same information that is displayed when you click the other link shown in Figure 10-17, See a list of programs you might want to install on your new computer. Figure 10-19 shows a summary of the categories.

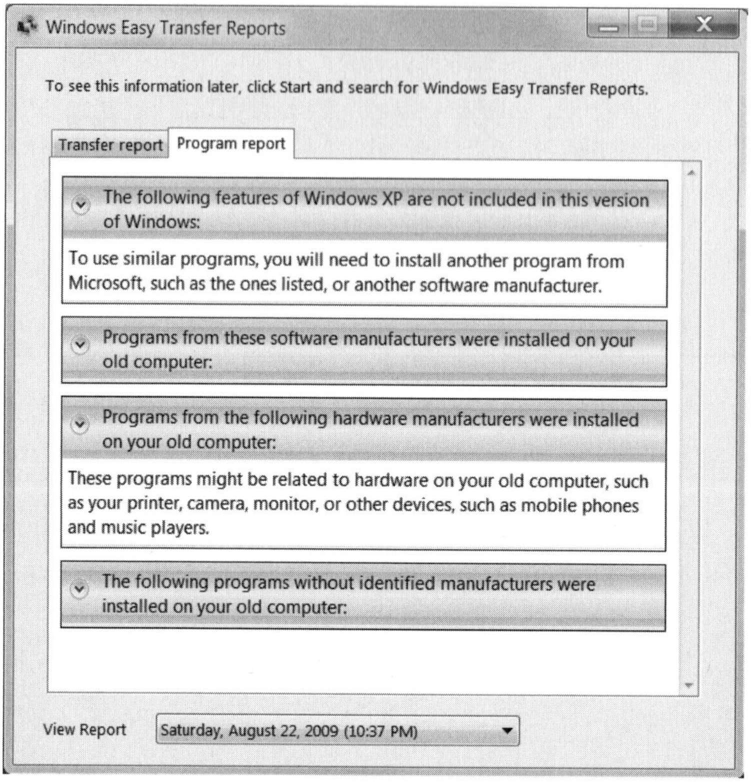

Figure 10-19. The program report provides a listing of programs that were installed on your old computer.

20. Click the down arrow on the left side of the category name to expand it and view the actual lists. Figure 10-20 provides an example of what type of information is displayed. If a program that was on your old computer is already installed on your new computer, a green check mark appears next to the program in the list.

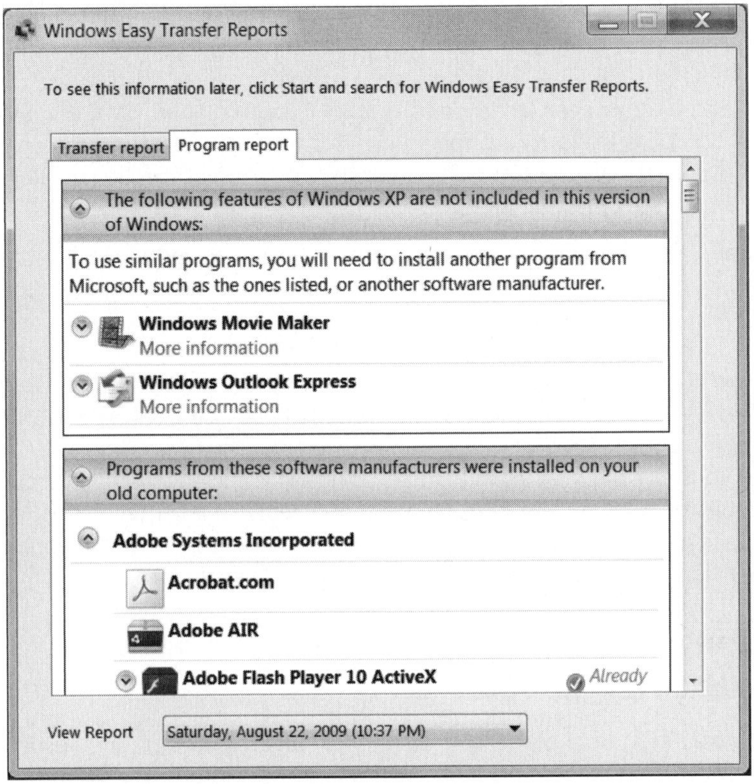

Figure 10-20. Some of the programs installed on your old computer may already be installed on your new computer. In that case, a green check mark with `Already` will appear next to the item.

Transferring files and settings via a network in real time

There are two ways you can use a network for Windows Easy Transfer:

- As a real-time direct-connection transfer between the old computer and the new, similar to using the Easy Transfer cable.

- As a storage location between your old and new computer, similar to using an external hard drive or USB flash drive. Transfer the files from the old computer to a network location, external hard drive, or USB flash drive, and then transfer the files from one of these storage locations to your new computer. This takes longer but enables you to break up the transfer process into two stages that can be completed at separate times and locations.

Typically, we think of a network as two or more computers connected to each other through a router or network switch. A network can also be two computers connected to each other directly through a special type of network cable, a **crossover cable**. Whichever of these network connections you use, you won't need to install hardware drivers as you do with an Easy Transfer cable. The transfer speed varies depending on your network and connection type. In practice, the fastest connections for Windows Easy Transfer are the Easy Transfer cable or a Cat5e crossover network cable. In actual testing for this chapter, they appeared to be about the same, though technically one is supposed to be faster than the other. A regular network connection appears to be a little slower than the Easy Transfer cable or crossover cable.

Setting up the network connection between the old and new computers

Both computers need to be able to talk to each other through the network connection. Otherwise, the information cannot be transferred between them.

To connect the old and new computers through a home network, follow these steps:

1. Connect each computer to the same workgroup, and router or network switch. A wired connection (Ethernet) is much more reliable in speed and quality. Avoid using a wireless connection for your transfer—the connection speeds are usually much slower than an Ethernet connection, and more prone to interruptions.

2. Make sure each computer has network sharing on. In Windows XP, you can configure this through File and Printer Sharing. In Windows Vista and Windows 7, use the Network and Sharing Center.

3. Start Windows Easy Transfer on the new computer. If you do not have Windows Easy Transfer installed on your old computer, follow the instructions on your new computer screen to install it.

4. Start Windows Easy Transfer on the old computer.

Here are the steps to connect two computers through a crossover cable:

1. Turn off both computers. Make sure they are close enough to each other that the cable can reach both of them.

2. Connect the crossover cable to the Ethernet jack on each computer.

3. Start both computers.

4. Start Windows Easy Transfer on the new computer. If you do not have Windows Easy Transfer installed on your old computer, follow the instructions on your new computer screen to install it.

5. Start Windows Easy Transfer on the old computer.

Choosing the connection method

Now it's time to pick the connection method you just set up:

1. After you have the Welcome to Windows Easy Transfer screen on both computers, click Next. Windows Easy Transfer lists the methods available to transfer files and settings to your new computer, as shown in Figure 10-21. Some options transfer the files and settings in real time directly from the old computer to the new computer. Other options transfer the files and settings to storage on a network share or external device, and then allow transfer to the new computer in a separate operation.

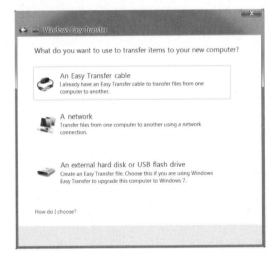

Figure 10-21. Windows Easy Transfer provides several options for transferring items to your new computer.

2. Click A network on both computers.

3. On both computers, Windows Easy Transfer asks which computer you are using now. Select This is my new computer or This is my old computer on the appropriate computer.

4. On the new computer, it will ask whether you need to install Windows Easy Transfer on your old computer. Click I already installed it on my old computer.

5. Both computers will display messages about getting or entering a Windows Easy Transfer key. Follow the instructions on both screens, as shown in Figures 10-22 and 10-23.

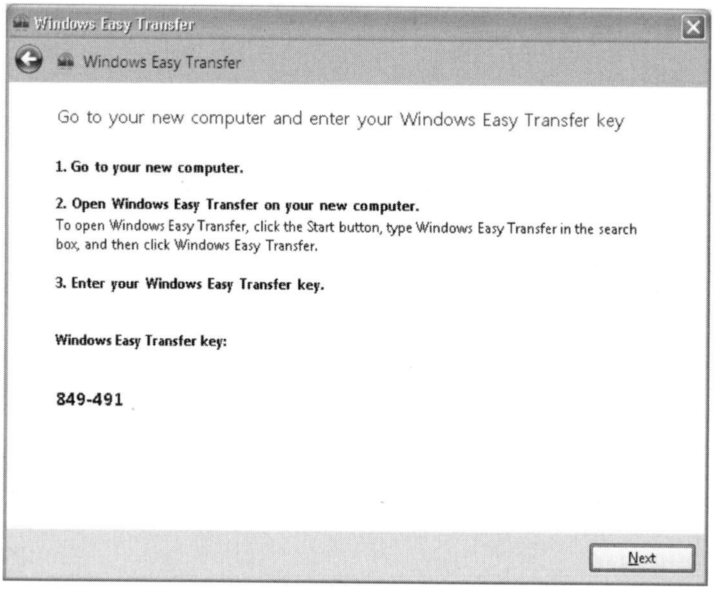

Windows Easy Transfer

Go to your new computer and enter your Windows Easy Transfer key

1. Go to your new computer.

2. Open Windows Easy Transfer on your new computer.
To open Windows Easy Transfer, click the Start button, type Windows Easy Transfer in the search box, and then click Windows Easy Transfer.

3. Enter your Windows Easy Transfer key.

Windows Easy Transfer key:

849-491

Next

Figure 10-22. On your old computer, Windows Easy Transfer provides the Windows Easy Transfer key.

6. Write down the key and then click Next.

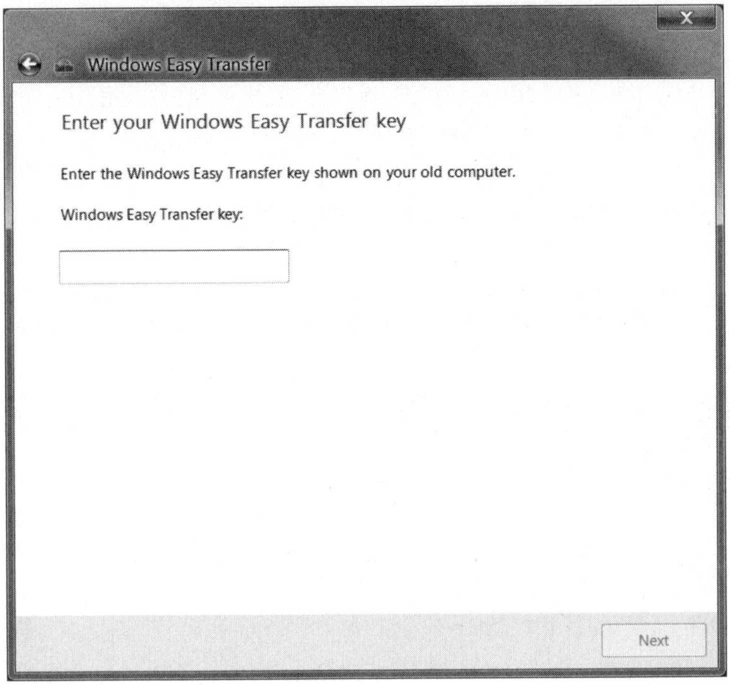

Figure 10-23. On the new computer, Windows Easy Transfer asks for the key from the old computer.

7. Click Next and then enter the key. After you have entered the Windows Easy Transfer key, Windows Easy Transfer will go through a series of screens in the following order to prepare for an actual transfer:

- Connection established
- Checking for compatibility
- Checking what can be transferred (new computer)
- Transferring files and settings (old computer)
- Choose what to transfer (new computer)

ExplainED

The rest of the transfer process via the network is identical to those for transferring via the Easy Transfer cable. To follow through the rest of these steps in detail, start at Figure 10-8.

Using a USB flash drive, external hard disk, or network location for Windows Easy Transfer

This method takes the longest of all, but is well-suited for doing a clean install of Windows 7 on an existing computer. Or you can use this process when the old computer and new computer are in different locations that cannot be connected directly to each other with a cable or real-time connection.

This is really a two stage process:

1. Creating a transfer file that contains your files and settings, and storing the transfer file on a USB flash drive, external hard disk, or network location

2. Transferring the Windows Easy Transfer file from the storage location to the new computer

Creating the transfer file from your old computer

First, create the transfer file from your old computer, as follows:

1. Install Windows Easy Transfer on your old computer. You may have to run Windows Easy Transfer on the new computer to obtain the Windows Easy Transfer installation files, and then copy them to a USB flash drive or an external hard drive.

2. Run Windows Easy Transfer on your old computer.

3. After the `Welcome` screen, when it asks, `How do you want to transfer?`, choose `USB flash drive or external hard drive`. Windows Easy Transfer scans the computer to determine transfer size and accounts.

368

4. Choose what to transfer from this computer, or accept the defaults and click `Next`.

Because this transfer isn't going directly from the old computer to the new computer, it is not as secure. Windows Easy Transfer offers the option to password-protect the transfer file, as shown in Figure 10-24.

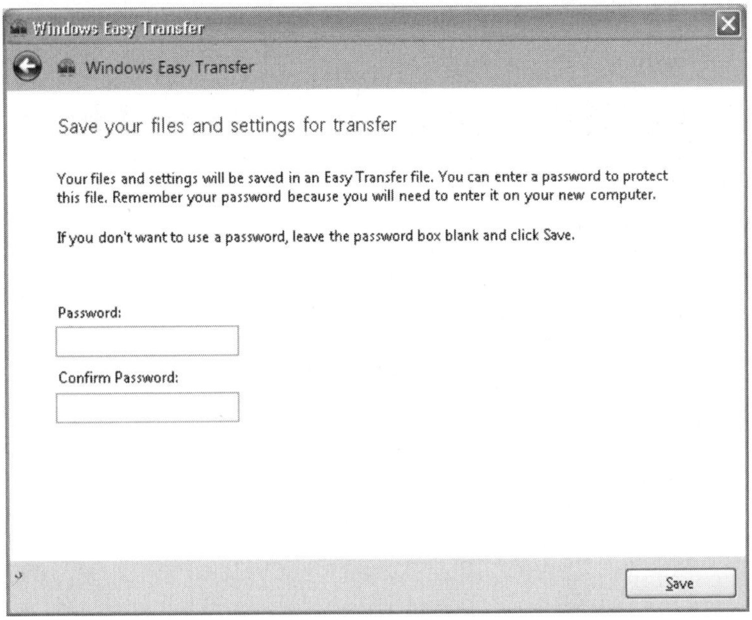

Figure 10-24. Password protection of the transfer file is optional. You can leave this blank if you want.

5. Specify a password or leave it blank.

6. Click `Save`. A dialog box is displayed so you can navigate to and select where you want the transfer files to go, as shown in Figure 10-25.

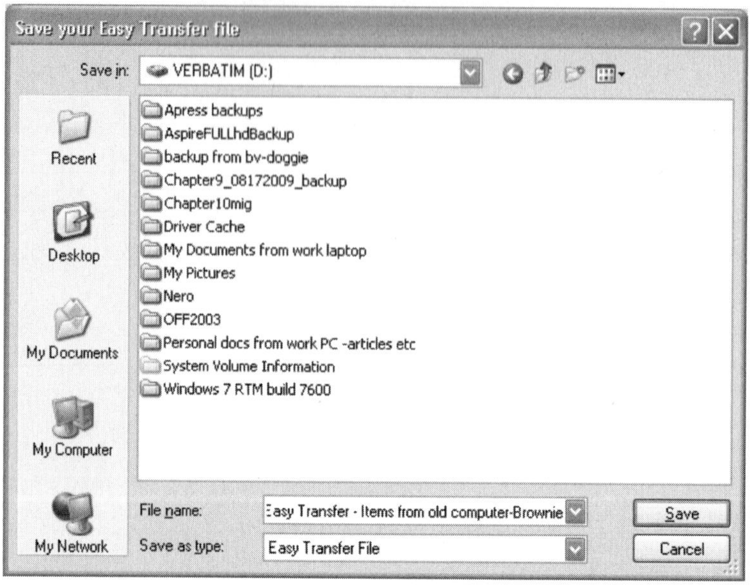

Save your Easy Transfer file

Save in: VERBATIM (D:)

Recent
Desktop
My Documents
My Computer
My Network

Apress backups
AspireFULLhdBackup
backup from bv-doggie
Chapter9_08172009_backup
Chapter10mig
Driver Cache
My Documents from work laptop
My Pictures
Nero
OFF2003
Personal docs from work PC -articles etc
System Volume Information
Windows 7 RTM build 7600

File name: Easy Transfer - Items from old computer-Brownie

Save as type: Easy Transfer File

Save
Cancel

Figure 10-25. You can specify a USB flash drive, external hard drive, or any network shared folder.

7. Specify the external hard drive, USB flash drive, or network location where you want to save the file. Windows Easy Transfer suggests a filename with the **.mig** extension, `Windows Easy Transfer – Items from old computer <old computer name>.mig.` **Click** `Save.`

The `Saving files and settings` screen appears. After a few minutes, the transfer time estimate appears, as shown in Figure 10-26.

370

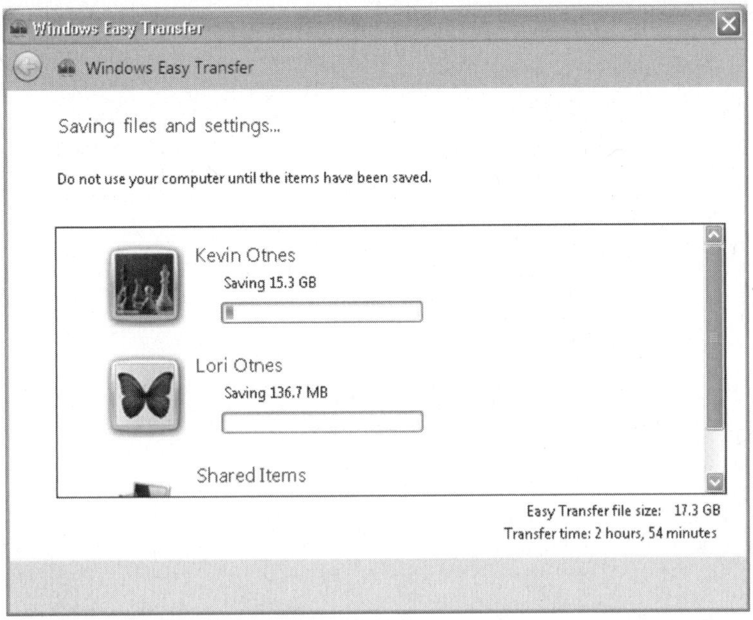

Figure 10-26. The transfer time estimate does not appear right away, and may change a few times in the first ten minutes after it appears.

When the transfer is complete, Windows Easy Transfer notifies you and provides instructions for the next steps, as shown in Figure 10-27.

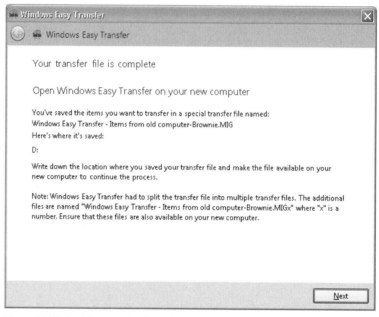

Figure 10-27. In this example, Brownie is the name of the old computer.

8. Write down the name of the transfer file or files, and where to find them.

9. Click `Next` and then click `Close`.

AdvancED

If you are doing a clean install of Windows 7 on your old computer, making it your new computer, perform the clean install now, before you transfer your files and settings. Note that after you do a clean install, everything that was on the hard disk will be gone permanently, except for what you previously backed up and what you included in the Windows Easy Transfer file.

Transferring the Windows Easy Transfer file from the storage location to the new computer

To finish the transfer, move the Windows Easy Transfer file from the storage location to the new computer:

1. On the new computer, attach the USB flash drive or external drive, or map to the network share where you stored the transfer file.

2. Open Windows Easy Transfer on your new computer.

3. When prompted `What do you want to use to transfer items to your new computer?`, select `An external hard disk or USB flash drive`.

4. When prompted, specify that this is the new computer.

5. When prompted `Has Windows Easy Transfer already saved your files from your old computer to an external hard disk or USB flash drive?`, click `Yes`.

6. Browse to the location where Windows Easy Transfer saved your files. By default, it opens to Computer. Besides browsing to devices attached to your computer, you can also browse to other network locations.

7. Look for a folder or icon named `Windows Easy Transfer—Items from old computer <old computer name>.mig`. When you open the file, Windows Easy Transfer checks for compatibility and what can be transferred.

8. Choose what to transfer to this computer. When the transfer is complete, Windows Easy Transfer displays the links to view the reports, as shown in Figure 10-28.

Figure 10-28. Use the Windows Easy Transfer reports as a guide to what programs you should install on your computer.

ExplainED

Windows Easy Transfer does not transfer programs, only settings and files. If you've had your old computer a long time, your Programs *list on your* Start *menu may have gotten quite large. The option* See a list of programs you might want to install on your new computer *can save you a lot of time trying to remember or write down all of the programs on your old computer. The report may also be useful in helping you figure out what programs you really need, based on the types of files you transferred.*

Carrying out post-migration tasks

Windows Easy Transfer saves you a lot of work moving your information from your old computer to your new computer, but there are still a few tasks to be done. Unfortunately, Windows Easy Transfer cannot transfer your *programs*, so you will need to reinstall them on your new computer. And you need to make sure you got everything you needed or wanted moved over to the new computer.

AdvancED

You may come across references in older Vista books to Windows Easy Transfer Companion, a download available from Microsoft when Vista was released. It sounded like a great idea—it would transfer your programs from your old computer to your new computer, and you would not have to manually reinstall them disc by disc. Unfortunately, Microsoft pulled it off their website and it is no longer available.

After the transfer is complete, take these steps:

- Start your new computer, and check that everything is there.
- Have each migrated user check his or her login. Each may have to create a new password.
- Reinstall your programs, using the transfer report as a guide.
- Reconnect printers and other devices, and make sure that they work. If not, you may need to reinstall the drivers. Check the device manufacturer's support website for updated drivers for Windows 7.
- Perform a full backup of your Windows 7 computer, and manually create a System Restore point.
- Check your mail and browser programs. Windows Easy Transfer should catch most of your preferences in the transfer. But sometimes the settings never find a home on your new computer because the old program is no longer used or supported on the new version of Windows. For example, Microsoft Outlook Express was a free mail browser program provided in Windows up through Windows XP. It is no longer supported in Windows, so you would need to find another program. Most mail and browser programs have their own import and export features so you don't lose your address book or bookmarks.

AdvancED

When you are in a hurry to get all your programs reinstalled, it's easy to ignore those messages that say You must restart your computer.... Don't ignore them. When you get a restart message, do that before you install any more programs. Most of the programs you reinstall should work fine in Windows 7 if they worked in Windows Vista. But occasionally some don't. If you install a bunch of programs at once, and then the next time you start your computer, you have problems, it may be hard to pinpoint which program is the culprit. Even if the installation program does not require a restart, it may still be a good idea to do so.

Using alternatives to Windows Easy Transfer

Some people do not want or need all of their settings and files migrated to their new computer. But they do want to save things such as their pictures, movies, and music. There are many tools and programs that you can use to transfer files between computers that don't require Windows Easy Transfer, such as The Tornado file transfer tool or Laplink. You can also use some of the same connection types used for Windows Easy Transfer.

What to do with your old PC

The Web, magazines, and newspapers have lots of articles on what you can do with your old PC, as well as what not to do. Here are just a few ideas:

- Use the computer as a print and file server for your home network. Hook up your printers to the PC, and then hook up the PC to your network. Then any PC on your network can print directly to the printers anytime. See Chapter 7 for more ideas.
- Don't dump your PC or monitor in the garbage or the dump. Computers contain lots of toxic chemicals that are hazardous to the environment, people, and animals. There are many low-cost or free PC recycling services, provided by the government and private industry.

- Be careful about passing down to another member of the family a PC that's just a little old and slow. If you are getting rid of your computer because it is slow or has other problems, it's not going to be any better for the person you give it to. And because it used to be your computer, that person may expect that you will know how to repair anything that goes wrong with it.
- If you are giving away or disposing of your PC, make sure the data on the hard drive is thoroughly erased. You can buy really strong software to erase your hard drive, or take it in to a shop that offers those services.

Exploring related information

After you've migrated all of your programs, files, and settings to your new computer, there are a number of other things you may want to do so you can get the most use and enjoyment out of it. Windows 7 provides many ways for you to customize which programs to use and how much personal preference information is saved on your computer and made available to programs and websites. *PC* stands for *personal computer*, right? So almost every chapter in *Getting Started with Windows 7* contains additional information about making your computer personal:

- Chapter 4 explains how to take advantage of the new themes, colors, and personalization provided in Windows 7.
- Chapter 2 provides more information about personalizing your user accounts. After you've migrated your user accounts and settings to the new computer, you may want to make use of the many features in Windows 7 that help you manage all of those settings.
- Chapter 7 provides information about sharing and keeping private your libraries and documents across your home network. This will also help fill in the gaps if you want to understand more ways to move files between computers on a network.
- Chapter 8 includes information about bookmarking your favorite websites, saving and storing personal contact information in e-mail address books, choosing which programs to use for your favorite tasks such as browsing, e-mail, listening to music, viewing pictures or video, or writing and viewing documents.
- Chapter 9 includes information about personalizing your security settings, passwords, and identity information.

377

Summary

Here's a review of what you've learned in this chapter:

- How to move files and settings from your old computer to your new computer with Windows Easy Transfer
- How to choose a connection method: Easy Transfer cable, Ethernet crossover cable, network connection, external hard drive, or discs to transfer the files and settings
- How to prepare your old and new computers for the transfer
- How to finish moving to your new computer by installing needed programs
- How to move things from your old computer to your new computer with alternatives to Windows Easy Transfer
- How to reuse, recycle, or dispose of your old computer

Index